Praise for *Tom Seaver*

"Tom Seaver is among the greatest pitchers of all time. He is also one of the most thoughtful and perceptive athletes I have ever known. Sadly, this deeply interesting man is now unable to provide us with a memoir of his own. The closest we will ever come is found here, from the Hall of Fame baseball writer who was exceptionally close to Tom and chronicled his entire career. Bill Madden renders Tom Seaver's story with the detail, insight, and care it deserves."

—Bob Costas

"In the mind's eye, Tom Seaver, the consummate power pitcher who transformed the hapless Metsies of my youth into the Miracle Mets of 1969, is forever reaching back for that last ounce of strength and thrust, his knee grazing the dirt of the pitching mound. *New York Daily News* columnist Bill Madden witnessed and chronicled it all—the misbegotten trade of The Franchise, the failure of the front office to ensure his place on the team after his return, and the cruel descent into dementia that forced him to withdraw from public life. Drawing on their longtime friendship and thirty hours of exclusive interviews with Seaver and his wife, Nancy, Madden has crafted a biography as terrific as its subject."

—Jane Leavy, author of *New York Times* bestseller *Sandy Koufax: A Lefty's Legacy*

"Tom Seaver mastered the craft of pitching about as well as any man who ever climbed a mound. A true virtuoso, he also was intellectually curious and very much in touch with the world around him. Precise. Creative. Thorough. Enthralling. The same descriptions apply to the work Bill Madden has done here. This is the biography an icon like Seaver deserves."

—Tom Verducci, *New York Times* bestselling author, and Fox and MLB Network analyst

"I've known Bill Madden since my playing days in New York. Never was there a more straightforward writer on the New York beat. He brings all his knowledge and experience to the fore in this terrific book. Add in his special relationship with Tom Seaver, and you have a must-read about one of the game's most intelligent and greatest players to ever put on a uniform. Bravo, Bill!"

—Keith Hernandez

"Bill Madden was the only person who could write this book of our dear friend Tom Terrific. Tom Seaver was Terrific. A Man's Man. Brilliant, funny, the best competitor I ever knew, and my friend."

—Johnny Bench

"For two years with the White Sox Tom fulfilled our very high expectations every time he pitched. What we learned about Tom went way beyond giving us a great chance to win. He is the smartest teammate we ever had and knew winning in all phases of the game! In our family culture, Tom quickly became one of our leaders with a personality that bonded with teammates on and off the field. This book by Bill Madden, who had a close personal relationship with him, captures all of that."

—Tony LaRussa

"A biography that bolsters Seaver's reputation as a thinker on the mound, who won by outleveling hitters in their mental preparation."

—Oskar Garcia, *New York Times Book Review*

"A vivid portrait of one of modern baseball's legendary players. . . . A fitting tribute to a great, memorable pitcher."

—*Kirkus Reviews*

"Madden shows readers more than a ballplayer: readers see a loyal friend, a devoted husband and father, a passionate opponent of the Vietnam War. . . . [A] superb bio."

—*Booklist* (starred review)

Tom Seaver

— A TERRIFIC LIFE —

BILL MADDEN

Simon & Schuster Paperbacks

NEW YORK   LONDON   TORONTO
SYDNEY   NEW DELHI

Simon & Schuster Paperbacks
An Imprint of Simon & Schuster, Inc.
1230 Avenue of the Americas
New York, NY 10020

First Simon & Schuster trade paperback edition September 2021

SIMON & SCHUSTER PAPERBACKS and colophon are registered trademarks
of Simon & Schuster, Inc.

For information about special discounts for bulk purchases,
please contact Simon & Schuster Special Sales at 1-866-506-1949
or business@simonandschuster.com.

The Simon & Schuster Speakers Bureau can bring authors to your
live event. For more information or to book an event, contact
the Simon & Schuster Speakers Bureau at 1-866-248-3049
or visit our website at www.simonspeakers.com.

Interior design by Paul Dippolito

Manufactured in the United States of America

1   3   5   7   9   10   8   6   4   2

The Library of Congress has cataloged the hardcover edition as follows:

Names: Madden, Bill, author.
Title: Tom Seaver : a terrific life / Bill Madden.
Description: First Simon & Schuster hardcover edition. |
New York : Simon & Schuster, 2021. | Includes bibliographical references and index. |
Summary: "Veteran sportswriter Bill Madden writes the definitive biography of a baseball and
New York sports legend, Tom Seaver, voted into the Hall of Fame by the highest percentage
vote ever at the time and still the most popular player in Mets history"— Provided by publisher.
Identifiers: LCCN 2020029441 | ISBN 9781982136185 (hardcover) |
ISBN 9781982136222 (trade paperback) | ISBN 9781982136215 (ebook)
Subjects: LCSH: Seaver, Tom, 1944– | New York Mets (Baseball team)—History. |
Baseball players—United States—Biography.
Classification: LCC GV865.S4 M34 2021 | DDC 796.357092 [B]—dc23
LC record available at https://lccn.loc.gov/2020029441

ISBN 978-1-9821-3618-5
ISBN 978-1-9821-3622-2 (pbk)
ISBN 978-1-9821-3621-5 (ebook)

*For Lillian, Steven, and Christopher
and in memory of Thomas Madden*

Contents

CHAPTER 1

300!

HE HAD ALREADY WON 273 GAMES IN THE BIG LEAGUES, ALONG with a record-tying three Cy Young Awards, a no-hitter, and *Sports Ilustrated's* Sportsman of the Year Award—not to mention having led the New York Mets to the most improbable World Series championship in baseball history—when Tom Seaver received the news that fateful morning of January 20 in 1984.

He was going to have to leave New York for the second time in his career.

Unlike the first time, 1977, when he was still in his prime, Seaver was thirty-nine now and coming off two successive losing seasons, which had already caused him to question privately whether it was time to start seriously considering life without baseball.

Other than miraculously regaining the lost two miles per hour on his fastball or winning the *Sporting News'* Comeback Player of the Year Award, Seaver had nothing more to prove when the Chicago White Sox shocked the baseball world that day by selecting him as the number one pick in something called the free-agent compensation draft, passing over hundreds of far younger established players and prospects.

"I just don't know if I want to do this," Seaver said to his wife, Nancy, that morning in the kitchen of their home, a converted barn snuggled within a parcel of seven heavily wooded acres in Greenwich, Connecticut. Leave home again? With his two daughters growing up? Why?

In recounting that conversation years later, Nancy Seaver said her husband's anger at the Mets for leaving him unprotected in the draft was tempered by his own self-doubt as to whether he had anything left in that durable right arm that had already logged more than four thousand innings across seventeen major-league seasons—and whether it was worth it to find out, in another city, in a different league with the designated hitter, halfway across the country from his home and family.

"I think he was questioning himself whether or not he needed to put himself out there again," Nancy said during an interview at Seaver's vineyard in Calistoga, California, north of San Francisco, in 2017. "Maybe it was time for him to come home and start to think about his future." But Nancy said she suggested that he give it a try. Go to the new team. "I started thinking, 'Well, we could live in the city. How fun that would be for the girls. We could actually live in a high-rise—we'd never done that before.'"

Seaver pondered what she had said, still uncertain about how much he had left.

"Well," he said, "maybe if I just get two hundred ninety wins. What's so wrong with that? Maybe I could be content with that."

Again, Nancy felt he was short-changing himself. What was twenty-seven more wins? He'd won twenty games in a season five times previously in his career and led the league with fourteen victories just three years earlier in the strike-shortened 1981 campaign.

"You have to go for the three hundred wins," she said, firmly. "If you don't at least try, it will always be in the back of your mind."

Looking back thirty-three years later, Nancy laughed. "I literally shoved the guy out the door. I said: 'You will never be happy if you have to wonder if you could ever get to three hundred wins.' I knew he wasn't finished."

Three years earlier, Seaver had told scribe Frank Deford of *Sports Illustrated*: "My one statistical goal is three hundred wins, but I'm not going to keep after it if I have to struggle. It's no fun to go out there and not pitch well. That would be too frustrating." He was thinking of two of the more recent three-hundred-game winners, Early Wynn and Gaylord Perry, both of whom had been in their forties and needed multiple starts to achieve three hundred. He wanted no part of that.

And much of the 1982 season, when he'd gone 5-13 with an ungodly 5.50 ERA in his last year with the Cincinnati Reds, and '83 when he'd pitched considerably better but still had another losing record (9-14) with the hapless (68-94) last-place Mets, had left him with nothing but frustration.

But perhaps more than anything, Seaver worried if he could fit in with a new team and new teammates, most of them ten to fifteen years younger than him. He had always been regarded as a true baseball Renaissance man, the out-of-the-ordinary clubhouse intellectual who was fond of citing Bernoulli's law to explain why a fastball rises; who eschewed reading the sports pages or the hunting and fishing magazines at his locker in favor of the *New York Times* crossword puzzle; and who organized bridge games in the clubhouse, as he explained to his teammates, "to stimulate your minds." He had learned bridge from his parents and brought the game to the clubhouse in his early years with the Mets. "It's a mental exercise," he would say, "just like the crossword puzzles I do every day. Both bridge and crosswords have you withdraw bits of information and recall things—just like you do with pitching."

There was another thing: he was no longer young. The game was changing, and so were the players He'd be moving on to another new team where he had to figure out if he could fit in. All around him, the kids were getting younger, their interests far different from his. Their music was louder, and they wore earphones. There was no conversation. No stimulation. It's important, he thought, how the new generations make you feel, in the same job you've been doing for twenty years.

But Nancy was right. He may have lost a tick or so off his fastball but nothing of his competitiveness. The White Sox were a far better team than the Mets, having led the major leagues with ninety-nine wins in '83, and it would be not unlike joining Cincinnati's All-Star-laden Big Red Machine in 1977, with Johnny Bench, Pete Rose, George Foster, and company. He and Bench had developed a very special pitcher-catcher rapport, much like what he'd enjoyed with Jerry Grote, who'd been his catcher with the Mets the whole ten and a half years he'd been with them. And Sox receiver Carlton Fisk was considered the American League "complete catcher" counterpart to Bench.

So, Seaver would go to Chicago—although not before an acrimonious contract extension negotiation with the White Sox owners—and begin that final quest for the one milestone that mattered to him. When he reported to the White Sox spring training camp in Sarasota, Florida, on February 20, he felt renewed. His bitter feelings toward the Mets had still not subsided—"what the New York Mets did was disrupt my family life," he told the Chicago press corps—but he'd had a full month to reflect on the benefits of going from a last-place team to a first-place team, and he'd gotten acquainted by phone with Fisk and White Sox manager Tony LaRussa; he'd seen firsthand how they went about their business, and concluded that the move might actually be a blessing.

"I knew in my heart I'd be pitching somewhere in 1984," Seaver told the Chicago media. "I can win sixteen to twenty games here." He went on to say how much he, a student of baseball history, was looking forward to pitching in the American League, especially at the White Sox's seventy-four-year-old Comiskey Park, venue of the infamous 1919 "Black Sox" World Series fix scandal, in which eight White Sox players were banned for life from baseball for conspiring to throw the 1919 World Series against the Cincinnati Reds. "I've never even been in Comiskey Park, or Fenway Park in Boston, where I've always wanted to pitch. This is going to be exciting for me."

As it was, he would win fifteen, but it was more than any other Sox hurler in '84, as the previous season's most successful starting rotation in baseball would all have off-years in '84—none more so than staff anchor LaMarr Hoyt. The twenty-nine-year-old righty went from leading the league with twenty-four wins and earning the AL Cy Young Award to a league-worst eighteen losses. (In the off-season, the White Sox traded Hoyt to the San Diego Padres for a promising twenty-one-year-old minor league shortstop, Ozzie Guillen.) Meanwhile, the old man of the staff was a model of consistency at 15-11, never missing a turn, while putting in 236⅔ innings, his most since 1978.

"I was very satisfied with that first year in Chicago," Seaver told the Chicago writers. "I was a different pitcher here, but I was still pretty darned good. I could still get batters out."

Left unsaid: Fifteen down, twelve to go.

He breezed through the first six weeks of '85 with four wins, one loss, and four no-decisions in his first nine starts, but pitched well in all but one of them, a no-decision, April 20, against the Red Sox at Comiskey in which he gave up five runs in five innings, including a pair of homers by Mike Easler and Tony Armas. Then from May 20 through June 30, he went through a spell of five losses in nine starts, but again pitched fairly effectively and ended June with a 7-6 record and a more-than-respectable 3.28 ERA. No longer the power pitcher with a ninety-six-, ninety-seven-mile-per-hour blazer, he was doing it now on guile, command, and smarts. Fisk marveled that Seaver was the brainiest pitcher he ever caught. After his bullpen session before one game in Minnesota, on June 9, Seaver saw White Sox pitching coach Dave Duncan shaking his head.

"You ain't got squat today," Duncan said, frowning.

"I know that, Dunc," Seaver replied. Then, pointing to the Twins' dugout, he added: "But *they* don't! Today we're just gonna have to fool 'em."

And he did, limiting the Twins to five hits and just one run in 7⅔ innings to run his record to 6-4 and reduce the magic number to three hundred to five. After the game, he said to Duncan, "Can you imagine if I'd had good stuff tonight, Dunc?" And they both laughed.

"One of the first things Tom said to me when he came over to us, and we were talking pitching, was there are three ways to get guys out: with velocity, location, or ball movement," Fisk related in a 2017 interview at the Hall of Fame.

"Of the three," Seaver said, "velocity is the least important. If I can have two—because you're not gonna feel a hundred percent every time you get on the mound—if I can have two of those elements, I can get guys out."

"That was his craft," Fisk said. "Getting guys out, the pitching part of the deal, working on hitters' tendencies—aggressive tendencies or nonaggressive tendencies. He was a master at changing speeds, running the ball, cutting the ball. He always knew what he was doing out there. It's like he could read the batters' minds. That was the fun part of him and I working together."

They could rag on each other pretty good, too, sometimes right in the middle of a game. Fisk recalled one instance when Seaver was having a particularly hard time with his breaking ball, bouncing it in the dirt, missing the plate by nearly a foot. After a couple of these errant pitches in succession, Fisk, who fancied himself a pretty good thrower, decided to retaliate. Retrieving one of the balls out of the dirt, he straightened up and fired the ball back to Seaver, nearly hitting him in the ribs.

"I could see that startled him," Fisk said. "Then the next inning, it happened again. He bounced another one, and I did the same thing, firing the ball back to him where I knew he'd have trouble catching it. This time he waves me out and I say to myself, 'Oh, boy, this is gonna be fun.'"

When Fisk arrived at the mound, Seaver was scowling.

"Okay, Fisky," he said, "who's pitching this game? You or me?"

"Well, with that shit you're throwing up there today," Fisk shot back, "I think I should be pitching and you should be catching!"

From June 20 through July 30, Fisk caught every one of Seaver's nine starts, in which he went 4-4 but at the same time lowered his ERA from 3.28 to 3.02—while achieving double digits in strikeouts only once.

"He was a wonder to watch," said Fisk, a Hall of Fame inductee in 2000. "As we got closer to three hundred, however, not once did we mention 'Oh, we've got ten left, we've got seven left.' We just kept at it. We knew in the back of our heads. He knew. But he kept his nose to the purpose. He never talked about it."

Even after Seaver gutted out a 7–5 complete game victory in which he gave up a couple of home runs and struck out only three against the Red Sox in Fenway Park, on July 30, for number 299, it didn't initially dawn on him that his next start would be against the Yankees—in New York! "I never looked ahead," Seaver said in a 2016 interview. "Someone pointed it out to me in the clubhouse afterward; I don't remember who. I just remember thinking, 'Well, isn't that gonna be nice. At least it'll be an easy commute for Nancy and the girls.'"

A few days before arriving in New York, Seaver was asked if he would feel any special revenge toward the Mets by winning his three hundredth game in their backyard. The passage of time had mellowed him. "I'm not going back with any idea of that," he said. "I have some very, very good memories of New York and its fans. When I left New York this last time, it was an honest mistake. There was no animosity leading up to the point where I was left unprotected. [Mets co-owner] Nelson Doubleday called me and apologized and told me he hoped I'd get my three hundredth real soon. So, it's not anything where I'm trying to show anybody up."

When the White Sox arrived in New York late Thursday night, August 1, for the four-game series against the Yankees, Seaver went home to Greenwich. Only when he was reading the newspaper at breakfast Friday morning did he learn that Sunday, when he would be making his hopefully historic start, had long before been designated "Phil Rizzuto Day" by the Yankees to honor their beloved former shortstop and longtime broadcaster by retiring his uniform number 10. So be it, Seaver thought; while the Rizzuto festivities were going on prior to the game, he would be otherwise indisposed.

Sunday, August 4, dawned to an unsettling commotion in the Seaver household. Somehow a bat—the flying kind—had made an unwelcome intrusion through a window in the old converted barn, arousing Tom and Nancy and sending them scurrying about to find a broom. Once one was located, Tom began flailing away at the bat until the creature finally winged off out the window whence it had come. Their rude awakening having subsided, Tom and Nancy went back to bed and were able to catch a couple more hours' sleep before the forty-year-old pitcher was to start preparing for the biggest day of his career.

It was a fitful morning, Seaver would later reveal, that had nothing to do with the bat invasion. His stomach was uneasy, and he could hardly get down an English muffin for breakfast. He had a headache, too. When he arrived in the visitors' clubhouse at Yankee Stadium later that morning, Jerry Reinsdorf and Eddie Einhorn, the White Sox owners, were waiting for him, along with a small group of reporters and a clubhouse man holding a case of baseballs for him to sign.

"How do you feel, Tom?" Einhorn asked.

"I've got a headache, and my stomach is queasy as hell," Seaver said, laughing. "Otherwise, I feel just great."

LaRussa knew otherwise. Between the ceremony to honor Rizzuto and Seaver's "homecoming" going for his three hundredth win, the White Sox manager could envision all the theater that was about to unfold in the House that Ruth Built. Privately, he was anxious and worried about his pitcher.

"I remember the atmosphere in the stadium like it was yesterday," LaRussa said in a 2017 interview. "At least half the fans were Mets fans, while the Yankees had all these formidable hitters, future Hall of Famers like Dave Winfield and Rickey Henderson, and there'd been so much buildup. I'm saying to myself, 'I know he's Tom Seaver, but this is so unfair to Tom to have all this attention and, likely, you know they're going to get him, and we're not going to play well, and it's just not going to be a storybook ending. How wrong was I?"

Shortly before two o'clock, Seaver began making his way down to the bullpen for his pregame warm-up session. By now, the Rizzuto Day ceremonies had taken on the air of the TV game show *The Price Is Right*, as one corporate CEO after another presented the sixty-eight-year-old Yankees legend with a slew of expensive gifts ranging from cars and boats to golf clubs, lifetime supplies of soft drinks, and a trip to Italy. It was John Campi, the longtime vice president of promotions for the *New York Daily News*, who supplied a welcome bit of levity to the interminable proceedings by coming up with the idea of presenting Rizzuto with a cow, adorned with a golden halo, in recognition of the signature "Holy cow!" phrase the Scooter was so fond of invoking throughout his broadcasts. Taking the reins of the cow from legendary *Daily News* cartoonist Bill Gallo, Rizzuto was suddenly jolted when the frisky bovine, who'd apparently had enough of all this shlock, stepped on his foot and knocked him to the ground. Fortunately, Rizzuto, who came up laughing, was not hurt, although years later he would frequently complain in jest about being upstaged on his own day by a cow and, of all people, an ex-Met, Tom Seaver.

"It's funny," said Reinsdorf in a 2017 interview, "I have absolutely no memory of the Rizzuto ceremony that day. That's how so consumed I was with Seaver."

Because the Rizzuto Day ceremonies dragged on as long as they did, Seaver twice had to stop throwing in the bullpen. It was not until 3:06 p.m., after the White Sox had come up empty despite two singles and two walks off the Yankees' Joe Cowley in the top of the first, that Seaver finally got to throw his first pitch. Among the near-sellout Yankee Stadium crowd of 54,032 were former president Richard Nixon, Baseball Commissioner Peter Ueberroth, and, sitting in a box right next to the visiting team's dugout, Nancy and their two daughters, twelve-year-old Sarah and nine-year-old Annie. Along with them was

Seaver's seventy-four-year-old father, Charles, who, a half century earlier, had achieved his own bit of sporting fame by going unbeaten for
the United States in its victorious 1932 Walker Cup golf match against
Great Britain. On his way out to the bullpen before the game, Seaver
stopped at the box and handed his dad a baseball.

He was not quite sure what kind of reception he would get, Yankee
Stadium being longtime hostile territory for anyone with a Mets pedi-
gree, and the day already devoted to Rizzuto. So, it was immediately a
great comfort to see so many people standing and applauding him as
he took the mound in the first inning. It was hard to differentiate Yankees fans from Mets fans, as they were all chanting "Sea-vuh! Sea-vuh!"
in the same New York accent.

Even though he found himself trailing, 1–0, after yielding an RBI
single to Ken Griffey in the third inning, he felt he had his good stuff.
Seaver was saved from a potential big inning in the fourth when, after
Yankees leadoff hitter Dave Winfield reached on an error by White
Sox third baseman Tim Hulett, Greg Walker made a diving stop on
Dan Pasqua's hard-hit ball to first, advancing Winfield. Seaver got Ron
Hassey to ground out on the right side, moving Winfield to third, then
hit second baseman Willie Randolph with a pitch, putting runners at
first and third. Reaching back to his '69–'73 youth, however, Seaver
struck out slugging New York third baseman Mike Pagliarulo to end
the inning.

Now he just needed a few runs—which the White Sox provided
after putting runners on first and third with one out to knock out Cowley in the sixth. Hulett doubled home one run off reliever Brian Fisher,
then Ozzie Guillen, Chicago's standout twenty-one-year-old rookie
shortstop, singled home the go-ahead run. Another single by Bryan
Little scored two insurance runs. In the clubhouse before the game, the

ever-ebullient Guillen shouted over to Seaver, "You gonna win today, Tom, and I gonna drive in the winning run for you! You wait and see!"

Bolstered with a 4–1 lead, Seaver retired New York in order in the sixth and seventh. His string of ten consecutive retired batters ended when the Yankees' Bobby Meacham singled to lead off the eighth. Seaver shrugged that off by striking out dangerous Rickey Henderson looking on a pitch down and outside. Afterward, Henderson would complain that home plate umpire Derryl Cousins was helping Seaver: "I wouldn't have played today if I knew they just wanted to give him the win that way," he moaned to the reporters.

After Griffey grounded into a force play, Don Mattingly, on his way to the AL Most Valuable Player Award, singled him over to third, giving the Yankees their first runner in scoring position since the fourth inning. That brought up Winfield, en route to a fourth consecutive season of a hundred or more RBI. Duncan, who had taken over as acting White Sox manager after LaRussa was thrown out of the game for arguing too vehemently an out call at home that ended the Sox's sixth-inning rally, hustled out to the mound for a conference with Seaver. LaRussa, before departing the premises (he would later creep back up the tunnel from the clubhouse to the edge of the dugout and watch the rest of the game from there), had instructed Duncan, "If he says he's got enough, let him stay, even though we'll have Bob James [the White Sox closer who saved thirty-two games in 1985] ready. He's always honest. Tom Seaver will never lose a game because of his vanity."

"You can't possibly be thinking of taking him out?" Fisk said to Duncan.

"I just want to know how he feels," the pitching coach replied. Then, looking at Seaver, he asked, "Have you got enough left?"

Seaver hesitated. As he would later admit, "I was caught up in the emotion of the day, and, at that point, I really didn't have a feel for how I was pitching."

"You're not done," Fisk said firmly. "You're Tom Seaver. You don't want someone from the bullpen coming in here. This is your *right*. You can get this guy. You're not leaving this game!"

Seaver nodded. "I'm okay, Dunc, really," he said.

Satisfied, Duncan retreated to the dugout, and Fisk resumed his place behind the plate. Later, he said, "If Tom had tried to take himself out of the game, I think I would have tripped him!"

As Griffey hovered off third, Seaver somewhat deliberately ran the count to 3-2 on Winfield before striking him out on what, in his later career, had become his signature out pitch. When everyone in the ballpark was expecting one of his vintage fastballs, Seaver threw a changeup. This one earned him a standing ovation from the crowd. Trotting off the field in giddy triumph, he rushed over to the corner of the dugout next to the box where his family was sitting, grabbed daughter Annie's hand, and said, "Three outs to go."

"Oh, good, Daddy!" she exclaimed. "Then we can go home and go swimming!"

Though they'd banged around a trio of Yankee pitchers for thirteen hits, the White Sox were unable to tack on anything to their 4–1 lead, leaving it up to Seaver to close the job with whatever he had left in the ninth. A hard-hit leadoff single off the right-field fence by the lefty-hitting Pasqua had the Seaver family all clenching their fists in silent prayer, only to feel momentary relief when the old man fanned Hassey on a fastball at the knees and got Randolph on a fly ball to right that required a running, leaping catch at the wall by All-Star Harold Baines. After Baines whirled and threw the ball back to the infield as Pasqua took second, Seaver, crouched behind third base to back up the throw, grinned.

"Congratulations," said third-base umpire Terry Cooney.

"Do you believe that catch?" Seaver said.

"You deserve it," said Cooney.

"I'll deserve it when I get one more out!"

But then he walked Pagliarulo on four straight balls to run his pitch count to 141, and this brought Duncan and Fisk to the mound again. Approaching the plate was thirty-six-year-old Don Baylor, still one of the most dangerous right-handed hitters in the league, pinch-hitting for Meacham.

"You okay?" Duncan asked.

"I'm okay," Seaver replied.

Though he surmised the walk to Pagliarulo had taken a little bit more out of him, Fisk expressed confidence his battery mate could finish. "You're pushing the ball," he said to Seaver. "Just relax. You've waited a long time for this." Then turning to Duncan, he said: "He's good, Dunc. Let him go."

"I was beat as hell," Seaver conceded later. "It was like I was levitating on the mound. I hadn't felt like that since 1969 when I was going for a perfect game against the Cubs. But there wasn't a chance in hell I was coming out. If you can't get up for one more out for your three hundredth win, then you never will!"

Duncan turned and headed back to the dugout, as Seaver began his staredown with Baylor, who now represented the tying run. It was 6:11 p.m., four hours and one minute after he'd first gone out to warm up, when Seaver threw his 142nd and final pitch of the game: a fastball close in on Baylor's hands. Baylor swung and lofted a high fly to medium left field. White Sox left fielder Reid Nichols moved in a couple of steps, then drifted back the same distance to camp under the ball and make the catch. It was over. Tom Seaver had just become the seventeenth pitcher in baseball history to win three hundred games. Final score 4–1, Seaver's uniform number throughout his major-league career. "Hel-*lo*?" Nancy would say later.

As soon as the ball settled into Nichols's glove, Ozzie Guillen leaped high into the air, screaming and waving his arms in exhilaration. After watching the catch, crouched down between the pitcher's mound and first base, Seaver turned and looked at Fisk, letting out a shout before jumping into his catcher's arms. "Seaves," Fisk said, joyously, "you'd have been nothing without me!" (Before he left the field, Fisk made sure to grab all the used balls from the game out of the home plate umpire's bag.)

After being mobbed in a brief scrum by his teammates, Seaver's attention quickly turned to Nancy, sitting in the dugout box and wiping away tears with a handkerchief. He broke away and rushed over to hug her and the girls, but he was a moment behind Guillen, who had decided to collect his reward for the game-winning hit by being the first to plant a smooch on Nancy and the Seaver daughters. "I said 'Congratulations' to all of them," Guillen explained to the media afterward, "because family is a part of your life. They felt real 'wow.' I was just real excited for a teammate and a good guy."

It was delirious bedlam, Seaver hugging Nancy and the girls and then his dad, as the entire stadium crowd remained standing and applauding amid more chants of "Sea-vuh! Sea-vuh!" and "Let's go Mets!

Let's go Mets!" In Chicago, his old team, the Mets, had just finished putting away the Cubs—twenty-year-old Dwight Gooden, their new Seaver, notching his eleventh straight victory to run his sophomore-year record to 17-3, with a microscopic 1.57 ERA—and watched the last two innings on the clubhouse TV. When Nichols gloved the final out, they erupted in cheers. "Tom is really a Met," first baseman Keith Hernandez told reporters. "He will always be a Met. We're very happy that he had the chance to do this historic thing in New York."

The last thing Yankees owner George Steinbrenner wanted was to see Yankee Stadium turned into a World Series–like celebration of an opposing pitcher—and a damned Mets icon, no less! "I congratulate Tom Seaver, but I'm not happy about being on the wrong side of history," Steinbrenner grumbled when approached in his box by reporters after the final out. "I'm happy for Tom, and I'm proud of him, but I wanted to beat him so bad today. I don't know if it bothered our players to lose, but it sure bothered me and [manager] Billy [Martin]." (That being the combative Billy Martin, who was in the fourth of his five tours as the skipper in the Bronx.)

Nevertheless, the Yankees' boss had taken the trouble to commission a special silver bowl commemorating Seaver's three hundredth win as a gift for him. His eyes reddened from a combination of tears and champagne, Seaver waved a bottle of the bubbly in the White Sox' clubhouse and shouted to his celebrant teammates: "We might want to do this more than once every nineteen years!" He then hoisted the bowl to show to the reporters. "This was really nice of George," he said. "The only thing is, how did he know I'd win my three hundredth here?"

"Oh," he said, scrutinizing the engraving on the bowl, "he didn't date it. I guess I'll have to do that myself."

"When do you think this will all hit you?" a reporter asked him.

"Probably in November," Seaver said, "when I'm out to dinner with my wife. I'll really be able to savor and appreciate it. Then I'll pour my heart out to her."

It had been a long, emotional day, one that began with his adventure with the bat and not feeling well, before gutting it out for three hours and twenty minutes in the most satisfying complete-game victory he would ever pitch. At last, the reporters had exhausted all their questions and began filing out. The day's hero would be right behind them; Nancy and the girls were waiting. But as he grabbed his sports jacket, across the room he spotted Lindsey Nelson, the Mets' lead broadcaster from their inception in 1962 to 1978, bedecked in one of his trademark blinding plaid sports jackets. Nelson had been been hired by WPIX, the local Yankees TV station, to do a one-game cameo while also hopefully sharing Seaver's greatest moment.

"Lindsey!" Seaver hollered. "Lindsey!"

Nelson, who was heading out the door, turned and waved.

"Lindsey!" Seaver shouted again. "Tell them I could throw the ball hard once. Tell the guys in my clubhouse too. They don't believe me."

"You could, Tom," Nelson said, pointing his finger at Seaver. "You sure could."

Much to Steinbrenner's chagrin, the next day's New York papers featured wall-to-wall coverage of Seaver's three hundredth, with Rizzuto's day pretty much reduced to large pictures of the beloved Scooter being knocked to the ground by the cow (much to the delight of John Campi). It was also the *Daily News*'s Mike Lupica who best summed up what the day had been all about:

"Tom Seaver still was something special to see on a summer

afternoon. It was Yankee Stadium, not Shea, and it was the White Sox for whom he was pitching, and not the Mets. But for three shining emotional hours yesterday, Tom Seaver said to a New York crowd: 'This is who I am. This is who I have always been.'"

Thirty years later, in August 2015, during one of my visits with Seaver at his vineyard in Calistoga, I asked him what, in retrospect, stood out most for him about that game. Doing it at Yankee Stadium, before a capacity crowd, including Nancy, the girls, and his dad, pitching a complete game? I prodded. It was none of that, he said.

"You know what?" Seaver said. "Winning three hundred games in the major leagues is a great achievement. But does anyone know what I did in my next start? No? Well, I won my three hundred first. I went back to work and said, 'This game is as important as the game five days ago.' I'm more proud of three-oh-one than I am of three hundred. There's such a motivation for three hundred. And I respected the game enough to understand that the next one is just as important, if not more so, than three hundred. Because it makes a statement. I loved it."

CHAPTER 2

Fresno

"YOU ARE ALL PART OF THIS. WE DID THIS TOGETHER."

On a warm, starlit evening in late July 1992, Tom Seaver's boyhood pals and coaches from Fresno, California, gathered around the big pool behind "the barn" (their affectionate term for the Seavers' reconstructed Victorian farmhouse in Greenwich) as he raised a beer in a toast to them. At Seaver's behest, they had made the three-thousand-mile cross-country trek from California, where they all still lived: his baseball teammates from Little League through high school, Russ Scheidt and Larry Woods; his high school baseball coach, Fred Bartels; his Fresno City College coach, Len Bourdet, and college teammates Don Reinero, his closest confidant, who coordinated the trip for everyone, and Brendan Ounjian; and his much-older Fresno neighbor on Arthur Avenue, Gary Kazanjian, whose shoe store at the end of the street had served as Seaver's "clubhouse"—a place where he and his buddies could hang out and talk about things they couldn't share with their parents.

He had invited them all to celebrate with him his induction into the Baseball Hall of Fame in Cooperstown, New York, a couple of days later. Standing alongside them at the festive gathering were Seaver's wife, Nancy, his two young daughters, Sarah and Annie, and his father, Charlie, as the retired pitching legend began recounting the journey that had taken him from the dusty, sunbaked fields of Fresno's hundred-degree summers to baseball's highest pinnacle.

"It was just a beautiful night, all of us back together again, celebrating Tom," remembered Larry Woods. "Just before barbeque time, Tom gave this little talk, going through each level of his career, from Little League, Babe Ruth, American Legion, high school, and college. It was highly thorough, and he made sure he didn't leave anybody out. There was no condescension like you might expect from a superstar athlete who long ago left his hometown behind. Instead, and in his speech at Cooperstown a couple of days later, he kept making the point that we'd all been an important part of his life—and we truly did feel a part of his life."

"We all felt special," agreed Brendan Ounjian. "Tom called each and every one of us to personally invite us to his induction. The day after the barbeque, he took us to Yankee Stadium for a private tour of the ballpark and tickets for the game. After taking us through Monument Park, where they have the plaques and monuments of Yankees immortals, he said: 'Okay, fellas, you're on your own for the rest of the day. I'm on my way to Cooperstown. I'll see you all there Sunday.'"

Fresno, California, in the late 1950s was a city of just over 130,000. Then and now it has served as the hub of the Golden State's San Joaquin Valley agricultural region. Seaver's dad, a world-class amateur golfer, was vice president of Bonner Packing, a raisin company in Fresno, and was said to be instrumental in raisins first being added to breakfast cereals. Upon embarking on building his vineyard in

Calistoga in the late nineties, Tom frequently made reference to friends and members of the media about agriculture and farming being in his blood.

Tom's mother, Betty, was also an excellent golfer, and she and Charlie spawned a family of athletes. Tom was the youngest of four. His brother, Charles Jr., was on the University of California varsity swim team. His sister Carol was a phys-ed major at UCLA, and his other sister, Katie, swam and played volleyball at Stanford University. Tom's parents constantly encouraged healthy competition in the Seaver household, be it golf, tennis, basketball, badminton, bridge, even dominoes. But his siblings, who like him excelled in school, were much older and were always able to outplay the much smaller Tom, no matter how fiercely he competed against them. He was glad to be included, but even then, at ages five through eight, he hated losing and didn't cotton to the notion of being the family mascot.

"Our family was always competitive, and even when my father was just working around the house, he wanted perfection, and he tried to instill that striving in all of us too," Seaver recalled in a 2015 interview.

Because his siblings were so much older, they were mostly out of the nest when Tom was in his formative years. His brother, Charles, whom he idolized for his creative intellect and individuality, introduced him to the rock 'n' roll music of Chuck Berry, Fats Domino, and Little Richard. Charles was the free spirit of the family. After college, he lived among the hippies in New York's Greenwich Village, was a social worker, taught at predominantly African American grammar schools in the Bedford-Stuyvesant section of Brooklyn, wrote poetry, and was an artist and a sculptor. At a lot of Tom's Mets home games, Charles would bring a group of underprivileged kids from Bed-Stuy to Shea Stadium to see him pitch. Tom was fond of telling the story of how Charles, after watching him win game four of the '69 World Series, rushed from Shea Stadium back to Manhattan to take part in an anti–Vietnam War rally in Bryant Park behind the New York Public Library. Priorities.

Tom's oldest sister, Katie, dated a Stanford classmate named Dave Guard, who was the founder of the Kingston Trio, the number one folk singing group of the late fifties and early sixties. Tom remembered around Thanksgiving 1955, Guard and another member of the Trio, Bob Shane, stopping over at the Seaver house in Fresno on their way back to Los Angeles from San Francisco. After dinner, they gathered around the family piano, and Seaver's folks said to Guard and Shane: "You like music, right? Let us play you a song."

With that, they opened the piano bench and pulled out a yellowed piece of sheet music with the song title scribbled in pencil: "Scotch and Soda." Listening to them harmonizing on the boozy, mellow lyrics, "Scotch and soda, jigger of gin / Oh, what a spell you've got me in," Guard and Shane were mesmerized. "Where did you get this?" they asked. Charlie and Betty explained they'd come across the song while on their honeymoon in Phoenix in 1932, in a backroom piano bar near their hotel. The piano player played it every night, and they quickly adopted it as "their song"—especially since scotch and soda happened to be Charlie Seaver's cocktail of choice. At the end of their stay, the piano player gave them the sheet music to take home with them, but he never bothered to sign it.

"Could we have this?" Guard asked Charlie. "I think we'd like to record it."

"That would be great," said Charlie. "We'd be honored."

According to Seaver, his folks had regretted never getting the piano player's name, but as soon as Guard and Shane got back to Los

Angeles, they registered the song at the copyright office, with Guard listed as its composer. They then included it, as a solo by Shane, on their first Capitol Records album in 1958, and as Shane said on numerous occasions, it became their most requested song ever.

"I was just a kid at the time and was much too busy playing baseball then to bother with the Kingston Trio, who weren't even a group yet," Seaver said.

Of all the family's sports and activities Tom especially loved baseball. He once said, "The thing I most appreciate about the game is that it is one of the few places left where a person like myself can show his individuality."

When Tom was eight, he was rejected for the North Fresno Rotary Little League team because he wasn't old enough—the age requirement was that a player had to be or turn nine years old during the course of the season, and Tom, who was born November 17, 1944, wouldn't turn nine until after the season. He vowed he would make the team the following year and, from there, become a pitcher who would get people's attention. He was determined to escape from the shadows of his older siblings and be somebody in his own right.

The family had seen how distraught he was at being turned down. In an effort to console and pump him up, his dad played pepper with him—Charlie would bat, and Tom would field—in the backyard every night after dinner. That was when Charlie began to see his son's exceptional athleticism. "From when he was a little kid, I could see he was a very competitive person," Charlie told the *Fresno Bee* in 1970. "Anything he did . . . I tried to teach him golf, handball, dominoes, bridge, baseball . . . he wanted to play well. He would study the rules, and he would listen when I would give him tips. Maybe it was because he was the youngest in the family, he wanted to compete so hard."

Longtime Mets broadcaster Ralph Kiner, a Hall of Fame outfielder who won seven straight National League home run titles from 1947 to 1952, remembered playing with Charlie Seaver in the Bing Crosby Pro-Am Golf Tournament at Pebble Beach when Tom was only ten and Charlie telling him: "I've got a good one coming."

The following spring in Little League, "Little Tommy Seaver" began to get noticed. According to his friend Russ Scheidt, Tom had originally been selected by another team. But Russ's father, knowing firsthand the boy's competitiveness and his will to win, urged Hal Bicknell, the coach of his North Fresno Rotary Club team, to work out a trade for him. "Tom was a helluva hitter," Scheidt said. "He was so small, but he had so much determination. As a pitcher, he barely topped fifty miles per hour, but he had all these other pitches, and he did magical things with slow speed."

For the first two years of Little League, Tom played all the positions and emerged as the team's best hitter, with ten home runs in 1956. But the following year, his last in Little League, he decided to concentrate solely on pitching—albeit hitting .540 in the process. He liked the idea of being in charge of the game, and he worked all spring on throwing strikes in the morning hours at the local junior high school field with his Little League teammates Scheidt, Cliff Harris, and Jeff Ring, and later on at team practice.

"I used to have him throw batting practice to me three, four times a week," said Harris. "My idea was that he would throw strikes and let me hit the ball. His idea was he would throw fastballs and then argue balls and strikes. One hundred-five-degree day, I'm in the cage, waiting for him to pitch, and instead of a fastball, he throws a curveball that breaks right down the middle of the plate. There was no way I could miss it, except I was completely fooled. As I fell to my knees, cursing him out, he stood on the mound and just laughed and laughed."

In the years that followed, that happened a lot. If there was one thing Tom Seaver was most proud of it was his ability to outthink hitters.

Actually, Seaver had been working on throwing strikes from the time he was six years old, when he and Scheidt—who lived in one of the houses on the other side of Arthur Avenue—would throw a baseball back and forth across the street to each other. Their parents had forbade each of them from leaving the property, so they knew that one errant throw into the street, and the game was over. "None ever did," Scheidt said assuredly.

When he wasn't playing baseball, Seaver and another neighborhood buddy, Mike Podsakoff, who played against him in Little League, spent hours hanging out in the shoe store at the end of the block. The owner, Gary Kazanjian, was fifteen years older than the two boys, but he shared their love of baseball and over time became like a second father to them. "Gary was just a real likeable guy," Podsakoff recalled. "We'd hang out there all day, just shooting the bull. Like Tom became an artist on the pitching mound, Gary was an artist making shoes, especially women's shoes. There was nothing to do in Fresno in the summers except play baseball, so we'd go down to the store in the morning and watch Gary carefully stitching and painting the shoes—he always had time for us. We could talk to him about everything, and he had a huge influence on Tom."

By the time he was twelve, in his final year of Little League, all the work Seaver had put in with his control and constantly developing different pitches was paying off. He won all seven of his starts in 1957 in dominating fashion. On June 20 he struck out sixteen of eighteen batters (Little League games were only six innings) in beating the North Fresno Lions, 6–1. Seaver remembered how he felt in complete control that day.

"When I took the mound, I looked around and saw my mom in the stands, where she always sat, and my dad behind the center field fence with our dog 'Little Bit,' and I was completely relaxed," he said. "I don't know how many pitches I threw that day, but I know it wasn't a whole lot because I threw strikes."

Seaver and Jeff Ring (who was 6-0) led North Fresno Rotary to a 13-1 record and the Spartan Little League Association championship in 1957—"Tom's first championship," said Ring, a three-sport (baseball, football, and basketball) standout who, all through high school, was considered a better prospect than Seaver until severely dislocating his shoulder in a recreational basketball game during his freshman year at the University of California.

"Even though we were teammates from Little League all through high school, we were rivals," said Ring, who hit .428, .432, and .409 in his three years on the Fresno High School varsity. "Tom was a good basketball player too, and he had this great, accurate arm, and it was too bad his folks wouldn't let him play football. I always said the best quarterback we had at Fresno High was the guy who didn't play."

Much as he'd excelled in Little League, by the time he was fifteen and beginning high school, Seaver found himself facing the same challenge all over again: at five foot six, 140 pounds, he was still one of the smallest players on the field; at the same time, his teammates and opponents had all grown taller and stronger and were no longer overpowered by his fastball.

In the 1950s, Fresno High was an athletic powerhouse. The 1958 varsity baseball team was ranked the number one high school team in the country and featured three players—pitchers Jim Maloney and Dick Ellsworth and catcher Pat Corrales—who all went on to success-ful major-league careers. Every regular on that team either signed a pro contract or earned a college scholarship.

Whatever dreams Seaver may have had for going pro or scoring a scholarship were quickly dashed when he failed to make the Fresno High varsity his sophomore year. Instead, he was completely over-shadowed by a hard-throwing five-foot-eleven junior right-hander, Dick Selma, who, ironically, wound up as a teammate with the Mets in 1967–68. They didn't have radar guns back in those days, but Selma's fastball and curve were superior to those of all the other local high school pitchers—with the possible exception of Wade Blasingame, a six-foot left-hander who went 26-0 in three years at Fresno's rival Roosevelt High School and signed a $125,000 bonus with the Mil-waukee Braves in 1961. The only times major-league scouts showed up at the Fresno High games were on the days Selma was pitching or Blasingame was pitching against them.

"Tom was a slow developer," said Podsakoff, "but he was able to dominate with finesse. He'd figure out a batter's weakness, and you were not going to get a pitch you could hit. He might not have looked the part physically, but you knew Tom would be competitive. Still, back then, no one would have predicted he'd ever be in the majors."

In a 1968 interview when he was with the Mets, Selma said: "Even when he was on the JV in high school, Tom was a heck of a pitcher, as contrasted to a thrower. He knew how to set up hitters even in high school, something I'm just learning now."

Despite a rather pedestrian 6-5 won-lost record as a senior, Seaver was selected by the *Fresno Bee* for the 1962 All-City team. As Jeff Ring said, "I can assure you all five of those losses were games in which Tom gave up only one or two runs." In the words of Fresno High coach Fred Bartels, he was still pretty much a "junk ball pitcher." Nevertheless, Bartels was impressed with Seaver's seriousness and pitch concentration on the mound—as opposed to his carefree, happy-go-lucky, sometimes mischievous demeanor off it. Bartels was a taskmaster, prone to profane outbursts when his players would miss a sign or screw up in the field or on the base paths—which Seaver was a master at deflecting.

"Tom was just so much fun," said Podsakoff. "If one of us made an error behind him, he'd turn around and walk toward us with his glove over his face and start yelling as if he were Bartels, 'How'd you fuck that one up?' Bartels never heard him, but that served to help us relax and get us back in the game."

Bartels was also the coach of Seaver's American Legion Baseball team, which advanced through several levels of the California state championships in the summer of 1961. On the bus to the American Legion playoffs in Ontario, California, Bartels overheard some of the players talking about betting. When they arrived at their hotel, Bartels issued a warning: "I don't want any of you guys getting involved in gambling here. You need to be concentrating on nothing but baseball." He did not know that his junk-ball pitching ace had decided to provide a little extracurricular activity for his mates in the form of a mouse race similar to the famous scene in the 1953 film *Stalag 17*, about a group of American airmen in a German POW camp during World War II.

"As we were strolling through town, we stopped at a pet store, where we bought a bunch of mice," recalled Jeff Ring. "Tom had come up with this idea that we would race these mice back at the hotel, and everyone would bet on them—just like in the *Stalag 17* movie with

William Holden. He thought that if he blew on the ass of his mouse, he could make it go faster. That was his plan."

There was only one problem: when the boys released the mice in one of the hotel's hallways, waiting to see which one would be the first to get to the other end, the mice all ran under the doors of the rooms along the way. Nobody won any money, but when Bartels later found out about the caper, he was annoyed but could also appreciate Seaver's leadership skills in organizing it.

Unfortunately, such attributes do not show up in the scouting reports, and when the school year ended, both Jeff Ring and Cliff Harris had landed baseball scholarships, to Stanford and Cal, respectively, but Seaver had no offers to turn pro or go to college. He knew why, and it ate at him. One day after one of their basketball games the previous winter, he'd expressed his frustration about his height to Ring. Citing the fact that his father and brother were both over six feet, and all the women in his family were also tall, he said, "I wish I knew when I was gonna grow."

Ring was confident it wouldn't be long, the reason being Seaver's hands, which, he said, even in Little League, were so much larger than everyone else's. They were in a pizza place and, to prove his point, Ring spotted one of the other Fresno High basketball players, John Loyer, and called him over to the table. The six-foot-four Loyer was headed to the University of Missouri on a basketball scholarship. Ring asked him to match his hands next to Seaver's. "It was truly amazing," Ring said. "Tom's hands nearly dwarfed Loyer's."

Reassuring as that little experiment may have been, Seaver had already determined he wasn't going to hang around Fresno waiting to grow. He had also told his parents that he was never going to allow them to subsidize his college education. If he couldn't get into college on a baseball scholarship, he would just find something else. The Vietnam War was just beginning in 1962, and Seaver knew that if he wasn't in school, he ran the risk of being drafted into the army for two years. After graduation, he'd spent a couple of months packing and shelving boxes of raisins at Bonner Packing—a job he detested. He thought about his options. His brother, Charles, had been in the marines, and, after reading up on the US Marines Corps Reserves, Tom was intrigued. He made the decision this would be his something else. Russ Scheidt was similarly adrift after high school, working in a local filling station, when Seaver approached him one morning.

"He told me he was signing up for Marine Reserves, and he wanted to know if I'd go with him," Scheidt said in a 2019 interview. "I said, 'Sure, why not?' I wasn't doing anything, and I actually looked forward to the marine experience."

Beginning June 28, 1962, Seaver and Scheidt spent the next six months in boot camp with the AirFMFPac (Aircraft, Fleet Marine Force, Pacific) Reserves in Twentynine Palms, California, which was about 330 miles southeast of Fresno. Despite the exhaustive and seemingly relentless mental and physical punishment from the drill instructors, after their training exercises every day Seaver insisted on getting in his pitching. "He'd pitch, and I'd catch," said Scheidt, "right in the middle of the Mohave Desert! I remember saying to myself, 'He's gonna go someplace.'" What was also apparent to Scheidt was that, with each passing week, Seaver was growing. When he'd arrived at Twentynine Palms, he was five foot nine, 150 pounds. When he got out six months later, he was six foot one, 210.

"I found out quickly that I'd have been a whole lot more comfortable going to school than in marine boot camp," Seaver told me in 2016. "But, of course, it was the best thing that ever happened for me.

When I came out, with all that extra height and weight, I found I could throw harder than ever before. The curveball and slider my dad had taught me now had something on them. I was a complete pitcher."

Cliff Harris remembered the day Seaver showed up at his front door after he returned home to Fresno. "My father had always called him 'little Tommy Seaver,' and there he was, four inches taller and nearly fifty pounds heavier. I saw the size, and I was amazed. I remember flashing through my mind: 'He's got everything he needs now.' "

"It was more than just the physical size," said Larry Woods. "It was the mental discipline. You could see he was much more focused."

Seaver would always say those six months in the Marine Reserves defined him as a person. "You know the saying, 'He came in as a boy and went out as a man'? Well, that was so true. Growing up, in Little League, Babe Ruth, and high school, I always prided myself in my preparedness on the mound and my ability to outsmart the hitters. I didn't know what it was to be truly mentally disciplined until I came out of the marines."

Back in civilian life, Seaver was eager to resume his baseball career and, more importantly, to find out what kind of pitcher he really was in this new body of his. As always, he had a plan. He would enroll at Fresno City College, majoring in dentistry—there always had to be a backup plan—and he would pitch for the Rams in hopes of performing well enough to get a scholarship from a Division I program, specifically, the University of Southern California (USC), a college baseball powerhouse under the legendary coach Rod Dedeaux. He called Fred Bartels and asked him if he would contact his friend Len Bourdet, the coach at Fresno City College, and tell him he was enrolling at the school and planning to play baseball. Bourdet was thrilled but wanted to see him on the mound. The next day, Seaver strolled onto the Fresno City College baseball field, where Bourdet and Bartels were waiting along with Brendan Ounjian, the Fresno City catcher. Bartels was astounded at how big he'd gotten. "Now *I* want to see him pitch," he told Bourdet, who himself had never seen Seaver pitch in person. Seaver took the mound and, for the first time he could ever remember, felt uneasy. "What if my control isn't there?" he asked himself. But then he reared back and fired a fastball—a fastball with such ferocity it stung Ounjian's hand, and he dropped it. Just as important, it was a strike. Seaver smiled in satisfaction. After firing off a dozen or so fastballs, along with a couple sliders, he looked at Bartels, who was shaking his head. "I think you've got something here, Len," he said to Bourdet. "This is a whole new Tom Seaver from the one I had. You're not going to have him for long."

According to Bourdet, Seaver was very up front with him about that.

"I couldn't believe how much he'd grown," Bourdet said in a 2019 interview, "and then he threw that first pitch, which had to be in the low nineties, and it was quite a surprise to my catcher. We talked afterward, and Tom was honest with me. He said he wanted me to know that he was only going to pitch one year at Fresno City and then transfer to USC. That was his plan, and I was good with that. Heck, I was just happy to have him for the one year. He was a stud by then."

Seaver had quite the year for the Rams, 11-2, with a fastball that was now peaking in the midnineties, along with the secondary pitches he'd been perfecting since high school. And all of a sudden, the scouts were coming. At the end of the season, the Los Angeles Dodgers offered him $2,000. It was flattering, especially in light of the snubbing he'd received after high school, but it wasn't what he wanted.

Other than having proved to himself that he had big-time college potential, Seaver's Fresno City College experience was made all the more enjoyable by the close and lasting friendship he formed with the

Rams' second baseman, Don Reinero. The five-foot-nine, 160-pound Reinero was the team pepper pot, always hustling, always stirring it up. Because he'd played against Seaver (for Roosevelt) in high school, they didn't hang in the same circle of friends then. They did, however, share in common the same fate of being deemed too small to warrant a substantial college scholarship despite having both been selected to the All-Fresno high school team in 1962. Seaver admired Reinero's scrappy, full-out style of play and relished his sense of humor. At last, a friend who could rank on people even better than he could.

"Reinero was the comedian among us," said Ounjian in a 2019 interview. "He could be merciless. After Tom made it big, he would constantly ask him: 'How much money you make today, Tom? C'mon, you can tell us! Don't be embarrassed!'"

"Tom always seemed to cultivate the little guys, like Donny, and, later with the Mets, Bud Harrelson," said Larry Woods. "I think he drew from their energy."

Seaver and Reinero also shared the same November 17 birthday. "That was something Don was always most proud of," said Reinero's wife, Joyce.

Throughout his career and after he retired, Seaver stayed in regular contact with all his Fresno friends, especially Reinero. ("Tom and Don were very, very close," said Bourdet.) In 1992, when Seaver was in his fourth season of handling play-by-play and color commentary on WPIX Yankees telecasts, he invited Reinero, Woods, and Clyde Corsby, the second baseman on their Little League team, to come up to Oakland for the weekend series between the Yankees and the Athletics. They played golf on Friday at the Olympic Club in San Francisco, and on Saturday Seaver brought them up to the TV booth to watch the game from there while he and Phil Rizzuto did the broadcast.

They were in baseball heaven, particularly Reinero, who immediately hit it off with his fellow *paisan* Rizzuto, who'd been his idol growing up. In between innings, Reinero and Rizzuto, fellow shortstops in high school, compared notes about being told they were too small to play in the big leagues. Rizzuto, five foot six and 150 pounds, told his favorite story about going to a Brooklyn Dodgers tryout camp in the mid-1930s and being told by manager Casey Stengel to "go home and get yourself a shoe box." Instead of becoming a shoeshine boy, Rizzuto went on to a Hall of Fame career with the Yankees in the 1940s and 1950s—the latter years for none other than Stengel. Reinero insisted to Rizzuto he'd been a better player than Seaver. "I was even bigger than him in high school; can ya believe that?"

"One of the great weekends of our life," said Woods.

And then on September 27, 1994, Don Reinero was riding his bike in the foothills of Fresno when a drunk driver struck him from behind, sending him spinning up in the air before landing headfirst on top of a car. He was taken to the hospital with permanent stage 3 brain damage that left him in a coma. Seaver, who had been let go by WPIX the previous March after five years in the Yankees' broadcast booth, was home in Greenwich when he heard the news. It seemed unfathomable. As soon as he could, he flew out to Fresno, where he hooked up with Woods to visit Reinero. Seeing his friend lying motionless, his eyes closed, hooked up to a ventilator and a feeding tube, was heartbreaking. Fighting back tears, Seaver knelt next to the bed, took off his 1969 World Series ring, and gently slipped it onto Reinero's finger. "I'm here, Donny," he said. "You've got to get through this."

But there was no response. As Woods related, even when Reinero later opened his eyes briefly, they couldn't tell if he recognized them. They stayed for about an hour, talking about old times on the Fresno baseball fields, hoping that maybe their friend could hear and signal some recognition. When they left the room, Seaver turned to Woods and said: "I don't want to have to see him like this again."

Still, he wouldn't give up hope. He wanted to stay in constant touch but rejected the idea of placing phone calls to Reinero and having someone—Woods or a family member—place the phone next to his ear. Not lasting enough, he said, and with no response on the other end of the phone, he'd have no idea if Reinero could even hear him. Then, over lunch with Rizzuto at the Hall of Fame inductions in 1995, he came up with an idea. Together they would make an audiotape on which they would talk in intervals to Reinero, pumping him up, telling jokes, promising to take him to the World Series as soon as he was able. Woods, who was in the radio business, edited the tape and brought it with him to the hospital to play for Donny. Sitting on the bed, he placed the small tape recorder next to the comatose Reinero's ear and held his hand. "Donny, I hope you can hear this," he said as he pressed the Play button.

It sounded like they were doing an actual broadcast together:

Seaver: Hi, Don. This is Tom Seaver, and I'm here in Cooperstown, New York. I'm with Phil Rizzuto, and we just saw one of the great moments of baseball and great moments of our lifetime—Mike Schmidt being inducted into the Hall of Fame—and it brought back a lot of great memories, and we just thought we would yak a little here for a few minutes with you and hope it would bring back a lot of great memories for you when you were here with all the gang from Fresno in 1992.

Rizzuto: Hey, Don Reinero. How ya doin'? Ya know, we little guys gotta stick together. You're a real battler, and you gotta battle through this. I hate to see this happen, and I know you can overcome it. You can't give up. You've gotta battle, Reinero! Now, I've gotta go out to the coast in two weeks on one of my infrequent trips out there—I've got to do it—but I'd love to see you.

Seaver: Maybe do the game together?

Rizzuto: Yeah. Absolutely. You'll be my guest, Reinero. Come up to the booth, and we'll talk on the air.

Seaver: Bring Larry Woods and Clyde Corsby along?

Rizzuto: Oh yeah. It was really a lot of fun meeting all you guys from Fresno with Seaver. Of course, Seaver's not a lot of fun. He's a pain in the ass. I know you're gonna be all right, Reinero, because I'd really like to see you.

Seaver: You know, Donny was a pretty good little ballplayer, Scooter. He was a pretty good hitter. He used to tease me that he could hit me like a drum.

Rizzuto: Did he really hit you?

Seaver: Well, that's a bone of contention. He was a good little infielder who could spray the ball around. We played against each other in Little League and high school and were teammates in Babe Ruth League and college.

Rizzuto: I know Seaver's a good friend of yours, Reinero, because he got me up here in this room after I just got back from the hot, sweaty ceremonies where they also inducted Richie Ashburn, another little guy! You know I hit more home runs than he did? Imagine that, Reinero!

Seaver: Speaking of sticking together, Scooter, tell Donny how well we worked together.

Rizzuto: Ohhh . . . when Seaver came to the broadcast booth, I almost quit! I said: "How the hell can I work with a Met?" But he grows on you, and you better listen to him, Reinero.

Seaver: The reason I went to work for the Yankees was because they offered me a job. I had one daughter in college and another on the way.

Rizzuto: I miss you, Seaver. It's amazing how many people I see who ask me, "Where's Seaver?" We worked great together. We didn't ever step on each other, and, Reinero, I know you're a good teammate, and you're gonna come out of this all right.

Seaver: Hey, Don, we've had a great time at the Hall of Fame here. It's a special time, and we were thinking about you, and we're pulling for you. And if Rizzuto says it, and gives you an order, you better get it done.

Rizzuto: Yeah, listen, Don, this is Scooter again. If you get through this, and I know you will, we're gonna go to the World Series. Or whenever you come to Oakland, you'll come up in the booth. We'll talk about Seaver—pump him up a little. I know your wife has been great, too, sticking with you through thick and thin, and I'm sure with a few prayers, and we'll light a few candles here and then, that you'll pull through.

Seaver: Good luck, Donny. I'll be by to see you when I get back to Fresno, buddy. And we'll work it when you get up north, we'll even get Rizzuto to buy you dinner—and he hates to do that!

Rizzuto: Oh, gladly. I *do* hate to do that.

Seaver: Donny, take care and say "hi" to everybody.

Rizzuto: So long, Donny!

As the tape was playing, Seaver and Rizzuto going on with their spiel, Woods said the most extraordinary thing happened.

"All of a sudden, Donny, who up to then had shown no sign of being aware of what was going on around him, started squeezing my hand, harder, harder, and harder until I could barely release it. And then his eyes opened, and he was crying."

Although there was no bringing him back—Reinero lived another fifteen years in the coma—Seaver's only solace was that, through the tape, he had at least been able to communicate to his friend how much he loved him and that his friend was able to know that.

CHAPTER 3

The Accidental Met

TRANSFERRING FROM FRESNO CITY COLLEGE FOR A SCHOLAR-ship at the University of Southern California was not quite the seamless transition Tom Seaver had envisioned. The distance from Fresno to Los Angeles is only 224 miles, but Seaver would be not able to complete that journey without first going through Alaska.

USC coach Rod Dedeaux ran the number one baseball program in the country. Under Dedeaux, the USC Trojans had already won national championships in 1958, 1961, and 1963, and would go on to win seven more before the great coach retired in 1986. In all, he sent fifty-nine players to the big leagues. The New Orleans native, then in his twenty-third of forty-five seasons as USC coach, was definitely interested in Seaver, kiddingly referring to him as "the *phee*-nom from San Joaquin," but Dedeaux needed to be sure he could compete with the big boys of college baseball. According to Seaver, Dedeaux told him: "I have only five scholarships to give out, and I'm going to hold one for you, but first I want you to go up to Alaska."

"Alaska?" Seaver asked.

"You're gonna love it, kid," Dedeaux said.

The coach had worked out an arrangement to send Seaver to the

Alaska Goldpanners of the Alaska Baseball League, an amateur collegiate summer league that had been founded in 1960 and served as a showcase for college and junior college players. Its founder, H. A. "Red" Boucher, was on the Fairbanks City Council and manager of the Goldpanners. Highly respected for his baseball acumen throughout the collegiate baseball community, Boucher over the years was able to recruit the best collegiate players to the Goldpanners, among them Rick Monday, Andy Messersmith, Graig Nettles, Bill "Spaceman" Lee, Steve Kemp, Floyd Bannister, Dave Winfield, Jim Sundberg, Terry Francona, and Kevin McReynolds.

So, once again, Seaver was being challenged to prove himself. He was only nineteen, and he was going to be facing more experienced and accomplished collegians two and three years older than he was. That was the whole idea for Dedeaux.

When Seaver got off the plane in Fairbanks in mid-June 1964, Boucher was there to greet him. "You won't be needing those," he said, pointing to the sweater and topcoat Seaver was wearing in expectation of spending a summer in near-freezing temperatures. The forty-three-year-old Boucher would also be putting him up with his family. On June 21, the summer solstice, Seaver pitched in the Midnight Sun Game, the traditional Alaska League opener, which began at ten thirty at night and usually ended somewhere around one thirty in the morning—all under the sunlight—at Fairbanks's Growden Memorial Park. Boucher used him both as a starter and in relief that summer, and Seaver thrived in the eternal daylight of Alaska.

"Alaska was something else," he told the New York baseball scribes a couple of years later. "You can't realize what a magnificent place it is unless you've been there. The weather in July and August is ideal—in the high sixties and seventies every day and no humidity. I remember one of my first nights there, I woke up at three in the morning and saw the sun coming through my windows, and I thought I'd blown my job. Playing night games without lights, that was really strange."

It was a continuation of Seaver's learning process. He appeared in nineteen games for the Goldpanners in '64, only five as a starting pitcher. He was 6-2, with a save and a 4.27 ERA, but with 70 strikeouts in 58⅔ innings. He put himself in the Goldpanners' record books in August when, at the National Baseball Congress World Series in Wichita, Kansas, he combined with Mike Paul (who would also go on to a major-league pitching career mostly with the Cleveland Indians and Texas Rangers) on a 6–0 no-hitter against Brandon, Nebraska, in the semifinals.

Boucher had chosen Seaver for the final roster spot for the NBC tournament over another future standout major-league pitcher, Ken Holtzman. Later in the same tournament, Seaver had an even bigger thrill, this one with his bat. After coming on in relief against the home-town Wichita Glassmen team with the bases loaded in the sixth inning, Seaver proceeded to walk the first two batters and then gave up a run-scoring single before finally retiring the side. He was therefore a little surprised when Boucher allowed him to hit for himself in the seventh after the Goldpanners had likewise loaded the bases. Going all the way back to Little League, he had always taken pride in his hitting, and the determined look on his face as he knelt in the on-deck circle must have convinced Boucher. Still, as he confessed later, even Seaver was happily stunned when he was able to reward his manager's confidence by hitting a grand slam. "Up to now, this is the highlight of my baseball career," Seaver told the media.

• • •

When Seaver returned home at the end of the summer, Dedeaux congratulated him on his successful season with the Goldpanners and welcomed him to the USC varsity—with a full ride. But leaving nothing to chance, Seaver enrolled at USC as a pre-dentistry major. He also joined the Sigma Chi fraternity, only to drop out because he disdained the *Animal House* party environment of fraternity life and moved into an apartment with Dedeaux's son Justin.

It was during spring practice the following March that one of his USC classmates, Jerry Merz, a phys ed major, recommended he start lifting light weights to increase his upper body strength. "It will help give you more velocity and avoid injuries to your arm down the road," Merz said. And it paid off as Seaver's fastball, which had regularly registered around ninety-two miles per hour with the Goldpanners, was now reaching the midnineties with USC.

Seaver began the 1965 USC season as Dedeaux's number three starter but by May had begun to establish himself as a potential pro prospect. A turning point was a game he started against the Trojans' alumni, some of whom had graduated to the big leagues. A bunch of pro scouts were there, and the first batter he faced was Ron Fairly—at the time the Dodgers' first baseman—whom he was able to retire on a weak pop-up with his slider. Jogging back to the dugout, Fairly shouted to Seaver within hearing distance of the scouts: "That was a pretty good pitch, kid!" Seaver was elated.

One of Seaver's 1965 Trojans teammates was Mike Garrett, the short but sturdy All-America running back on the USC football team who would go on to win the Heisman Trophy as the outstanding college player in the nation that fall and then spend eight successful seasons in the American Football League and the National Football League. The story Seaver loved telling—and which Garrett later confirmed—involved an impromptu but epic pitcher-batter face-off between the two during a preseason intramural game. During batting practice they were joking around, and Seaver began jabbing Garrett.

"You're nothing but a dead fastball hitter," he said, "and that's all I'm gonna throw you when I face you today. I'm gonna strike you out on three pitches."

"Feel free," said Garrett. "But be prepared. There won't be but one pitch."

As Garrett came to the plate in the very first inning, Seaver shouted from the mound, "Remember, only fastballs!"

True to his word, Seaver's first pitch was a fastball up and away, which Garrett swung at and missed. The next pitch, another fastball, was up and in. Again, a swing and a miss. Seaver was now thoroughly juiced up for his third pitch. The fiercely determined Garrett dug in, squeezed his bat harder, and began his stride. But instead of the anticipated heater, Seaver's pitch seemed to float to the plate—a changeup!—thoroughly fooling Garrett. With an unbalanced swing, way out in front of the ball, he fell to one knee and couldn't get up.

"You son of a bitch!" Garrett screamed, pounding his bat in the dirt. On the mound, Seaver convulsed with laughter.

"Maybe the greatest strikeout of my career, better than Mays, better than McCovey, better than Aaron!" he told Garrett when the two happened to meet up at an NFL game between the New York Jets and Kansas City Chiefs (for whom Garrett was then playing) at Shea Stadium in 1969.

Seaver finished the 1965 USC season with a 10-2 record, 2.47 ERA, and 100 strikeouts in 105⅔ innings. With each succeeding start, he pitched with more and more confidence, and his teammates could sense that. By the end of the season, he was the acknowledged Trojans leader. Both he and Dedeaux were well pleased at how the quality of his pitches and his self-confidence had come around. As a reaffirmation of that, on June 8, the Dodgers selected Seaver in the tenth round of the major-league draft.

In those days, the only players who were offered big money were the ones taken in the first or second rounds. Accordingly, the Dodgers' offer was only $2,000. The twenty-year-old talked it over with his father, and they both agreed it wasn't nearly enough for him to leave college. They elected to wait until the January 1966 winter draft, which was for all the players who were either not drafted in June or failed to sign. In the meantime, Seaver was more convinced than ever that his career plan was right on schedule.

"I learned more in one year at USC under Coach Dedeaux than I would have in two or three seasons in the low minors," he said years later. "Most of all, I learned concentration and to stay in the game mentally."

With no assurance of what the January draft might bring, Seaver elected to return to Alaska and join the Goldpanners late in their 1965 season. One of his teammates was another right-handed power pitcher, Danny Frisella, who would become one of his teammates with the Mets from 1967 through 1972. Once again, he stayed at Red Boucher's house. As part of the deal, the Goldpanners players were required to work local jobs. Frisella drove a lumber truck, and Boucher appointed Seaver to be the Growden Memorial Park groundskeeper, mowing the grass and watering the infield. He appeared in only eight games for the Goldpanners in '65, six of them starts, striking out fifty-one in 45⅔ innings and posting a 1.95 ERA. More importantly, now there were at least a dozen scouts at every game he pitched.

A dozen years later, while moonlighting during the postseason as an ABC-TV broadcaster for the 1977 World Series, Seaver paid tribute to Boucher. He and the other announcers had been talking about the Goldpanners, and Seaver said, "If you're watching, Red, I want to express my appreciation for the opportunity you made available to me and the time you spent helping me as a Goldpanner. It was a vital step in my progress."

On January 29, 1966, in the secondary phase (for previously drafted players) of the baseball winter draft, Seaver was selected by the Braves, who'd left Milwaukee over the winter and set up shop in Atlanta. He was elated to be drafted by the Braves because his favorite player was Hank Aaron, who was already well on his way to becoming a Braves immortal. He was even more excited, however, when the Braves ponied up a $40,000 bonus, plus an additional $11,500 to complete his college education, to sign him.

Seaver inked a contract a few days after the draft and looked forward to starting his professional career. That night, his parents held a farewell barbeque for him at the house in Fresno, with all his high school teammates and buddies in attendance. "Say hello to Hank Aaron for me," said Russ Scheidt with a trace of wistfulness.

But it was not to be—at least not quite yet, and not with the Braves. Shortly before signing, Seaver had played a couple of games for USC that he thought were exhibitions, against California Polytech University and San Fernando State College. They were, in fact, part of the Trojans' official schedule. Another major-league team, later revealed to be the Dodgers, called this to the attention of the Office of the Commissioner of Baseball, maintaining the signing was illegal because Seaver had already begun his second year as a collegian and therefore was ineligible to be drafted. Rules were rules, and Commissioner William Eckert had no choice but to void Seaver's contract with Atlanta.

Though Braves publicity director Jerry Sachs issued a statement saying the signing was "an honest mistake" and that the Braves "didn't realize those early games constituted intercollegiate matches," Eckert fined the club $500 for signing a player still in college. At the same time, the National Collegiate Athletic Association (NCAA) declared Seaver ineligible to pitch for USC because he had signed a pro contract.

Suddenly Seaver found himself in no-man's-land: not only still undrafted and without a pro contract but also ineligible to return to college. Charlie Seaver was furious. His son had done nothing wrong, and yet he was being screwed by everyone. After discussing the situation with some of his powerful friends in sports and the legal profession, he wrote to Eckert threatening to sue Major League Baseball if this issue with his son was not rectified immediately. The commissioner's written response didn't offer any promise of resolving it. So, Tom took it upon himself to call Eckert's office, pleading with his assistant, Lee MacPhail, for a solution. The commissioner finally agreed that the matter had to be remedied and issued a bulletin inviting any of the nineteen other clubs willing to match the Braves' offer of $51,500 by April 1 to participate in a drawing for Seaver. Only three sent wires of intent: the Cleveland Indians, the Philadelphia Phillies, and the New York Mets.

Late in the afternoon of April 3, Seaver, who'd been waiting by the phone with his parents, got a call from MacPhail informing him that Eckert was in the process of pulling one of the three telegrams out of the hat of the commissioner's aide, Joe Reichler. In the days leading up to the lottery, he'd thought a lot about which team he'd most like to pitch for. All of them were thousands of miles away from Fresno on the other side of the country. In that respect, he was curious as to why the Dodgers hadn't chosen to take part, especially after they'd drafted him the previous June and were widely believed to be the ones who'd blown the whistle on the Braves. While not admitting they were the whistleblowers, Dodgers general manager Buzzie Bavasi revealed to the *Long Island Press* beat writer Jack Lang in 1967 that he had intended to send a wire to Eckert about Seaver but got sidetracked by the increasingly rancorous contract negotiations he was having with his two pitching aces, Sandy Koufax and Don Drysdale, in their unprecedented dual holdout that winter.

On the surface, aside from their geography, none of the three participating teams was particularly appealing. The Phillies hadn't been to the World Series since 1950, the Indians not since 1954, while the Mets, born as a National League expansion team in 1962, had lost more than a hundred games in each of their first four seasons and were generally regarded as the worst team in baseball. Still, when MacPhail announced that Eckert had just plucked the Mets' telegram out of the hat, Seaver smiled.

"Guess which team, Mom?" he said.

"Oh my God! Not the *Mets*?" Betty Seaver shrieked in mock horror.

But Seaver was secretly happy with the outcome. It didn't matter to him that the Mets had been a laughingstock their first four years of existence. He'd had nothing to do with that. What intrigued him was the prospect of going to a team that could only get better and that offered him the opportunity to move quickly through the minor leagues and, hopefully, play a key role in turning it into a winner.

Before he could embark on his professional career, however, there was one other matter Seaver needed to sort out. Over the course of the last two years, he had fallen in love. He had first taken notice of Nancy McIntyre, a beautiful, slender, athletic California blonde (by way of Kansas), when he was playing basketball for Fresno High and she was a cheerleader for rival McLane High. He made a mental note to pursue her when the time was right—which turned out to be the spring of 1964, when both of them were at Fresno City College. He'd seen her periodically around campus and was working up his nerve to ask her out, but he also knew that she had most recently been dating his Fresno CC Rams catcher, Brendan Ounjian.

"I'd only dated Nancy for a few months, and it had been a while since we broke up, when Tom told me he was planning to ask her out, but he wanted to make sure there'd be no hard feelings if he did," Ounjian said. "I was frankly a little surprised he would ask me that, but that's the kind of guy Tom was."

Not long after that conversation, Seaver and some pals were drinking beer after playing a game of slo-pitch softball when one of them spotted Nancy, standing by herself, on the other side of the field. "There she is," one of them said to Seaver. "I dare you to run over there and tackle her." Fortified with a few beers, Seaver instantly accepted the challenge, racing across the field and flinging himself full force into Nancy, knocking her to the ground, breathless. It should have been the end of the relationship right there, but for some reason, after picking herself up, Nancy was more astonished than angry, especially when, after apologizing, Seaver then had the audacity to ask to take her out for coffee.

"First I said 'No,' and then I said, 'Yes, I'll go out with you, but under the condition that you must bring me home immediately,'" Nancy recalled in a 2017 interview. "And that was it. I think we wound up staying out until two o'clock in the morning, just talking. We walked on the golf course by his house. He was just so interesting and charismatic and so polite. I had so much fun with him. He talked about things that were a lot more serious than I was. He was a lot more mature than I was. I was originally a Kansas girl who moved to California when I was eleven. He would talk about life and the world, and this was something I hadn't really thought about. If it wasn't in Kansas or Fresno, it was a little out of my realm."

They started seeing each other regularly and would go on more walks on the golf course, talking about their goals. Tom made no secret of his love for baseball and his designs on getting a scholarship to USC after a year of pitching for Fresno City College. But just in case, he said, he also had thoughts of being a dentist or a veterinarian. He was hoping that baseball would pay for his schooling and that, if all went right, he would maybe get a job in the major leagues.

"He wanted me to watch him play," Nancy said, "and I said, 'Okay, I'll bring my pom-poms and watch you play.' He never said, 'I'm going to be a big baseball star.' He said he just wanted to *see* what he could do."

They dated off and on that year, and in the spring Nancy went to his games. She dated others when he went off to the Goldpanners that summer, but she knew that he was the one. And the feeling was mutual. At USC the following year, Tom called her every other day.

"What are the girls like there?" she'd ask.

"Nothing like you," he said. "They're boring. All they want to do is party and shop for clothes."

He liked her down-to-earth wholesomeness. There was nothing artificial about her. They just clicked. Then his plans all began coming together. Now, in a couple of weeks, he was to report to the Mets' minor league spring training complex in Homestead, Florida, but before departing, he used part of his bonus money to buy Nancy an engagement ring.

Nelson Burbrink, the Mets' Southern California scout who signed him after firmly recommending they get into the lottery for him, met with Seaver when he arrived in Homestead and assured him that no matter how he pitched in spring training, the team was prepared to start him out at a high level of the minors in '66. It turned out to be the very highest level: the Triple-A Jacksonville Suns of the International League. As evidenced by the Jacksonville club, which was composed mostly of retread former major leaguers, the Mets, in their first four years under the direction of aging general manager George Weiss, had been slow to develop young talent.

After an enormously successful career as general manager of the Yankees, in which they won ten American League pennants and seven World Series in his thirteen years at the helm, Weiss was forced into retirement after the 1960 season, only to be resurrected a few months later by Joan Whitney Payson, scion of the prominent Whitney family of philanthropists and thoroughbred horse racing royalty, and an avid baseball fan who'd been a minority stockholder in the New York Giants before buying the Mets as a National League expansion team. Weiss was sixty-seven and made, as his first hire, another oldster, seventy-one-year-old Casey Stengel, his manager with the Yankees from 1949 through 1960. It was a popular move with the fans, as was, initially, Weiss's decision to select older, mostly recognizable players in the 1961 expansion draft—among them former National League All-Stars Richie Ashburn and Gus Bell, while also acquiring ex–Brooklyn Dodgers Gil Hodges, Charlie Neal, Roger Craig, and Don Zimmer. All of them were past their prime. That decision, along with largely ignoring in the draft younger unprotected players in the established teams' farm systems, probably set the Mets back at least three or four years.

So they were an aged team from the beginning, playing their first two seasons in the Polo Grounds, a relic in Upper Manhattan, and without the great scouts and player development people who had served him so well with the Yankees all those years, Weiss made mostly poor choices in accumulating amateur talent, none worse than the record $100,000 bonus in 1964 he gave Dennis Musgraves, a right-handed pitcher out of the University of Missouri who went on to appear in only five games in the majors.

There were just a few genuine prospects on the '66 Jacksonville club: shortstop Bud Harrelson; a versatile good-hitting infielder, Ken Boswell; and the California golden boy who attracted all the media attention when Suns manager Solly Hemus gathered the team at Homestead. (Boswell would go on to become an integral player on the '69 world championship Mets team.)

"I remember watching Tom, surrounded by reporters in the clubhouse that first day and wondering what kind of guy he was," said Harrelson in a 2012 interview. "We all knew he'd gotten big money, and then we went out to take batting practice, and he's pitching, and I'm thinking he's probably gonna want to show off his hard stuff. But instead, he just laid 'em up in there for all of us, and that really impressed me. Wasn't long after we became the best of friends."

Seaver soon began to demonstrate to the Mets that their $51,500 investment was going to be money well spent. In his first professional start, he beat the Rochester Red Wings, the top affiliate of the Baltimore Orioles, 4–2, striking out eleven, then followed that with a two-hit shutout over the Buffalo Bisons, the Cincinnati Reds' triple-A team. "That's about the best first-year pitcher I can ever remember," Bisons manager Red Davis told the media glowingly, "and I've been in baseball for eighteen years now. We may be watching one of the great ones of our time." Added veteran Buffalo first baseman Tim Harkness, who'd previously played in the majors with the Dodgers and the Mets and had gone down swinging for the final out of the shutout: "His fast-ball just exploded when it reached the plate."

Hemus, manager of the St. Louis Cardinals from 1959 to 1961, was blunt in his assessment of the twenty-one-year-old prodigy, whom he called "Wonder Boy," in an interview with the *Sporting News*: "He's the best pitching prospect in the minor leagues. 'Wonder Boy' reminds me of Robin Roberts the way he throws, only he's faster than Roberts. He has a twenty-one-year-old arm and a thirty-five-year-old head." Roberts, about to enter his nineteenth and final season, won twenty or more games for the Philadelphia Phillies from 1950 through 1955 and would be enshrined in Cooperstown in 1976.

But as well as he'd been pitching, Seaver was feeling miserable in Jacksonville. He desperately missed Nancy. After winning his first three games, he lost the next four in a row. Minor league baseball was much different from the college game. There wasn't the same camara-derie. Here it was all business, with players fighting for their careers. He knew what he needed to get untracked, and it was her. Returning to his tiny room in the Roosevelt Hotel after a game one night, he sat down at the desk and began writing her a letter. Originally, they had planned to get married in September, after the season. According to Nancy, Tom formally proposed to her shortly before leaving for Jack-sonville "in his crummy Chevy with no heater." But he needed her with him now. In the letter, he expressed his loneliness and asked her to join him, and they would be married. Before sealing the envelope, he enclosed a one-way airplane ticket to Jacksonville. The letter sent, he followed it up with a phone call.

According to Nancy, "He told me, 'I'm going to send you a ticket to Florida. Will you come . . . here . . . and marry me?'"

After a brief pause, she blurted "Yes!" And she said she would. They both talked to their parents, but as Nancy said, there was no question. The day after the ticket arrived, she was on the plane to Florida. When she arrived at the Jacksonville airport in her white knitted skirt and carrying her Samsonite traveling luggage, Tom was waiting for her—to take her directly to Sam M. Wolfson Park for a Suns' twi-night double-header.

They were married on June 9, 1966, in Jacksonville, but it wasn't easy. There was a religion problem. Nancy was Catholic and Tom was Protestant. According to Nancy, they initially visited a Catholic church but before agreeing to marry them, the priest insisted that Tom take instructions on the Catholic faith. This was too much pressure for him and they instead found a Protestant minister who agreed immediately to perform the ceremony. Before doing so, however, he felt he had an obligation to at least inform the priest. "Father, if you won't marry these two nice young people then I will," the minister said, to which the priest quickly changed his stance. "The priest, seeing he was about to lose some business, told us to come on back over and he would marry us, which is what we did," Nancy said. "The minister came with us and served as the best man!"

Two nights later, Seaver, who wore number 21 for the Suns, ended a string of seven tries for his fourth win by once again dominating Buffalo in a complete-game four-hitter. For Tom, it was a relief and a comfort to have Nancy with him as he strove to impress the Mets brass for the next two months, all the while dreaming of what it would be like to pitch to the likes of Hank Aaron, Willie Mays, and Roberto Clemente. For Nancy, it was an abrupt introduction to all the uncertainties, insecurities, and loneliness of a baseball wife. They were married only three days when the Suns went on a two-week road trip. Alone in a strange city, with no friends, Nancy struggled to cope with her anxiety and homesickness. Occasionally, Tom would call from the road, but mostly he wrote letters to her, almost every day, and while they were comforting, they could not compensate for all the empty hours.

She also wasn't naïve. They'd moved into an apartment complex where some of the other players were staying, and she'd heard the wives talk about what went on with the players when they were on the road: the female baseball groupies, the parties. It gnawed at her. It was after the second or third long road trip that Tom came home and found her crying. When she expressed to him her fears, Nancy said he reminded her of all the reasons why she married him. "We both knew what a strain baseball can be on a marriage," he said, "but you have to trust me, and I know you do. Being apart for long periods of time is hard—hard for both of us—but I will never betray that trust."

In mid-July Seaver was joined in the Jacksonville rotation by Bill Denehy, a strapping six-foot-three, two-hundred-pound right-hander who was promoted after excelling at Double-A Williamsport in the Eastern League with a 9-2 record and 1.97 ERA. A native of Middle-town, Connecticut, Denehy had signed with the Mets out of high school a year earlier for a bonus of $22,500 and made a rapid rise through their system. If Seaver was regarded as the organization's West Coast pitching phenom, Denehy was its East Coast counterpart.

"By the time I got there," said Denehy in a 2019 interview, "there were a few other future major leaguers who'd joined the team: Tug McGraw, before he developed his screwball, [pitcher] Floyd Weaver and [second baseman] Ken Boswell. The three of them took me in and let me stay with them in their apartment. Actually, what happened was, Tug agreed to give me his bed, and he got himself a mattress and slept on the floor in the walk-in closet. It was like he was in a cave."

Tom and Nancy were in the same apartment complex, although

Denehy said they saw very little of them. "Sitting around the pool, which Tom never used, we use to joke, 'Why would he want to hang out here with us when he's got Nancy up there?' " Denehy said with a laugh.

Although they were both power pitchers, Denehy said there was definitely a contrast in styles. "Tom essentially had two fastballs—one rising and one sinking—plus a great slider, all with really good control," he said. "I, on the other hand, was just the opposite. I was always high and wild."

As it was, Denehy didn't pitch well for Jacksonville, appearing in only ten games, five of them starts, before developing a sore arm. Seaver finished the season with a perhaps respectable but hardly sensational 12-12 record and 3.13 ERA. The next spring, they were both invited to the Mets' major-league camp in Saint Petersburg, Florida, amid much hype and anticipation.

"Going into spring training, we were '1-A' and '1-B,' " said Denehy. "The scouts said you could flip a coin as to who was better."

But while they both would make the team as part of the initial '67 Mets starting rotation, Denehy's tenure was to be short lived.

Bothered by a sore shoulder, he pitched poorly (1-7) and was demoted back to Jacksonville in June, never to return. His one claim to Mets fame was being selected by the Topps Chewing Gum Company to appear next to Seaver on its "Mets 1967 Rookie Stars" baseball card. The card, number 581 in the '67 Topps set, features side-by-side headshots of Denehy and Seaver with a yellow border, and at first glance they look almost identical.

The following November, however, Denehy would inadvertently be a party to a trade that would have a major impact on Seaver's career.

CHAPTER 4

A Splash at the Show

ALTHOUGH FEW COULD HAVE REALIZED IT AT THE TIME, ESPE-cially the way the writers were regaling everyone with stories about the ineptitude of Casey Stengel's lovable losers, the Mets were about to begin a transition to respectability when Seaver arrived on the big league scene in the spring of 1967. And their transition would be largely because of him.

It had taken a couple of years longer than originally planned, but George Weiss, seventy-two, finally retired as Mets president after the 1966 season and was replaced by forty-nine-year-old Bing Devine, the former St. Louis Cardinals general manager. Despite having been the architect of their 1964 world championship team, Devine was un-ceremoniously fired by Cardinals owner Gussie Busch in August that season and a few months later was swooped up by the Mets as Weiss's assistant and heir apparent. It was Devine who lobbied Weiss to enter the ad hoc lottery for Seaver, and who, along with Player Development Director Johnny Murphy, presided over the amateur drafts that netted future pitching stalwarts Nolan Ryan in 1965 and Gary Gentry in 1967.

Prior to Weiss's long-awaited departure, the seventy-five-year-old Stengel was also forced to retire as Mets manager after fracturing his hip in a fall, on July 25, 1965, but he remained around the team that season and in spring training the next couple of years in the role of special advisor. Stengel was succeeded as manager by his polar opposite in terms of personality: the quiet, amiable Wes Westrum, who'd been one of his coaches. The front office's selection of Westrum, a superb defensive catcher for the New York Giants in the 1950s but who had no previous managerial experience, was a bit of a surprise, if only because the popular Yogi Berra, who'd won an American League pennant in 1964 as manager of the Yankees before being fired the day after losing a hard-fought seven-game World Series against those Devine-built Cardinals, was also on Stengel's staff. The dull, plain-spoken Westrum was largely devoid of humor—other than the unintentional kind with his periodic malapropisms such as "That was a real cliff dweller" after the Mets battled back for an extra-inning win against the Phillies in July in one of his first games as manager.

It was perhaps for this reason the Mets beat writers continued to quote Stengel and make repeated references to the frequent inept play of his teams in their stories. Such was the case with Greg Goossen, hailed as one of the organization's top catching prospects in '67 spring training. Whatever abilities Goossen might have had were nullified by the oft-repeated statement Stengel had made about him when he showed up as a twenty-year-old the previous spring. Though he was big and strong and had the looks of a ballplayer, Stengel saw quickly that the kid had holes, too many of them, and in his assessment of Goossen to the writers, he said: "And we have this fine young catcher named Goossen, who is twenty, and in ten years . . . uh . . . he has a chance to be thirty." (Stengel was correct in his assessment of Goossen, who hit just .202 with 2 HR and 15 RBI in 238 at-bats before they unloaded him in the 1968 expansion draft.)

Seaver went about his business in his first big-league camp, working hard on his control and on developing his secondary pitches in hopes of sufficiently impressing Westrum into taking him north with the club for the season. But he felt a bit uneasy listening to all the Mets jokes. Particularly dismaying to him was the frequent term "Amazin's," which the writers had pinned on them in reference to Stengel's favorite expression during their historically bad 120-loss maiden season in 1962.

Seaver could not understand what was so funny about being called "Amazin'," since Stengel had used it in reference to their play being amazingly bad, not amazingly good. The rookie would listen to the veteran Mets beat writers—Jack Lang of the *Daily News*; Maury Allen and Vic Ziegel of the *New York Post*; and Steve Jacobson of *Newsday*—going on with their tales of Stengel and the "lovable losers" of 1962 to 1965: the baserunning blunders of defensively challenged first baseman "Marvelous Marv" Throneberry, the squat (five-foot-nine, 185-pound), monosyllabic catcher Clarence "Choo-Choo" Coleman (of whom Stengel once said he never saw a catcher so fast at retrieving passed balls), and the versatile "Hot Rod" Kanehl, who led the league in hustle and could play seven positions, none of them well. But instead of laughing along with the writers, Seaver often found himself biting his tongue. He wanted no part of this. One day during spring training, he approached Ron Swoboda, a promising but still-learning power-hitting outfielder whom the Mets had rushed to the big leagues in 1965 before he was ready, and expressed his feelings.

"I don't know about you, Ron, but I'm not comfortable with all this 'lovable losers' stuff everyone keeps talking about around here," Seaver said. "I've been on winning teams my entire life, going all the way back to Little League, and I don't intend to be part of a losing team now."

Years later, Seaver told me: "When I came to the Mets, there was an aura of defeatism on that team; a feeling of 'Oh, let's just get it over with,' and I could just not accept that. I was unaware of the legend of Marvelous Marv Throneberry. I probably got a few people mad, saying what I did, but people pay money to see professional baseball played well." Strong as he may have felt about that, the fact was New York fans fell in love with the Mets' ineptitude. Once the Mets moved into Shea Stadium, their attendance soared from 1.1 million in '63 to 1.7 million in '64, and despite finishing last for the third straight year, they handily outdrew the Yankees (1.3 million), who were on their way to their fifth straight World Series.

"Tom was a Hall of Famer from the day he showed up for that first spring training in 1967," Swoboda reflected in a 2019 interview. "He was full of confidence and intelligence, and he didn't change, and that rubbed off on everyone. He had the intelligence to figure out what he needed to do on days when he didn't have his best stuff. His demeanor was always the same. He wanted—and intended—to win."

One day that spring, Seaver, Swoboda, and a couple of the pitchers, "Fat Jack" Fisher (who would go on to lead the National League in losses for the second time in three years in 1967) and Jack Hamilton, a right-handed reliever whom Devine had purchased from the Detroit Tigers in one of his first deals in 1965, were sitting around the clubhouse talking about movies—specifically, an imaginary Mets movie starring . . . them.

"Who would play us?" they asked one another. It was decided that the rotund comedian Jackie Gleason would be an ideal Fisher, while Hamilton expressed his preference for the cool crooner Dean Martin playing him. They all agreed caveman cartoon character Fred Flintstone epitomized the hulking, slack-shouldered Swoboda. As for who might most resemble Seaver, they somehow came up with child actor Spanky McFarland, the smooth-faced, mop-haired leader of the popular *Little Rascals* film shorts of the 1930s. Of all the characters, the Spanky reference to Seaver stuck, and that became his nickname around the Mets' clubhouse for the next ten years.

Meanwhile, despite a wide-open competition for the last two spots in the Mets' rotation behind the veterans Fisher and Bob Shaw (who'd both tied for the club lead with eleven wins in '66) and Don Cardwell (who won thirteen games for the Pirates in '66 and came over in a Devine trade along with the highly touted five-foot-eight, 160-pound switch-hitting center fielder Don Bosch), Westrum was slow to test Seaver's limits, using him in brief middle-inning relief stints his first three or four spring training outings.

"I had set no time limit for making it to the big leagues, but I believed that eventually I could get there because I felt I was good enough," Seaver told me. "There were no self-declarations that if I didn't make it in two, three years, I would quit and try something else. At training camp, I was ready to be sent back to the minors if they felt I needed the extra work because I believed in the absolute integrity of major-league baseball. To be honest, I had not been overly impressed with myself my first year of pro ball at Jacksonville. A record that shows you won as many games as you lost is not one you can accept or be happy with."

When it came to the rookies in camp, Westrum's prime focus was on Bosch, if only because his boss, Devine, had made such a point of the twenty-four-year-old's supposed multiple skills, as the key player in the Pittsburgh deal. The new general manager had sacrificed Dennis Ribant, the Mets' most effective starting pitcher in '66. But Bosch was, first, a late arrival at camp, and when he did arrive, his diminutive physique left Westrum dumfounded.

"Oh my god," the manager said off the record to the writers, "they sent me a midget! He doesn't even look like a ballplayer!"

In fact, he wasn't. There was nothing about Bosch's game that warranted such glowing scouting reports, some of which had even said he possessed the defensive prowess of Willie Mays. (Indeed, the writers surmised it was no accident that Bosch was given Mays's uniform number, 24.) But the heralded rookie was at best a mediocre center fielder, frequently letting the corner outfielders call him off on fly balls. Moreover, Bosch couldn't hit a lick—from either side of the plate. Though he would start the season as the everyday center fielder and leadoff man, by June 4, Bosch was hitting only .161 and was sent back to Triple-A Jacksonville. Following the 1968 season, a carbon copy of '67 (.171 BA, 3 HR, 7 RBI in 50 games), the Mets sold him to the expansion Montreal Expos, and he was out of baseball a year later, with a lifetime batting average of .164. As for Bosch's supposed blinding speed, in his four-season career, he attempted only seven steals, getting caught four times.

Fortunately for Devine, the emergence of Seaver that spring as a true rookie standout diverted everyone's attention from the colossal flop Bosch. After one relief outing, in which he held the Minnesota Twins to two hits over three innings, concluding it with a strikeout of future Hall of Famer Harmon Killebrew, the most feared home run hitter in the American League, Westrum decided it was time to start Seaver. He pitched five innings of one-run ball against the Kansas City A's and, more impressively, another five scoreless innings against the defending 1966 world champion Baltimore Orioles. By the end of the spring, Seaver had pitched better than all the Mets' starters, and Westrum made the decision to bring him north with the team, along with his fellow big-bonus rookie "stablemate" Bill Denehy, to fill out the starting rotation behind Cardwell, Fisher, and Shaw.

Westrum thought the twenty-two-year-old Seaver had shown more "pure stuff" than any of the veterans and for a while considered giving him the opening-day assignment against the Pittsburgh Pirates. But after consulting with Devine, they concluded this might put undue pressure on their valuable pitching prodigy and opted instead to tap the veteran Cardwell, with Seaver pitching the second game at Shea Stadium, the Mets' futuristic new ballpark, which opened in Queens in 1964, adjacent to the World's Fair.

It made no matter to Seaver, who was ecstatic over just making the team. After being informed by Westrum, he rushed back to the apartment where he and Nancy were staying in Saint Petersburg. The good news, he told her, was that they were going to New York, to the Show, the big leagues! The not-so-good news was that he was going to have to remain with the team on its trek north, which included two more stopover exhibition games against the Orioles, in Jacksonville and Durham, North Carolina, while she, in turn, was going to have to drive to New York by herself and then find them an apartment near the ballpark in Flushing, Queens.

"I said, 'I can do that,' but that was very scary," said Nancy, who was just twenty-two. "Driving into New York, it was like going to a foreign country. I couldn't believe that people hung their laundry outside the high-rise buildings. And the traffic, that was also stunning. Flushing was very crowded and very noisy."

Nevertheless, she was able to find them a small basement garden apartment for $125 a month that had a tiny backyard with a dry fountain. At first, she was reluctant to venture far from the apartment for fear of getting lost. Then she had a visit from one of her girlfriends from back home in Fresno who knew her way around New York, and together they'd drive Nancy's car to Shea Stadium, park in the players' lot, and catch the number 7 train to Manhattan. "It was all great fun," Nancy said, "and I was no longer intimidated by the big city."

On the morning of Thursday, April 13, 1967, Seaver awoke with a nervous stomach. Nancy had prepared him a breakfast of scrambled eggs and bacon, but all he could do was to nibble on the bacon while going over in his mind all the Pittsburgh hitters' traits and stances he'd studied. Two days earlier, the Mets had lost the season opener to the Pirates, 6–3, behind Cardwell, to add just a little more pressure to his first major-league start. Upon arriving at Shea, Seaver found Bud Harrelson waiting by his locker. "Your day," the wiry shortstop said. "Go and get it." From across the room somebody— he couldn't tell who—shouted: "Hail, Spanky!" Suddenly he began feeling more at ease.

The first batter Tom Seaver faced in the major leagues, Matty Alou, slammed a double to right field. Disconcerting as that might have been, the rookie got the next two batters, Maury Wills and Roberto Clemente, on infield groundouts, and, after issuing a walk to home run threat Willie Stargell, struck out Donn Clendenon to end the inning and strand Alou at third.

In the second, Mets second baseman Jerry Buchek staked Seaver to a 2–0 lead with a homer, but the Pirates came back to tie it with solo runs in the third and fourth on RBI singles by Clemente and Wills, respectively. The score remained even when Seaver ran into trouble with one out in the sixth, surrendering a double to the opposing pitcher, veteran Vern Law, before hitting Alou with a pitch. At that point, Westrum strolled to the mound to talk with his young pitcher. He'd been impressed with the kid's debut—eight strikeouts in 5⅓ innings—but he could sense Seaver was beginning to lose it. As much as he wanted to stay in the game, with a chance for a victory in his first major-league start, Seaver did not protest when the manager signaled to the bullpen for reliever Chuck Estrada.

The Mets went on to win the game on an RBI double by pinch hitter Chuck Hiller in the eighth. Though Estrada wound up with the victory, Westrum afterward praised Seaver's effort. "He showed me a lot, and I think if you ask them" (he pointed in the direction of the Pirates' clubhouse) "they'll say the same thing. That's a pretty good lineup he held to only two runs."

But major-league win number one would have to wait.

There were only 5,379 fans at Shea when Seaver took the mound for the second time, April 20, to face the Chicago Cubs. His opponent, the wily thirty-seven-year-old lefty Curt Simmons, was in the final year of his career but was still capable of keeping a team at bay for five or six innings—which is what he did on this day. The score was locked at 1–1 going into the sixth when the Mets got to Simmons and provided Seaver a welcome cushion, on a single by their increasingly impressive-hitting young outfielder Cleon Jones, followed by a sacrifice bunt, an RBI single by the veteran third baseman and 1964 National League MVP Ken Boyer, a double by Tommy Davis (like Boyer, a former National League All-Star acquired in trade by Devine), and a sac fly by Swoboda.

Buoyed by the 3–1 lead, Seaver stranded a couple of Cubs base runners in the seventh. But when he gave up a leadoff single to shortstop Don Kessinger in the eighth and retired second baseman Glenn Beckert on a hard-hit liner to left field, once again, here came Westrum, along with Boyer over from third and Harrelson from short.

"How do you feel, Tom?" Boyer asked.

Looking at Westrum, Seaver wanted to say he was fine. But he also didn't know if he had enough to get through another inning, and right now he was the winning pitcher of record.

"I'm pooped, Wes," he admitted, while also noting that the next Cubs batter, outfielder Billy Williams, a future NL batting titlist and Hall of Famer, had tripled in the only run off him in the third.

Rookie Don Shaw, Seaver's road roommate, came in and got Williams to hit into an inning-ending double play, and then, after the Mets scored three more runs in the bottom of the inning, retired the Cubs in order in the ninth.

Westrum would later tell the writers that what impressed him just as much that day as Seaver's 7⅓ innings of one-run, five-strikeout, walk-free ball was his honesty. "He could have selfishly told me he was okay, and I probably would have left him in, but he knew he was about out of gas, and that wouldn't have been fair to the team," the manager said.

Five days later, Seaver faced the Cubs again, this time at Wrigley Field. He pitched ten innings, yielding only four hits and one unearned run for a 2–1 victory. He was 3-1 with a 2.21 ERA for his first six major-league starts when he faced the Braves—and his boyhood idol Hank Aaron—in Atlanta on May 17. In their first encounter, with one out in the first inning, Seaver got Hammerin' Hank to ground into an inning-ending double play on a sinking fastball. The next time up, leading off the fourth, Aaron struck out looking. In 2016 Seaver remembered strutting back to the dugout after the inning, being giddy with joy.

"You can just imagine how I felt at that time, having retired Henry on a double play and a strikeout looking," he told me. "Growing up, the Braves had always been my favorite team because Henry was my favorite player. Henry was always first with me, and I don't find it strange at all that a white boy who wanted to become a major-league pitcher would most identify with a black hitter. I thought of Aaron as excellence. He was so much fun to sit and watch because he was so damn consistent, dedicated, and yet capable of making the game look so easy to play. Confidence flowed out of him."

That was never more evident than in his next at-bat, in the sixth, with the Mets nursing a 3–1 lead. After a one-out single by Felipe Alou, Aaron clubbed a long home run to left field to tie the score. The pitch was the same sinking fastball Seaver had struck him out on two innings earlier. Seaver had always prided himself in remembering hitters' tendencies and weaknesses and then capitalizing on them. On this occasion, he learned a lesson that hitters, especially hitters like Bad Henry, also remembered.

Meanwhile, the rookie pitcher helped his own cause with the bat, going 3-for-3 with a pair of run-scoring doubles off Braves starter Bob Bruce. The contest remained tied until the bottom of the ninth when catcher Joe Torre, playing with a broken index finger, led off with Atlanta's third homer of the night for a 4–3 win. (Over the course of his career, Aaron was 18-for-82, .220, with 5 homers and 14 strikeouts against Seaver.)

In a July 2017 interview, at the Hall of Fame, Aaron recalled those first impressions he had of Seaver.

"Tom was just so dedicated. He came up to the big leagues knowing what baseball players were all about. I can't think of anyone else in my twenty-three years in the big leagues who was as competitive as he was," he said. "I remember that first time we faced him, somebody on our team said, 'This kid coming out of California, right out of college, he's not ready for the big leagues.' And then I went up to the plate, and I said, 'I don't think you're right. This kid is ready for the big leagues and probably ready for the Hall of Fame.'" Aaron laughed. "He was that good. I don't know who his teacher was, but to me I would have to say he was more than ready for the Show."

Seaver made it a point of getting to know Aaron, and, through the years, they talked often, particularly about what might have been.

"He seemed like he wanted to meet me, and I wanted to meet him," Aaron said. "We had a great relationship. It was not one of those deals where we shook hands and he said, 'Well, I'll take it easy on you.' We were friends until he put on that uniform and got on the mound, and then I was his enemy. I had heard all about him because of that draft that came as a result of the Braves' illegally signing him. I think we would have won a few championships if he'd been a pitcher on our Braves ball club, don't you?"

In five starts in May, Seaver pitched three complete games, winning two of them and giving up more than three runs only once. On July 3 he hurled his ninth complete game of the season, a 5–3 victory over the Giants at Shea Stadium, giving him a 7-5 record with a 2.70 ERA. After the game, he learned he was the lone Mets player to be selected to the All-Star Game in Anaheim, California, on July 11.

"When Seaver came into the big leagues, he came in pitching," said Billy Williams in a July 2018 interview at the Hall of Fame. "And if you picture him, when he threw the ball, he always dragged his knee—that knee would always go to the ground, and he threw the ball low. He seldom gave you a good pitch to hit. And he knew how to get people out."

As Ron Darling, a standout starter for the Mets from 1983 through 1991 and later a baseball TV analyst, observed: "Because of the way Tom was built, stocky, strong, six foot one, he had the ability to do a thing that we call the 'drop and drive.' Every pitcher wants to do it, but few can because you have to be built a certain way. I'm six feet, Tom was six one. I could never drop and drive because it was just too hard to get that low. When you watched his body, he was just so powerful from the waist down and was able to use his lower half."

Despite the quiet admiration he was receiving from his peers, when Seaver arrived at the National League clubhouse and looked around the room at the sight of Aaron, Clemente, Mays, Drysdale, Orlando Cepeda, Juan Marichal, Bob Gibson, and Ernie Banks all suiting up as his teammates for the day, he felt like Alice in Wonderland. Only two years earlier, he'd been pitching for USC, and now here he was in the presence of some of the greatest players baseball had ever known— as an equal, no less, at least in the minds of the players, coaches, and managers who had selected him to the All-Star Game.

It took only a couple of minutes to jolt him back to reality. As Seaver was looking around the room for his locker, Lou Brock, the speedy St. Louis Cardinals outfielder and soon to be the preeminent base stealer in baseball, approached him. "Hey, kid," Brock said, "mind fetchin' me a Coke?"

At first, the embarrassed Seaver didn't know what to say, so he dutifully went over to the soda cooler, pulled out a Coke, and brought it back to Brock. "Here you are, Lou," he said, putting out his hand. "By the way, I'm Tom Seaver."

Now it was Brock who was momentarily embarrassed. Then they both laughed. But Seaver never let Brock forget the unintentional slight. Every year at the Hall of Fame inductions in Cooperstown, whenever he'd see Brock in the lobby of the Otesaga Hotel, he'd holler out: "Hey, Lou! Fetch me a Coke, will ya?"

"Being in that clubhouse and seeing all those guys who, as a baseball fan, I always had the impression were super beings, not human, I was really in awe of it all," Seaver recalled to me in a 2016 interview. "But my biggest thrill, before the game itself, was when Sandy Koufax came into the clubhouse to visit his old friends and sat down beside me." The three-time NL Cy Young Award winner, who led the league in ERA from 1962 through 1966, had shocked the sports world by retiring in November. Though just thirty-one years old, Koufax had been bedeviled by chronic arthritis in his valuable left arm, and he quit the game to prevent injuring himself permanently. Now he was trying his hand as a baseball announcer for NBC-TV. "All of a sudden," marveled Seaver, "here we are talking like two ordinary guys, and he's chatting with me like I'm his equal."

Before the game, Seaver told the New York writers he didn't expect to see any action. Back in those days, the leagues played the All-Star Game to win, and it was not uncommon for starting pitchers to throw at least three innings. As Seaver pointed out, with Gibson, Drysdale, Marichal, and Ferguson Jenkins, all future Hall of Famers, not to mention four or five other starting pitchers with far more experience than he had, it didn't figure there would be enough innings for the rookie.

As it turned out, there were.

In what became the longest All-Star Game in history (until matched in 2008), the Americans and Nationals engaged in a 1–1 stalemate into the fifteenth inning. While National League manager Walt Alston made use of all of his heralded aces, including Marichal, Gibson, Drysdale, and Jenkins, plus two others, Mike Cuellar of the Houston Astros and the Philadelphia Phillies' Chris Short, once it got to the eleventh inning, his American League counterpart, Hank Bauer, handed the ball to Catfish Hunter of the Oakland A's, and left it with him. In the top of the fifteenth, Hunter finally buckled, yielding a one-out solo home run to the Cincinnati Reds' Tony Perez.

As soon as the ball cleared the fence, Alston signaled down to the bullpen for Seaver to start warming up. For the Mets rookie, it was a "Who, me?" moment. After being assured that Alston wanted him and not veterans Claude Osteen or Denny Lemaster to protect the game, he jumped up and began throwing, his heart pounding and his stomach churning. Nancy and his parents were in the stands, and he could only imagine what they were thinking, seeing him warming up in anticipation of getting the save in his first All-Star Game.

As Seaver came out of the bullpen, he remembered jogging past Clemente in right field, and trying his best to slough off the pressure he was feeling by yelling, "Let's get three and go home here!"

"That's right, rook," Clemente replied. "Go get 'em, *keed*!"

Then as he got to the infield, he said to Pete Rose at second base, "How about you pitching and me playing second?"

The Cincinnati Reds' star, in the middle of his third straight .300 season, laughed.

"That's okay. I'll stay where I am. You'll get it done," he said assuringly.

After retiring leadoff hitter Tony Conigliaro on a fly to left, Seaver peered down at his Boston Red Sox teammate, Carl Yastrzemski, wagging his bat at the plate. The menacing left-handed hitter would go on to achieve the rare Triple Crown, leading the league in batting average (.326), home runs (44), and runs batted in (121), and, almost anticlimactically, win the 1967 American League Most Valuable Player Award that season. As Seaver told me years later: "I wanted no part of Yastrzemski, and there was no way he was getting a pitch to hit."

He didn't. After walking Yaz, Seaver retired Detroit catcher Bill Freehan on a fly to Willie Mays in center and closed out the game in spectacular fashion by striking out White Sox outfielder Ken Berry, pinch-hitting for Hunter, on a high, midnineties fastball. "That," said Seaver, "was my new highlight of the day. In the clubhouse afterward, the Aarons, Mayses, and Cepedas were all coming up to me and shaking my hand, and my eyes, I'm sure, were as big as saucers." He was especially taken by the raucous celebration in the NL clubhouse afterward. Even though it was only an exhibition, and most of them had played in numerous All-Star Games, the National Leaguers, who were in the process of winning nineteen out of twenty All-Star contests from 1963 through 1982, took it seriously. On the plane flight home, Seaver said to Nancy, "Those guys are all winners. They take pride in winning. That's what we've got to start instilling with the Mets."

Whether or not it was just his imagination, Seaver began to sense the Mets played harder when he pitched. He wasn't the only one who took winning to heart, as evidenced in his April 25 extra-innings win against the Cubs at Wrigley Field. Seaver was pitching a 1–0 shutout when, with two outs in the ninth, Bud Harrelson botched a grounder to short by Ron Santo, allowing the tying run to score. The next inning, Seaver led off with a single, was sacrificed to second by Cleon Jones, and scored the go-ahead run on a single by Al Luplow. After retiring the Cubs in order in the bottom of the tenth for the complete-game victory, he came into the clubhouse and found the disconsolate Harrelson sitting alone at his locker, his head buried in his hands. "These guys *do* care," Seaver thought. "At least some of them do."

Seaver, 9-8 after the All-Star break, ended the 1967 season at 16-13, making him the first Mets starter to surpass thirteen wins. His 18 complete games, 251 innings, 179 strikeouts, and 2.76 ERA also set Mets records. In 8 of his 13 losses, he gave up 4 or fewer runs. Seaver was finishing up classes back at USC when, on November 20, three days after his twenty-third birthday, the Baseball Writers' Association of America overwhelmingly elected him National League Rookie of the Year, 550 points to 300 points over runner-up Dick Hughes, a right-hander who'd gone 16-6 for the world champion St. Louis Cardinals.

For Seaver, it had been a very good first year in the major leagues.

For the Mets, however, it was still too much of the same. After finally escaping the cellar in 1966 and losing fewer than a hundred games for the first time, they regressed to 61-101 and found themselves back in tenth place for the fifth time in six years. Throughout the season, Devine tried mightily to make improvements with what seemed like a deal a week. Most of them were a matter of shuffling one bad player for another, but there were a couple that would bear dividends in the future.

On May 16 Devine had sent retread outfielder Larry Eliot to the Kansas City Athletics in exchange for Ed Charles, a thirty-three-year-old third baseman who had spent most of his prime years in the minor league system of the Milwaukee Braves. Though he batted only .238 for the Mets in 1967, Charles demonstrated leadership qualities that prompted Devine to deal the fading third baseman Ken Boyer to the White Sox in July in exchange for a player to be named later who turned out to be catcher–third baseman J. C. Martin. Both Charles and Martin would go on to play key roles in the greatest of all Mets seasons two years down the road.

Change was indeed in the wind as the '67 Mets' season ended. On September 21, after waiting to no avail for the Mets to offer him an extension, Westrum resigned as manager. He was also not unaware of the recurring speculation among the Mets beat writers that the popular and flamboyant Whitey Herzog, who'd been the club's third-base coach in 1966 before moving into the front office as player development director, was being groomed for the manager's job. At the same time, there were rumors that a repentant Gussie Busch, realizing the error in firing the man responsible for most of the players that had won him championships in 1964 and now 1967, was seeking to lure Devine back to St. Louis. Fueling those rumors was the fact that Devine had never sold his house there or bought one in New York.

It was probably for that reason that Mets board chairman M. Donald Grant, who had exerted more and more authority after Weiss's retirement, eventually put Devine's assistant, Johnny Murphy, in charge of hiring a new manager. Grant had already decided who the new manager was going to be, and it was not going to be the strong-willed Herzog. Rather, he was set on bringing back the beloved former Brooklyn Dodgers first baseman Gil Hodges, who'd finished his playing career with the Mets in 1962 and '63 before being traded to the Washington Senators so that he could replace Mickey Vernon as their manager.

As much affection as Grant and Mrs. Payson, the Mets' owner, had for Hodges at the time of the trade, they felt they could not stand in his way to becoming a manager when the Senators approached them in late May '63, seeking his services. And despite not having had any previous experience, Hodges proved to be quite adept as a manager. Under his direction, the Senators showed gradual improvement, from last place in '63, to ninth in '64, eighth in '65 and '66, and a tie for sixth in '67.

To the Mets, however, Hodges was the perfect choice. After two and a half dismal seasons under the bland, colorless Westrum, they needed a manager with instant popularity and credibility in New York, one who would excite their fan base. Hodges, a Dodgers hero who'd married a local Brooklyn gal, Joan Lombardi, and had now gained immense respect throughout baseball as a manager, checked all those boxes. Plus, he desperately wanted to come home.

Despite all this, the Senators were not inclined to let him out of his contract, which posed a huge problem for Grant. For one thing, Washington resented the inference from the Mets that Hodges had effectively been "loaned" to them back in '63 and now was the time for them to return him. Because Senators general manager George Selkirk had been a teammate of Johnny Murphy's with the Yankees back in the 1930s , Grant dispatched Murphy to Washington to work out a deal. And after much haggling, Selkirk finally agreed to free Hodges in exchange for Bill Denehy, who was still considered a top Mets pitching prospect, and $100,000.

"What the Senators didn't know was that I was damaged goods," Denehy told me in 2019. "I had hurt my arm in May, which turned out to be a torn rotator cuff, which the Mets didn't disclose. They'd just sent me to the minors, where I got a couple of cortisone shots. Even though they'd been teammates with the Yankees, Murphy and Selkirk really didn't like each other. Mr. Murphy told me he had offered three different players, but the Senators insisted on me."

According to Denehy, his injury occurred when he threw a hard slider to Willie Mays in his fourth start of the '67 season. Over the next twenty-six months, he said, he received fifty-seven shots of cortisone. Many years later, he was told that nobody should take more than ten shots of the anti-inflammatory steroid hormone in a lifetime and anyone exceeding that amount risked considerable damage to his eyes. In January 2005 he awoke one morning unable to see out of his right eye, which was determined to be the result of a torn retina. The condition worsened gradually to the point where, by 2019, Bill Denehy, then seventy-three, was legally blind.

"In my case, it was a matter of the team doctors back then not knowing the full extent of the dangers of cortisone—and the pressure exerted on them from ownership and upper management to get me back on the mound," he reflected.

Denehy's 1-7 record with the Mets in 1967 was pretty much the extent of his major-league career. The man who had once been labeled 1-B to Seaver's 1-A (or vice versa) as the Mets' top pitching prospects in 1966 pitched a total of two innings in three games for the Senators in 1968. After that, he bounced around the minors with four different teams before resurfacing briefly in the majors in 1971 with a 0-3 record for the Detroit Tigers. Later, he would often joke to friends that between him and Seaver, they had 312 wins in the majors. But Denehy did have the distinction of being the player the Mets traded to get Gil Hodges, as well as being forever linked to Seaver through that famous Topps Mets 1967 Rookie Stars baseball card, one of which, graded in near-mint condition, sold in an October 2018 auction for $6,987.

Once the Hodges deal was finally agreed upon, the Mets wasted no time in making it official. Two hours before the sixth game of the 1967 World Series between the Cardinals and the Boston Red Sox, they announced they'd signed Hodges to a three-year contract at $60,000 per to be their new manager.

Seaver followed all these developments with great interest. He liked Westrum all right, felt he'd been treated more than fairly by him, but frankly never viewed him as any sort of inspirational leader. It seemed to him Westrum was more of a caretaker for a bad team, who would inevitably be replaced once the Mets started to become good. The hiring of Hodges was an indication to him that perhaps that time was finally at hand.

And, typically, he'd done his research on Hodges. A six-foot-one, two-hundred-pound bear of a man, Hodges was said to have legendary huge hands—just like Seaver—and before fully embarking on an eighteen-year career in the big leagues as a perennial All-Star first baseman with 370 homers and seven straight 100-RBI seasons, he'd spent two years with the Marine Corps in the South Pacific in World War II.

He served as a gunner in the Sixteenth Antiaircraft Battalion, assigned first to the island of Tinian and then, in the final months of the war, with the assault troops in the fierce, protracted battle for the Japanese island of Okinawa, for which he was awarded the Bronze Star.

Without ever having met him, Seaver said: "This is a guy I can't wait to play for."

CHAPTER 5

Gil and the Miracle Workers

AS EXPECTED, TWO MONTHS AFTER THE 1967 SEASON, ON DE-
cember 5, Bing Devine resigned as Mets general manager to heed the
call home to St. Louis after Cardinals owner Gussie Busch offered him
back his old job as head of their baseball operations. Before he left,
however, Devine made one more trade that would impact the coming
seasons—acquiring outfielder Art Shamsky from the Cincinnati Reds
for utilityman–pinch hitter Bob Johnson—and laid the groundwork for
what became another one of the most important trades in Mets history.

With Devine's departure, team president M. Donald Grant el-
evated player development chief Johnny Murphy to Mets GM. Once
on board, Hodges began working closely with Murphy on personnel
decisions for the coming year and, in particular, pushed hard for the
completion of trade negotiations Devine had begun with the Chicago White Sox. The deal, which Murphy was able to conclude at the
baseball winter meetings in Mexico City in December, brought center
fielder Tommie Agee and infielder Al Weis from Chicago in exchange
for "Fat Jack" Fisher and the former All-Star outfielder Tommy Davis,

who turned in a fine offensive performance his one season in New York: .302 BA, 16 HR, 73 RBI, leading the club in all three categories. Despite experiencing a tail-off in 1967 after winning American League Rookie of the Year honors in '66, Agee had impressed Hodges with his all-around skills. Reportedly, Hodges told Murphy, "As I see it, our biggest need here is a center fielder who can provide us defense and power. Agee will do that."

In the weeks leading up to his first spring under Hodges, Seaver staged a minor contract holdout with the Mets while finishing up his classes at USC. He received a B in argumentation and debate and an A in radio and television news. In the latter course, among the world topics he was assigned to cover was the escalating war in Vietnam, on which he composed an editorial questioning the United States' involvement.

"I took the view that it's the wrong war," Seaver said. "It's basically a civil war and a guerilla war, but now we're committed and in too deep and at an ungodly cost." (A year later, the ex-marine would be quoted publicly on Vietnam, which would garner a whole lot more attention.)

Toward the end of the semester, Seaver received his new contract from the Mets, calling for a modest raise from the $12,000 he'd earned in his rookie year. He sent it back, politely informing Murphy that, after talking it over with his dad and his lawyer, they all agreed he wasn't being paid enough. This caused considerable consternation among the Mets' hierarchy, as the last thing they wanted was to get into a public contract dispute with their new star.

Murphy happened to have some business in California to attend to, so instead of conducting further negotiations with Seaver through the mail and over the phone, he paid a personal visit to him in Los Angeles, contract in hand. Seaver was impressed the GM made such an effort—but was even more impressed when, after a brief negotiation, Murphy agreed to double his salary to $24,000 for 1968. "I don't have the salary figures of the other clubs," Murphy told the Mets scribes, "but Tom may very well be the best paid player in the majors today with just one year of experience. That's okay. In our minds, he deserved it."

Upon arriving in Saint Petersburg for spring training in mid-February, Seaver immediately felt a whole different vibe. For one thing, it was mostly just eighteen pitchers and four catchers under the watchful eye of Hodges—wearing the familiar number 14 uniform he'd made famous with the Dodgers and then as an original Met in '62—and his four coaches. In previous Mets camps, there'd be any number of nonroster players roaming the fields and vying for time in the batting cages. But this spring, Hodges made it known from the outset that he'd have little time for players who weren't going to be on the team. On one of the first days of camp, the new manager was leaning on the batting cage watching one of the pitchers throwing, when a reporter came up to him and informed him that Kevin Collins, a marginal utility infielder who'd spent most of the '67 season at Triple-A Jacksonville before undergoing shoulder surgery, had just arrived at camp. "Is that so?" Hodges said to the *Daily News*'s Jack Lang. "I don't know too much about him. Isn't he the kid who had some shoulder trouble?"

When informed that he was, Hodges shrugged. "Well, he can do anything he wants, just as long as he doesn't get in our way." (Collins did make Hodges' team in '68 but hit just .203 as a utility infielder and was traded to Montreal the next season.)

Later, Murphy, the old Yankees reliever from the 1930s, spoke glowingly to the Mets beat writers of the new spring training regimen under Hodges. "This is the way it used to be in the Yankees camps I was in under Joe McCarthy," the GM said. McCarthy, who piloted the

Bronx Bombers to seven World Championships from 1931 through 1946, "didn't want a bunch of nonroster extra players around, and he didn't think it necessary to have a lot of minor league managers, scouts, and instructors. I anticipate a different year because Gil is going to run a different type of club. I'm already seeing it in the meetings with the players. They are tired of losing. They are tired of the Mets image and tired of being the butt of jokes."

Hodges's fewer-is-better philosophy, in which he eschewed the constant shuffling of players back and forth to Triple A, continued all season, with the Mets using a total of thirty-four players in 1968 as opposed to fifty-four the year before.

Seaver, taking it all in, could not help but be impressed. Hodges was running this spring training with the regimentation and efficiency of, well, marine boot camp, without the nonstop physical abuse. And while Hodges was clearly the camp's drill sergeant, he was the quintessential quiet man, an imposing figure, observing wordlessly, hands in his back pockets, as his coaches hollered out instructions and conducted the drills.

On the first day of full squad workouts, Hodges addressed the team and laid down his rules: Jackets were to be worn around the Colonial Inn, where the team was staying for spring training, and ties would be worn with coats on the road. No swimming in the ocean or the pool, and nobody was to wander back to the clubhouse during workouts without permission. Hodges went on to say he had no objections to card playing, with the exception of poker. And anyone missing the team bus could take a cab at his own expense.

"I also don't believe in petty fines like a dollar, two dollars, or three dollars," Hodges said. "But I do believe in minimum fines of, say, twenty-five dollars."

As Dick Young wrote in his column in the *Daily News*: "Til now, nobody has spanked the Mets, and maybe it's time it started. Or else we're liable to have a spoiled brat on our hands if we don't already. . . . I think when there were 77,000 fewer customers at Shea Stadium last year, M. Donald Grant and the rest of the people who watch Mrs. Payson's money so closely realized it, and that's why they broke their necks to get Gil Hodges."

All of this was in direct contrast to the relatively lax Mets camps under Wes Westrum and Casey Stengel. But what was just as eye-opening that spring for Seaver as the new attitude was the proliferation of live arms that had suddenly appeared. In addition to his old Fresno City College teammate Dick Selma, who'd started a few games for the Mets in 1967 before being tried as a closer, there were three other hard-throwing right-handers—Gary Gentry, Jim McAndrew, and Nolan Ryan—plus a strapping, strong-armed left-hander, Jerry Koosman, with a midnineties fastball and sweeping curve. All were vying to jump from the minor leagues to a spot in the Mets' rotation. One was more impressive than the other, but where did they all come from?

The six-foot-one, twenty-three-year-old Gentry was a third-round draft pick out of Arizona State University in 1967 and went right to Double-A Williamsport, where he posted a 1.59 ERA with 77 strikeouts in 79 innings in 10 starts. McAndrew, an eleventh-round draft pick from the University of Iowa in '65, had led the Double-A Eastern League in ERA (1.43) at Williamsport in '67, while Ryan, the "baby" of the bunch at twenty-one, had been a twelfth-round draft pick out of Alvin High School in Texas in '65. Ryan threw harder than all of them, his fastball registering regularly in the high nineties, as he led the Class A Western Carolinas League in wins (17-2) and struck out a phenomenal 272 batters in 183 innings pitching for the Greenville Mets in 1966.

In the opinion of the Mets' hierarchy, however, the six-foot-two, 210-pound Koosman was the furthest along developmentally, having led the Class-A New York–Penn League in ERA (1.36) in '66 and similarly dominated at Triple-A Jacksonville in '67 with a 14-12 record, 2.24 ERA, and 232 strikeouts in 233 innings. After observing his smooth, low-to-the-ground drop-and-drive delivery so similar to Seaver's, it was easy for Hodges to envision a lefty complement to his righty ace atop the '68 rotation.

Unlike the others, who all came through the amateur draft, Koosman, a farm boy from tiny Appleton, Minnesota, had taken an unconventional route to the Mets. After pitching in what he called "beer leagues" in Minnesota upon graduating from high school, he was drafted into the army when he was eighteen and stationed at Fort Bliss, Texas. While there, he pitched for the Fort Bliss team against other army teams, averaging eighteen strikeouts per game. His catcher, John Luchese, was a native of Queens, and he called his father, John Sr., who was an usher at Shea Stadium, to tell him about this country boy with the low-nineties blazer and drop-dead curve. The elder Luchese passed on his son's informal scouting report to Mets GM Joe McDonald, who dispatched his Texas area scout, Red Murff (who also signed Ryan), to take a look at Koosman.

With scouts from the Twins and the Phillies also now watching him, the young southpaw was hoping for a sizeable signing bonus. But after watching Koosman strike out twelve batters in the first game he scouted him, Murff offered him a bonus of only $2,000. Koosman turned down the offer. A few days later, after having watched him a second time, Murff got on the phone to New York and came back with an offer of $1,900. According to Koosman, the offers from the Mets kept going down, not up, and when it got to $1,600, "that's when I decided

I better take the Mets' offer, or else I was going to end up owing them money!"

Word spread quickly through spring training about this bumper crop of big, strong-armed young pitchers in the Mets' camp. Whether or not it was just a coincidence, it seemed to Seaver that there were an inordinate number of scouts sitting behind home plate for the Mets' spring training games as opposed to last year. "The enthusiasm on this club is just oozing out," he told the New York scribes. "We've got a lot of good young pitching here. And with the defense Tommie Agee will provide in center field, we're bound to be better."

And then disaster hit—with a sickening thud.

The Mets played their first spring training game, March 9, against the Cardinals, who trained on the other side of Saint Petersburg and shared Al Lang Field with the Mets. Bob Gibson started for the Cardinals, and before the game Cleon Jones approached his fellow Alabaman, Agee, with a word of warning. "Be on the alert with Gibson," Cleon, in a 2019 interview, remembered telling his friend. "He likes to test new players in the league, especially the ones who might have some ability. He wants to challenge you to see how you'll react."

"It's no big deal," Agee said. "I faced guys like that in the American League."

"No, you haven't," said Jones. "There is only one Bob Gibson."

Undeterred, Agee led off the game anticipating a fastball and determined to hit it hard and far. Instead, the pitch came right in at his head and the Mets center fielder was unable to get out of the way. It struck him on the side of the head, sending him crumpling to the ground, momentarily dazed. A wobbly Agee was helped off the field and taken to the hospital, where it was determined that he had suffered a concussion. For the Mets, Gibson's "Welcome to the National League" pitch would have devastating consequences. The aftereffects plagued Agee all season. After starting out 5-for-16 in his first four games, Agee went into a 0-for-34 slump that left his batting average at a dismal .104 by May 6. For the '68 season, he hit just .217 with five homers and seventeen RBI in the worst year of his career.

While Agee lay on the ground, being tended to by the Mets' medical staff, Seaver, sitting in the dugout, turned to catcher Jerry Grote and said firmly: "I'll take care of this when the situation is right."

Seaver and Gibson matched up only one time in 1968, on May 6, and it was a dandy, both of them going the distance in a 2–1 eleven-inning game won by the Cardinals when Lou Brock tripled off Seaver to lead off the eleventh and later came home on an RBI single by Orlando Cepeda. Although Grote insisted Seaver retaliated soon after against Gibson, vividly recalling the circumstances, there was no reporting of any hostilities between the two in that particular game. "I forget exactly what precipitated it," Grote said in a 2019 interview, "but Tom waited for Gibson to come up to bat and then threw at him three times. Gibson was ducking him, and Tom shouted, 'Look out. You're going to get hurt!' Tom was the next batter for us in the next inning, and I think he timed it perfectly like that. When he came up to bat, Gibson threw one behind him, and Tom yelled, 'Now you're *really* gonna get hurt!'" Very likely the game to which Grote was referring was the first matchup between Gibson and Seaver in 1973, April 12 at Busch Stadium in St. Louis, which was not long after Gibson had punished the Mets' John Milner with a pitch in the back in a spring training game in retribution for his having hit three doubles off him earlier. In that game, Gibson's Cardinals battery mate Tim McCarver recalled Seaver sending Gibson sprawling in the dirt with a pitch at his head and Gibson screaming: "You're not that damn wild!" According to McCarver, Seaver shouted back: "Neither were you when you hit Milner!" Said Grote: "Tom showed us he was serious that day and I don't remember Gibson ever throwing at our guys again."

Just prior to the start of the season, Seaver had been holding court with the Mets beat writers when someone asked him about the so-called sophomore jinx. It was a question that made him bristle because he despised even the suggestion of negative thinking. "If you're asking me if I'm worried about not being able to equal 1967, I can tell you I'm not looking forward to a season like that," he said, then paused for effect. "I'm going to be better than that, I hope, and if I'm not, I'll be very disappointed." He went on to say the reason he believed he would be better was having a better knowledge of the hitters. "The more I see them, the better I get to know them, although there are still some hitters I can't get out."

One of the hitters he'd had a particularly hard time with his rookie season was Art Shamsky of the Reds, who just happened to be standing nearby as Seaver spoke. Pointing to Shamsky, now a teammate, he said, "There are two less hits right there I won't give up."

He would prove to be right about being better in 1968, but his optimism about the Mets finally finding winning ways in Hodges's first year fell far short of expectations because of the most anemic hitting in the league. Seaver came to realize that early. In his first eleven starts in '68, he had an ERA of 1.91—and a won-loss record of 2-5. Only twice in those eleven starts did the Mets score more than three runs. Things finally began to turn around for him in June, when he went 5-0 with three shutouts and, along with Koosman (who was on his way to a 19-12 rookie season) and Grote (who raised his average 87 points from 1967 to .282 in '68), earned a second straight selection to the National League All-Star Game. The game was played at the

Houston Astrodome, and this time Seaver had no doubt he would get to pitch. When his time came, called upon for the seventh inning, with the Nationals clinging to a 1–0 lead, he got Baltimore Orioles second baseman Davey Johnson on a grounder to short, then struck out Carl Yastrzemski before giving up a scorching double to Minnesota outfielder Tony Oliva off the arcade in left-center. Recovering quickly, he struck out Cleveland catcher Jose Azcue to strand Oliva. Then, returning to the mound for the eighth inning, he got to experience the thrill of a lifetime by striking out an aging, faded Mickey Mantle, who was pinch-hitting for the pitcher in his final All-Star Game—and final season—on three straight fastballs.

Many years later as Seaver and I were strolling through the plaque room at the Baseball Hall of Fame, we stopped in front of Mantle's, and Seaver said: "Striking out Mickey in the All-Star Game was one of my all-time moments, just because of who he was and what he meant to me. I never said anything to him about it. I just kept it to myself."

Seaver finished the 1968 season strong, winning six of his last nine starts while only twice giving up more than three earned runs. Around that time Jack Lang, the *Daily News* beat writer, began referring to him as "Tom Terrific" in his game stories. It was a nickname that would endure. The disappointing Mets season notwithstanding, there was much personal satisfaction for Seaver in finishing at 16-12. Although his won-loss record was nearly identical to that of his rookie year, his 2.20 ERA, 205 strikeouts, 40 walks, and an 0.978 WHIP (walks and hits per innings pitched) were considerable improvements over 1967 (2.76 ERA, 170 strikeouts, 78 walks, and a 1.203 WHIP).

Nineteen sixty-eight became known as the "Year of the Pitcher." There were 339 shutouts thrown in the majors, the American League hitters' collective slugging average of .340 was the lowest since 1915, and the Cardinals' Gibson posted the lowest ERA (1.12) in baseball since 1914. In the American League, the Tigers' Denny McLain won 31 games, a feat no pitcher has achieved in the fifty-two years since. But as far as Seaver's former USC coach, Rod Dedeaux, was concerned, his guy was far superior to Gibson if only because of the degree of difficulty. "I speak at a lot of banquets, and I manage to stun a lot of people when I say Tom Seaver is the best pitcher in baseball while I'm admitting the existence of another pitcher named Bob Gibson," Dedeaux told the *Los Angeles Times* in April 1969. "But I'm serious about Seaver. Look at it this way: last season, Tom won sixteen games for the Mets, and all year long he pitched only two games that might have been considered below par. He is amazingly consistent. If he'd been pitching for a club with all the offense and great defense of the St. Louis Cardinals"—who easily won their third National League pennant in five years and came within one game of winning the 1968 World Series against the Detroit Tigers—"it is very possible Seaver would have won thirty games."

Seaver did feel a certain emptiness about the overall 1968 Mets season, though, in which, despite winning the most games in their history (73-89), they were a mere one game from finishing last again. "Our record wasn't good," he told me in a 2016 interview, "and that bothered me because we had better players and a better manager, and I was getting impatient."

As the season wore down, with the Mets also well on their way toward the worst record in the National League in games decided by one run (26-37), Seaver could see the toll it was taking on Hodges. On September 24 the team was opening a two-game series in Atlanta against the Braves when Seaver saw his manager, standing behind the cage for pregame batting practice (which he normally would have been throwing himself), lean over suddenly and then sit down.

When Hodges got up and walked slowly back to the dugout, Seaver noticed his face had a grayish pallor to it. It would later be revealed that, sometime in the first inning, Hodges told pitching coach Rube Walker he was feeling weak and was going back to the clubhouse to lie down. In the clubhouse, he started experiencing chest pains, prompting Mets trainer Gus Mauch to immediately call a doctor, who determined Hodges needed to be taken to the hospital. It wasn't until the next day, when Hodges's wife, Joan, could get to Atlanta from New York, that the Mets announced that the tough, stoic ex-marine had suffered a heart attack, leaving his future as a manager uncertain.

"We were all just stunned," Seaver said. "Even though it had been another losing season, the improvement was measurable, and Gil's fingerprints were all over it. The biggest thing we did were the ABCs. We made the plays defensively, and the pitchers cut down on their mistakes. The new guys, Koosman, Ryan, and McAndrew, weren't afraid. We did the ABC's because Gil demanded it. He was just . . . *there* . . . and he didn't have to speak many words because when he did, he got it across."

And now, as they finished the season, he wasn't there.

The night after Hodges was stricken, Seaver shut out the Braves, 3–0, on a three-hitter for his sixteenth win. It would not be until a few weeks after the season that the Mets players learned Hodges had been given a clean bill of health by the doctors and would be able to resume managing—with a few conditions: he was told he had to drastically change his diet and give up his three-packs-a-day cigarette habit. As far as the stress that was part of the job, well, the Mets players were the only ones who could alleviate that.

Over the winter of '68 –'69, a lot of changes took place in baseball. At the December winter meetings in San Francisco, William Eckert, the man responsible for setting in motion the process that made Seaver a Met, was relieved of his duties as baseball commissioner and replaced by Bowie K. Kuhn, an attorney for the National League. Other big changes were afoot: after having expanded again, from twenty teams to twenty-four, by adding new franchises in Montreal and San Diego to the National League and Seattle and Kansas City to the American League, Major League Baseball announced a new two-division format. Each league would be divided into an East Division and a West Division of six teams apiece, and the two first-place finishers in their respective divisions would face off in a best-of-five league championship series for the right to go to the World Series. Finally, in a rules change that was clearly the genesis of Gibson's microscopic ERA in '68, the baseball lords elected to lower the mound elevation from 15 inches to 10 inches—a huge revision akin to expanding the nets in hockey.

Come February, Hodges was anxious to get back to running his ball club again. Much as he would have loved for Murphy to have added another strong hitter for the Mets lineup, who hit only eighty-one homers in '68 with Ed Charles leading the team with just fifteen, he'd seen enough progress in 1968, especially in the pitching department, to give him confidence that 1969 would be a breakthrough season for the Mets. Unfortunately, when he arrived in Saint Petersburg in early

February, Hodges found the strains of "Take Me Out to the Ballgame" had been usurped by Frank Loesser's classic ballad "Spring Will Be a Little Late This Year": the players were staging a spring training hold-out in a dispute with the owners over payments to their pension fund.

Seaver was one of the leaders of the fledgling Major League Base-ball Players Association, which was formed in 1966 when the players elected Marvin Miller, the former principal economic advisor and chief labor negotiator for the United Steelworkers, as its first execu-tive director. Miller quickly established himself as a force to be reck-oned with for the baseball owners and, using the pension issue as his primary cause célèbre that spring, was able to negotiate the players' first collective bargaining agreement. On Miller's instructions, the players all traveled to their spring training sites but did not report to camp, while their new union boss negotiated with the owners in New York. As the unofficial team leader, Seaver organized an informal daily "minicamp" for the Mets players, mostly pitchers and catchers who had reported early, at a public baseball diamond in South Saint Petersburg Beach. The sessions were short, consisting mostly of pitchers throwing and fielding, but as Seaver said later, the camaraderie that came out of them spilled over for the entire season in 1969.

The ministrike was settled on February 25, when new commis-sioner Kuhn interceded and helped bring the sides together on a new deal in which the owners agreed to contribute $5.45 million annu-ally to the players' pension fund and raise the minimum player salary from $7,000 to $10,000. "That was when we knew we'd picked the right guy in Marvin," Seaver recalled in a 2016 interview. "Through the years, all the gains he made for the players—free agency, salary arbitration—he had as much impact on baseball as anyone ever. It's just a shame he was never elected to the Hall of Fame." (That would finally be rectified when Miller was elected by the Modern Era veterans committee in 2019.)

So, the players' holdout had been worth it, but it also made for a truncated spring training in which the normal three to four weeks of conditioning programs for the pitchers were cut in half. At least in Mets camp, however, nobody seemed to care. Hodges was back, and optimism prevailed throughout—with Jerry Grote setting the tone.

"It was early on, those first few days of spring training, and Grote was the first one to predict we could win it all in '69," Seaver said. "He said with our pitching, and our defense up the middle, with Agee in center field, Buddy Harrelson at short, and him behind the plate, we had all the right ingredients."

"I did say that," Grote confirmed, "but I also said we need one more RBI guy."

Before camp broke, Johnny Murphy thought he might have succeeded in acquiring one from Atlanta: twenty-eight-year-old, Brooklyn-born Joe Torre, who, since becoming the Braves' starting catcher in 1963, had averaged twenty-one homers and eighty runs batted in per season, while hitting above .290 four times. On March 17 Murphy engaged in intense negotiations with Braves GM Paul Richards, who had become disenchanted with Torre's players' union activism and personal contract demands. In the end, however, Murphy found Richards's firm asking price from the Mets—Nolan Ryan and Amos Otis, a top-prospect center fielder—excessive. Later in the day, Richards traded Torre to the Cardinals for future Hall of Fame first baseman Orlando Cepeda, the 1967 National League MVP.

Murphy, too, had heard about Grote's remark, and while he wanted to agree with him, his thirty-five years of baseball experience had taught him to be cautious about making bold predictions, especially when it came to pitchers. "It's true we've got some fine young arms," Murphy said, at the outset of spring training, "but outside of Seaver and Koosman, no one yet has proved himself."

It was perhaps for this reason that Mets pitching coach Rube Walker, a Dodgers teammate of Hodges in the 1950s and also his pitching coach in Washington, had approached the manager in 1968 with the idea of abandoning the traditional four-man rotation in favor of a five-man unit. They experimented with it at the end of the season after the emergence of Ryan and McAndrew, and determined to go full blown with it in '69. The expanded rotation would include Seaver, Koosman, holdover veteran Don Cardwell, and any combination of the young power-arm righties—Gentry, Ryan, and McAndrew—all of whom had pitched well enough in the spring to earn spots. This, said Walker, would allow them to bring along the kids gradually, keeping them stronger over the long haul of the 162-game schedule, while also conserving their arms for the September stretch. It was Walker's belief that there were only so many pitches in an arm, which is why he also forbade them from doing any additional throwing between starts without his permission. (By the midseventies, every team in baseball would adopt the five-man rotation.)

Before Hodges and Walker settled on the rotation, however, there was one other young pitcher who thought he should be part of it and on whom they needed to make a decision. Tug McGraw, a flaky, fun-loving left-hander with a taste for John Jameson Irish whiskey, had been a largely ineffective starter in brief trials with the Mets from '65 to '67. The previous spring, he'd been forbidden by Hodges from working on what would become his most effective pitch, the screwball, and instead spent the entire '68 season at Jacksonville. When he arrived at spring training in '69 sporting a mustache and a long, shaggy General

Custer hairstyle, Hodges told him: "Shave the former and clip the latter." But the more the Mets' skipper observed McGraw's much refined screwball, the more he began to think there might be a role for him on the team after all—not as a starter but as a potential closer. Hodges believed that to be good reliever, you had to have the arm strength and durability to pitch on multiple days and have one true "out" pitch, usually an overpowering fastball or slider, or a sinkerball. It did not hurt, either, in Hodges's eyes, that McGraw had done a six-month stint, like Seaver, in the marine reserves in 1965, and that, because of it, he probably had the mental toughness required to be a closer. Though McGraw's screwball might have been an unconventional out pitch, Hodges thought it would be worth trying if McGraw was amenable. On the last day of spring training, he called him into his office and made him a proposition.

"I know you feel you should still be a starter," Hodges said, "but right now we've got our full quota of starters. I do think you've got a good chance to be an excellent late-inning reliever, which is what we need, so I'm going to give you a choice. You can go back down to Jacksonville and remain a starter or stay up here and be a reliever in New York."

"I'll stay here," McGraw replied.

McGraw would later tell the media, "With Gil running the club, you always felt sane, even if you were insane." And though he did get to start four games in 1969 in Rube Walker's rotating five-man rotation, the irrepressible "Tugger," with his patented screwball, would go on to become one of the most consistently effective closers in baseball over the next decade.

Alas, the spring of good feelings was quickly dampened by the cold reality of the regular season, where the Mets had yet to discover how to win. If they thought drawing the new expansion Montreal Expos as their first opponents of the season would be a cure-all for their opening day futility—winless in seven tries thus far—they were to be sadly mistaken.

For the second straight opening day, Hodges handed Seaver the ball, but unlike 1968 in San Francisco, when he pitched into the seventh inning and left with a lead, Tom Terrific and his mates flopped in front of the 44,541 Shea Stadium patrons. A fielding error by second baseman Ken Boswell, a walk, and a two-run double into the right-field corner by Bob Bailey put Seaver in an immediate two-run first-inning hole. In the second, however, a rejuvenated Tommie Agee bailed him out temporarily with a three-run double off Expos starter Jim "Mudcat" Grant.

But Seaver was clearly not on his game, allowing the Expos to tie it in the fourth on a home run by, of all people, their relief pitcher Dan McGinn, who had just replaced Grant. It was the first and only home run of his five-year major-league career. Though the Mets came back again with another three-run rally in the fourth, Hodges decided Seaver had had enough after five innings and turned the game over to his bullpen. From there, the contest evolved into a wild slugfest, with the Expos ultimately prevailing, 11–10, in the franchise's very first game. The Mets, meanwhile, were now 0-for-8 in openers. (In contrast to the Mets' continuing Opening Day futility, all four new expansion teams won their first games in '69, while in '62, the Mets' National League expansion "cousins," the Houston Colt 45s, also won their opener.)

"My God, that was ridiculous," an embarrassed Seaver told the writers after the game. Although the Mets managed to win the next two games against Montreal, they closed out the opening home stand by being swept three times by the Cardinals. When they lost the first game of a doubleheader to the Cubs on April 27, they were 6-11.

On June 3, when Seaver, with a one-inning save by McGraw, beat the Dodgers, 5–3, the Mets climbed over .500 (24-23) for the first time that season. It was their sixth win in a row. Despite the happy milestone, there was little jubilation in the clubhouse, probably because they'd remembered back on May 21, when Seaver evened the club's record at 18-18 with a 5–0 shutout over the Braves, he'd scolded reporters afterward for making a big deal of it.

"Five hundred is nothing to celebrate," Seaver said. "That's only mediocrity. We didn't come here to play .500 ball this season. I'm tired of all the old jokes about Marv Throneberry and Rod Kanehl. We're here to win. You know when we'll celebrate? When we win the pennant."

Though he expressed his feelings in the midst of a scrum of reporters, Seaver made a point of speaking loud enough to be within earshot of his teammates, dressing in silence. "That was one of those moments during the '69 season," said Ron Swoboda, "when Tom took the lead and delivered an emphatic message."

The next day, Jack DiLauro, an unheralded left-hander on the '69 Mets, who had been recalled from Triple A just a few days earlier, pitched nine shutout frames against the Dodgers in his first major-league start, and New York went on to win, 1–0, in fifteen innings. They won four more in a row after that—including Seaver's June 8 start, in which he struck out fourteen San Diego Padres—to run the longest winning streak in their history to eleven games and catapult them from fourth place to second behind the Chicago Cubs in the National League East.

For the first time, the Mets could start to think of themselves as legitimate contenders. Then, at the June 15 trading deadline, Johnny Murphy certified that by finally filling the Mets' long-standing need for a big bat in the middle of the order, acquiring Donn Clendenon, a thirty-three-year-old right-handed-hitting first baseman, from the Expos. To get Clendenon, who'd averaged seventeen homers and seventy-six runs batted in over the previous six seasons, Murphy had to sacrifice five prospects, only one of whom, right-handed starter Steve Renko, ever went on to achieve any success in the majors. In an interview I conducted with Seaver in July 2015, he called the Clendenon trade the turning point of the '69 season:

"Clendenon brought us a spark, no question. We looked at that deal and said, 'We can win now.' We were averaging something like three and a half runs a game, and we'd needed a big bat from the time I got there. Clendenon was absolutely the right guy. Not only did he get a lot of big hits for us, he was an instant leader in the clubhouse. He was a college grad, with great insight on the game, who had a wonderful sense of humor and could also needle the hell out of guys."

In his first sixteen games with the Mets, Clendenon drove in either the lead run or the winning run. The Mets won eight of their next ten games after the trading deadline, to stand at 38-28, five games behind the Cubs following a doubleheader sweep of the Phillies on June 24. But when they then proceeded to lose four in a row, falling back to eight games behind, Seaver felt it was time to take it upon himself to try to lighten the growing tensions in the clubhouse.

In the aftermath of a particularly ugly 7–4 June 28 loss to the Pirates at Shea, in which they committed two errors and Mets pitchers allowed two runs to score on wild pitches, Seaver, seeing his teammates sitting glumly at their lockers, heads bowed, grabbed a bat, stood up on a chair, and rapped for attention.

"Gentlemen," he proclaimed, "after watching that performance tonight, I would like to take this opportunity to announce my retirement from baseball!"

After a momentary stunned silence, everyone, the writers included, burst out laughing. The next day, with the help of eleven hits from his teammates, Seaver hurled a complete-game 7–3 win over Pittsburgh, striking out ten.

In early July the Mets first began to put some serious heat on Chicago. Coming off a road trip in which they had taken six of eight from the Cardinals and the Pirates, they'd shrunk their deficit to five and a half games when the first-place Cubs arrived at Shea Stadium, July 8, for what would be the first "big" series in Mets history. There was already plenty of animosity between the two teams, stemming from a beanball war between Seaver and Cubs right-hander Bill Hands back on May 4 in Chicago. That skirmish had been ignited when Seaver hit Cubs All-Star third baseman Ron Santo with a pitch, and Hands retaliated by plunking Seaver in the back when he came to bat in the bottom of the inning. Not done, however, Seaver drilled Hands in the stomach in *his* next at-bat, prompting the umpires to swiftly intervene, issuing warnings to both benches, as Wrigley Field fans were about to riot.

Adding to the drama was the presence of Leo Durocher as Cubs manager. Durocher, who had managed both the Dodgers and Giants in New York, was looked upon as a villain by the jilted fans of both those departed teams, and his reputation for ordering his pitchers to deliberately throw at opposing batters had earned him universal contempt around the league. That was okay with Durocher, who took special pride in the credo attributed to him, "Nice guys finish last."

In the first contest of the midweek three-game series, Koosman was trailing, 3–1, in the ninth when the Mets rallied for three runs off Cubs ace Ferguson Jenkins to win the game and set the stage for what would become the most memorable—and heartbreaking—game of Tom Seaver's life.

With the Mets now having closed to within four and a half games of first place, Seaver's Wednesday-night start against Ken Holtzman was already a sellout, but attendance quickly exceeded the ballpark's official capacity of 55,300. The largest crowd ever to watch a Mets home game crammed into every nook and cranny of Shea—59,083—50,079 of whom were paid. The other 9,000 were "walk-up" fans with standing-room-only tickets, as the New York City Fire Department, whose job it was to prevent overcrowding at public events, pretended not to notice. Foremost in the crowd, at least as far as Seaver was concerned, was Nancy, sitting in her accustomed box seat behind the Mets' dugout. Alongside her was Seaver's dad, Charles.

As he warmed up in the bullpen before the game, the electricity in the air was inescapable for Seaver. These were the kinds of games that if you couldn't get your competitive juices flowing, you weren't human. Pressure? The only thing Seaver was feeling was a little stiffness in his shoulder, and that, if nothing else, just made him feel all the more anxious. In the game plan he'd gone over with Grote, it was decided he would throw fastballs almost exclusively, working in an occasional curve or changeup but essentially challenging the Cubs' batters with location.

After a one-two-three first inning that ended with a strikeout of Billy Williams, whom he always considered one of his biggest nemeses, Seaver felt his shoulder loosen up. And when the Mets immediately provided him with a 1–0 first-inning lead on a leadoff triple by Agee and a double by Bobby Pfeil, the platoon third baseman, the anxiety he'd been feeling abated as well. It was game on now, and in the second, he struck out the side: Santo, Ernie Banks, and veteran outfielder Al Spangler. Then in the bottom of the inning, Tom Terrific helped himself with his bat, singling to right after two successive infield errors by the Cubs for one run, before Agee doubled in one more for a 3–0 lead and ending Holtzman's night.

For the next six innings, Seaver was both masterful and overpowering, retiring every Cub he faced, with nary a hard-hit ball, the two exceptions being Santo's fly ball to Agee on the warning track in center in the fifth and Cubs shortstop Don Kessinger's high drive down the left-field line off a curveball in the seventh that was gloved by Cleon Jones. After Seaver fanned Banks and Spangler again to end the eighth, for his tenth and eleventh strikeouts, Mets radio announcer Bob Murphy pronounced: "Ladies and gentlemen, after eight innings, Tom Seaver is walking into the dugout with a perfect game." With that, the Mets' radio station in Hackensack, New Jersey, WJRZ-AM, cut to a Chevrolet commercial in which, ironically, the announcer was heard intoning: "Dream the impossible dream."

Nobody was feeling the excitement of the moment more than Bud Harrelson, Seaver's roomie, who was watching the game from a bar in upstate Watertown, near the Canadian border, where he was fulfilling a two-week army reserve hitch at Fort Drum. "I felt like I was being pulled into the TV screen," Harrelson would say later. "I had so much pride in the team and in Tom that I guess I lost my head. When he went to the mound in the ninth inning, I did something only a kid is supposed to do. I turned around to the guy standing next to me, and I yelled, 'Hey, I *know* him! I know Tom Seaver! Tom Seaver is a friend of mine!'"

When Cubs catcher Randy Hundley dropped a bunt in front of the plate to lead off the ninth, the crowd howled. But the ball rolled directly to Seaver, who scooped it up efficiently and threw over first for the twenty-fifth out. Next came Jimmy Qualls, a light-hitting platoon center fielder, who had previously flied out to right and grounded out to first.

"The first two times up, Qualls had hit the ball decently," said Grote in a 2019 interview. "So before we went out for the ninth, I said to Tom, 'You want to stay low and away with Qualls,' because that's the way we'd gone over it before the game, and Tom hadn't been able to do that those first two times."

Out in center field, Agee considered moving a little more toward left to guard against the switch-hitting Qualls, who was batting lefty, from dunking an opposite-field hit into left-center. Agee would say later that because Qualls, a rookie, was the one Cubs batter whom Seaver had never faced prior to the game, "If there was anyone who could break it up, it was this guy."

On Seaver's first pitch, a fastball waist high, Qualls swung and lined a clean single between Agee and Jones in left-center field. Seaver turned, and as soon as the ball struck the outfield grass, he slumped, head down, in despair. In the stands, the television cameras instinctively panned to Nancy, who was wiping away tears. At first, the crowd jeered Qualls (who later revealed that he had received threatening letters when he returned home to Chicago), and then they rose to give Seaver a resounding ovation that shook the stadium.

"Tom was disappointed, but he didn't show any real emotion after the hit because that wasn't his way, and he still needed to get two more outs," observed Grote. "I didn't go out to talk to him because he knew he just got the pitch up."

For Qualls, it was the twelfth of just thirty-one hits he would have in his sixty-three-game big-league career, but it had earned him a place in Cubs immortality.

In the clubhouse, after he retired the last two batters to secure the shutout and the win, his fourteenth, Seaver told the reporters, "I was up for a big game. My heart was beating so much, and the feeling was almost out of my arm. . . . It was within my grasp. . . . You just don't get another chance. . . . I can't measure the disappointment."

Waiting for him outside the clubhouse door, Nancy was still crying when Seaver emerged fifteen minutes later. "What are you crying for?" he said to her. "We won the game. That's all that matters."

It would be a while, only through reliving it over in his mind, before he was able to appreciate the magnitude of his near-perfect performance that day—and what might have been but for one ill-placed fastball. In 2019 Nolan Ryan, author of a record seven no-hitters over the course of his twenty-seven-year career, told Steve Marcus of *Newsday*: "I had twelve one-hitters, and five or six of them I lost in the ninth inning, but Tom was something special that night." And even Durocher grudgingly praised his effort, saying, "He'll probably never be that fast again as long as he lives."

Over the '69–'70 winter, Seaver collaborated with the celebrated sportswriter and TV commentator Dick Schaap on a book, *The Perfect Game: Tom Seaver and the Mets*, in which he allowed himself to air all his feelings. "I wanted that perfect game more than I'd ever wanted anything in my baseball life," he admitted. "I didn't want to believe that I'd come so close and lost it. Never in any aspect of my mind, in baseball or outside, had I experienced such disappointment."

And nearly fifty years later, in a conversation at his vineyard in Calistoga, his assessment of that night still hadn't changed. "The Qualls game will always be the biggest disappointment of my baseball career," he told me. "That was the greatest game I ever pitched."

Seaver lost his next two starts, including a 5–4 decision to the Expos in Montreal. The next day, the Mets split a doubleheader with the Expos, and when they arrived at the airport for their flight home to New York, they were informed it was delayed at least an hour. They had two choices: sit out the delay in the waiting area or go to the bar. Most of them chose the latter, which was most opportune, since it enabled them to watch the Apollo 11 moon landing of Neil Armstrong and Buzz Aldrin on the bar TV. And as Art Shamsky remembered, the irony of their present circumstances, given what the Apollo astronauts had just accomplished, did not escape them.

"It was Ed Charles who said, 'Look at this: they can put a guy on the moon, but we can't get a plane to fly us home to New York!'" Shamsky related later on in the season. "But then Swoboda, who was the space nut of our group and had spent a lot of time in Houston and met John Glenn"—the first US astronaut to orbit the Earth—"came up with a kind of rallying cry for us, saying, 'Hey, if they can land a man on the moon, we can get to the World Series.'"

Still, it would be a while longer before Seaver and the Mets began making like miracle workers. They closed out the month with four straight losses at Shea, including a 16–3, 11–5 doubleheader thrashing from Houston on July 30. If Gil Hodges had one ironclad rule, it was that he demanded 100 percent effort, 100 percent of the time. He was already seething privately from having watched the Mets get slaughtered in the first game, and now, in the third inning of the nightcap, the Astros had batted around against Gary Gentry for seven runs.

At that point, the manager finally removed Gentry and brought in Ryan, who gave up a line drive down the left-field line by the Astros' lead-footed catcher Johnny Edwards. Cleon Jones was slow to retrieve the ball, allowing Edwards to make it to second. A minute or so later, Hodges emerged from the Mets' dugout, called time out, and began a slow walk past Bud Harrelson at shortstop into left field, where he confronted Cleon. After a few words, Hodges turned and headed back to the dugout, with Jones walking a few steps behind him.

"We were all wondering what happened," Seaver said in a 2016 interview. "Was Cleon hurt? But there he was taking Cleon out of the game in front of fifty thousand people, and I know how embarrassing that must have been for Gil to do it. But there'd been issues with Cleon before, and he wanted—he knew we really couldn't win without Cleon—and like a doctor, he was trying to get the patient to kick it. When they got back to the dugout, neither one of them said anything, but if Gil had intended to send us a message, he accomplished it. And Cleon could have gone the other way. "

The message, at least as it was interpreted then, was that even though Jones may have been the Mets' best player—he was hitting .346 at the time and vying with the Pirates' Matty Alou for the batting title—Hodges was not going to tolerate what he perceived to be a lack of hustle. Fifty years later, at a press conference in Port Saint Lucie, Florida, kicking off the golden anniversary of the '69 season, Jones finally revealed to reporters his side of the story.

"I know everybody here wants to get to the fact that he walked out onto the field to get me," Jones said, "but nobody knows but Gil Hodges and myself what really happened. Edwards hits the ball down the left-field line, I go over to get the ball, and he ends up on second. Gil didn't like what was happening. When he got out there, he said to me, 'Are you all right?' I said, 'I'm fine,' and he said, 'Well, do you think that ball should have been a single?' I said, 'No. Look down.' Both his feet and my feet were under water. It had rained pretty good that day, and I reminded him of a talk we'd had a week before about a bad ankle I had from an old football injury that was starting to puff up on me. He then said: 'You know what, Jonesy? You shouldn't even be out here,' and I said, 'Fine.' "

Hodges never confirmed any of that or offered any reason for keeping Jones out of the starting lineup for the next three days, leading to speculation that this was further punishment.

"It was unfortunate for Cleon that Gil had made an example of him," Seaver said, "but even if it was by design, I think Cleon had to know that Gil loved him."

The big push began at last in mid-August. Their pesky 1962 expansion "brothers," the Astros, who had swept them three straight twice previously in May and at the end of July, did it again on August 11, 12, and 13, in Houston, dropping the Mets to third place for the first time since June 2, ten games behind the front-running Cubs. Returning home, the Mets were rained out Friday, the fifteenth, making for a Saturday doubleheader. Seaver, pitching game one, shut out the Padres on four hits, 2–0. In the nightcap, McAndrew and McGraw followed suit on a four-hit 2–1 win.

By then, however, Mets fever had started to subside in New York, and the front-page news that weekend was about a three-day "peace and music" rock festival in upstate New York. More than four hundred thousand people had crowded into a cow pasture in the town of Bethel, some forty-three miles southwest of Woodstock, which was turned into a quagmire from torrential Friday-night rains. The Woodstock Music & Art Fair, featuring many of the top rock and folk performers of the day, went on anyway and soon became the stuff of legend in the "peace and love" antiwar movement in the summer of '69. No one imagined the doubleheader sweep of the Padres would be the start of a 29-7 Mets run.

It could be argued that the tide turned with Durocher's refusal to rest his veteran regulars, as well as the residue of Rube Walker's five-man rotation. Seaver and Koosman, especially, responded to the extra days' rest when it counted most. From August 26 to the end of the season, Seaver hurled eight consecutive complete-game victories, while Koosman was 9-2 with seven complete games from August 1 to the end of the regular campaign, finishing 17-9 with a 2.28 ERA. The final demise for the Cubs, who had been watching fitfully as the Mets kept winning and whittling down their lead to almost nothing, was the two-game series at Shea, on September 8 and 9, when Koosman and Seaver each pitched complete game victories over them.

In the first game, Monday night, the beanball hostilities from back on May 4 in Chicago resumed when Cubs starter Bill Hands threw a pitch right at Agee's head, leading off the first inning. Ron Santo, who was leading off the bottom of the second, instinctively knew he was going to be the victim of retaliation but was nevertheless unable to avoid Koosman's first pitch right on his elbow.

"Hands was trying to intimidate us—that was right from Durocher," Koosman said in a 2019 interview. "So, I didn't waste any time. The 'hit' was so loud I thought at first I'd broken Santo's arm. Later, in the eighth inning, Hands threw at me, and I yelled at him, 'You don't throw hard enough to hurt anyone!'"

Agee, meanwhile, got his pound of Hands's flesh with a retaliatory two-run homer his next time at bat in the third, to send Koosman and the Mets off to a 3–2 victory and bring them to within a game and a half of first place. Finally showing no ill effects from the beaning by Gibson that hampered him all of '68, Agee had the kind of season in '69 that Hodges had envisioned when the Mets originally traded for him: he batted .271 with 26 homers and 97 runs scored and provided superb defense in center field.

The next night, a series of events left the Cubs totally demoralized. As if Seaver's efficient five-hitter wasn't enough, Durocher's decision— critics called it a panic move—to start Jenkins on just two days' rest backfired badly when the Mets battered the Cubbies' ace for six runs, including homers by Clendenon and Shamsky, in the first five innings.

But it was in the top of the fourth when the Cubs were really shaken. Glenn Beckert's one-out double gave Chicago its first base-runner against Seaver. With dangerous Billy Williams at the plate, the game was suddenly interrupted by a black cat that came out from under the stands, circled around Santo in the on-deck circle, and paraded in front of the Cubs' dugout before retreating from whence it came.

"We're looking at this cat, and we figured it came from somebody in the stands," recalled Williams in a 2017 interview at the Hall of Fame. "Here it is, circling around Santo, and everybody said, 'What the hell, we're done now.'"

"The black cat was just so funny," said Koosman. "The poor thing was terrified. But we all felt sorry for Fergie. Leo left him in even though he was pitching on two days' rest and clearly didn't have it. Actually, the whole Cubs team was tired from all those day games at Wrigley Field and Leo not resting them."

Chicago, which had already lost four in a row coming into Shea, never recovered. The team lost eleven out of twelve from September 3 through September 15, and on September 24 the Mets clinched the National League East Division when Gentry shut out the Cardinals, 6–0, in front of 54,928 delirious fans. Chicago, which once led the Mets by ten games, would finish a distant second, eight games back. That brought the Mets' season attendance to 2,175,373 in '69, double that of the Yankees' 1,067,986. No sooner had the Cardinals' Joe Torre grounded into a double play to end the game, the fans came pouring out of the stands onto the field and began frantically scooping up handfuls of turf. Meanwhile, the Mets players had to literally scramble for their lives, pushing through the rampaging mob, to get to the safety of the dugout.

After the game, Seaver and Nancy celebrated with a quiet late dinner at their new home in Greenwich and stayed up to watch the *Tonight* show with Johnny Carson. It had been a season full of small miracles, and it wasn't over yet.

"It was such a wonderful time," Nancy reminisced. "I guess we just didn't realize what was happening. I mean, I understood what was happening on the field, and that was the most exciting thing in the world—you know, to be the underdogs, the new kids on the block. But it was a wonderful time for a lot of young people to pull together. Tom was as excited about it as everybody else. They were a young team, and they were very close, and they loved winning, and the winning was such a surprise."

CHAPTER 6

The Little Team That Could—Was Us

"YOU DON'T HAVE TO BE ANYTHING MORE THAN WHAT GOT you here."

A few hours before game one of the 1969 National League Championship Series, on Saturday, October 4, Gil Hodges was addressing the Mets in the visitors' clubhouse at Atlanta Stadium. While the young team might have been feeling a bit jittery at the prospect of participating in this first-ever championship series for the National League pennant, its manager was a picture of steely calm, reminding his men they'd earned this right with their determined play throughout the season, winning one hundred games (not to mention ten out of twelve from their NLCS opponents, the 93-69 Atlanta Braves), and need not apologize to anyone for being here.

Still, the Braves, under manager Lum Harris, had been just as hot as the Mets down the September stretch. Entering the last month of the season stalled in fourth place, they won seventeen of their last twenty games, including ten in a row. By midmonth, they'd caught and then passed the first-place San Francisco Giants, then fended them off the rest of the way to finish three games ahead in the National League West.

As much as Hodges's words were always reassuring for him, Seaver was unable to assuage the knot he felt in his stomach as he prepared himself mentally to take the ball for game one. Even though he'd finished the season with ten straight victories for a 25-7 record and stingy 2.21 ERA, it had been a week since he'd pitched, and he worried about being overrested. The twenty-four-year-old spent the night before going over the Braves' hitters in his head, particularly their formidable middle of the order: Orlando Cepeda (.257 BA, 22 HR, 88 RBI), Rico Carty (.342, 16, 58), and his idol, Hank Aaron (.300, 44, 97). He'd hardly eaten any breakfast, and the late four o'clock game time only added to his anxiety.

For his part, Hodges sought to combat Seaver's opponent—the often baffling right-handed knuckleballer Phil Niekro, who'd won twenty-three games in the regular season—by inserting into his lineup four left-handed batters: Wayne Garrett at third base, Ken Boswell at second, Ed Kranepool at first, and Art Shamsky in right field.

Nonetheless, the quick 2–0 lead the Mets staked Seaver to in the second inning failed to ease his discomfort on the mound. Grote could sense that by the way his battery mate was rushing his pitches.

"I remember Jerry telling me I needed to get my arm higher," Seaver explained in 2016, "but when I did, my pitches were coming in higher, and the Braves were hitting them."

Carty led off the second with a double and later came around on a sacrifice fly. Then in the third, second baseman Felix Millan and outfielder Tony Gonzalez hit successive one-out doubles, bringing Aaron to the plate. "All I was thinking then," said Seaver, "was that I can't let Henry beat me." That would be wishful thinking. Aaron stroked the Braves' third straight double of the inning to put them ahead, 3–2.

The Mets regained the lead for Seaver the following inning when Kranepool singled, Grote walked, and Seaver's road roomie, Bud Harrelson, tripled to right. But when Gonzalez homered leading off the fifth to tie the score, 4–4, it was clear Seaver was not on his normal game. His pitches were still coming in uncustomarily high, and the Braves were taking advantage. Was it the extra rest? If there was one thing resolute about the 1969 Mets season, it was that when Seaver took the mound, they could almost always count on a *W*. Now, in the biggest game of the year so far, they'd twice given him leads he couldn't hold.

The score remained tied into the seventh when Aaron, who'd lined out hard to Harrelson at short in his third at-bat after the Gonzalez homer in the fifth, was at the plate. How to keep Bad Henry from hurting him again? Instead of challenging him with a fastball, this time Seaver chose to try to cross him up with a slow outside curve—a decision he immediately regretted when Aaron deposited the pitch deep over the left-field fence for a 5–4 Braves lead.

So much for the projected low-scoring game between the two best pitchers in the National League. Niekro, who'd also had a week's rest, didn't have his best stuff, either, his knuckleball misbehaving way too much. This was further evidenced in the eighth when the Mets struck back with a leadoff double by Garrett and a game-tying RBI single by Cleon Jones on a knuckleball that didn't break. The rally continued: Shamsky singled, Jones stole third on an aborted bunt attempt by Boswell and scored on a throwing error to the plate by Cepeda on Kranepool's grounder to first. With two outs and two runs in, the Braves elected to intentionally walk the light-hitting Harrelson to load the bases. Now that the Mets had taken Seaver off the hook, Hodges was taking him out of the game, sending up J. C. Martin to hit for him—and Seaver felt relieved when the reserve catcher broke open the game and completed the kayo of Niekro with a bases-clearing single.

In retrospect, it was one of the ugliest and most unsatisfactory wins of Seaver's career, particularly in light of the game's importance. Afterward, he admitted to reporters about being nervous, causing him, he said, to rush his pitches and get his delivery out of sync. But the bottom line was that the Mets still won, proving, Seaver joked, that "God truly is a Met."

His two other heralded "young gun" rotation mates, Koosman and Gentry, fared far worse in their first postseason starts. Despite being gifted an 8–0 lead in the fourth inning of game two, Koosman was driven from the mound by a five-run Braves uprising in the fifth and was unable to get credit for an eventual 11–5 Mets victory. Back home at Shea the next day, the Mets completed the three-game sweep despite a third straight subpar starting pitching performance, in which Gentry was pulled by Hodges with runners at second and third and no outs in the third inning with the Braves leading already, 2–0.

This was the game when it was said that Nolan Ryan came of age. Relieving Gentry, the twenty-two-year-old Texan, he of the hundred-mile-per-hour heater, was able to work his way out of the bases-loaded jam and pitch the rest of the game, fanning seven in seven innings. The Mets would come from behind to win the game, 7–4, and clinch the pennant, hammering Braves starter Pat Jarvis for homers by Tommie Agee in the third, Boswell (with one on) in the fourth, and Garrett (with one on) in the fifth. But it was Ryan, more than anyone else, who earned Seaver's admiration that day.

"What Nollie did, finishing that game out like that, was huge," said Seaver in 2017. "He'd had issues with blisters during the season, and he'd missed time with National Guard duty, but that was another example of Gil showing faith in us to do things we weren't sure we were capable of. What made Gil such a great manager was that everyone on the team always had to be ready for whatever came up during the course of the game. The marine in him taught him to always be prepared."

Before the season, the Las Vegas oddsmakers had tabbed the Mets, who'd never come close to a winning season, 100-to-1 long shots to win the National League pennant. Well, the 100-to-1 shot had just come in, and now its reward was a World Series matchup against the Baltimore Orioles, winners of a major-league-high 109 games in the regular season. Baltimore, too, had just put away its opponent, the Minnesota Twins, in like manner in the American League Championship Series. So once again the Mets found themselves heavy underdogs, to an Orioles team with two former American League MVPs in Brooks Robinson, a magician with the glove at the hot corner and still a threat at bat (.234 BA, 23 HR, 84), and outfielder Frank Robinson, who at age thirty-three put up a .308 average, banged 32 homers, and knocked in 100 runs, and a future MVP in first baseman Boog Powell (.304 BA, 37 HR, 121 RBI) the following year. In addition, Baltimore boasted a starting rotation to match New York's in quality and depth. The quartet of Dave McNally, Mike Cuellar, Jim Palmer, and Tom Phoebus had combined for seventy-three wins in '69.

After the Orioles wiped out the Twins in three games, Frank Robinson proclaimed, "Bring on Ron Gaspar and the Mets," a disparaging reference to the Mets' reserve outfielder *Rod* Gaspar. When one of his Oriole teammates, Merv Rettenmund, corrected him—"It was "*Rod* Gaspar, not Ron, stupid"—Frank reportedly retorted, "Okay, bring on the Mets and Rod Stupid!"

The Orioles were clearly not impressed by the mystique surrounding the Mets and all the improbable ways they'd won ballgames in '69. "If somebody upstairs is guiding the Mets as we're being told, then all I can say is He is guiding us better," quipped Orioles manager Earl Weaver, "because we won a hundred nine games to their hundred." To that, Frank Robinson chirped in again, "The World Series might go five, or it just might go four. The Birds haven't decided yet."

After the Mets' NLCS sweep, Hank Aaron, in a 2018 interview at the Hall of Fame, recalled walking through LaGuardia Airport in New York and running into a couple of Orioles scouts. "One of them said, 'Oh boy, they handled y'all pretty good,'" Aaron reported, "and I said, 'Well, sure they did, but they had something to handle us well with. When you get to see Seaver, Koosman, Gentry, and Nolan Ryan, those guys can get anyone out.' They said, 'We'll see about that,' and I said: 'You sure will, 'cause I'm going home!'"

The Mets paid no heed either to the cocky statements from the Orioles and instead were enjoying the World Series atmosphere. At the workouts the day before the Series was to start at Baltimore's Memorial Stadium, Seaver and Gentry decided to have some fun with the media, most of whom knew little about them as opposed to the star-laden Orioles, who, three years earlier, had swept the Dodgers of Sandy Koufax, Don Drysdale, and Maury Wills in the '66 Fall Classic. According to Seaver, the two decided to switch uniform jerseys, Gentry wearing Seaver's 41 and Seaver taking Gentry's 39. Much to their delight, the Baltimore reporters did not know the difference. One of them approached Gentry, wearing Seaver's jersey, and, coincidentally, asked him a question about Gentry.

"To be honest," Gentry said, "I think Gary Gentry is a lousy pitcher." Immediately, a group of stunned reporters began gathering around "Seaver," scribbling furiously in their notebooks as he continued saying outrageous things—until a writer from the *New York Times* happened by and, spotting Seaver standing nearby, hollered, "Hey, Tom! How ya doin'?" The group looked at him curiously, and then at Seaver, wearing number 39. "Sorry, guys," Seaver said, laughing. "We just wanted you to get to know us better."

In the hours before game one on Saturday, October 11, Seaver was feeling the same kind of queasiness in his stomach as he had before his game one start in the NLCS against the Braves. For one thing, he'd again had hardly anything to eat. The lines for breakfast in the coffee shop of the antiquated Sheraton-Belvedere Hotel, where the Mets were staying, were so long, he and Harrelson simply gave up and got on the first team bus to the ballpark. After a while, one of the clubhouse boys fetched Seaver a roast beef sandwich, which was hardly satisfying, as he consumed himself with going over the Orioles' hitters one by one. It had been exactly one week since his last start in the NLCS.

After Orioles starter Mike Cuellar (23-11, 2.38 ERA) set down the Mets in the top of the first, Seaver trudged to the mound with his familiar plowboy gait for his first World Series start. How ironic, he thought, that the first batter he should face in his first World Series start was fellow USC grad and Rod Dedeaux protégée Don Buford, the Orioles' pint-sized (five-seven, 160 pounds) left fielder. In fact, the Trojans' coach had flown in from California to see both of his former stars. Buford, a .291 batter in 1969, with eleven home runs and nineteen stolen bases, was much more of a speed guy than a power threat, and, as such, Seaver's plan was to go right after him with fastballs inside. His first pitch, a fastball just a tad inside, was a ball. On his second pitch, another inside fastball, Buford stroked the ball high and deep to right-center. At first, Seaver thought it was going to be a relatively easy fly ball out. But then he saw Swoboda turning and shielding his eyes with his glove before leaping and tumbling to the ground as the ball disappeared over the right-field wall.

"What the hell happened out there?" Seaver asked himself.

Swoboda was livid with himself, especially after hearing later that Buford, as he was rounding the bases, had shouted to Harrelson at short: "You ain't seen nothin' yet!"

Early in his career, Swoboda was generally regarded as a below-average defensive outfielder, and as he wrote in his 2019 memoir, *Here's the Catch: A Memoir of the Miracle Mets and More*, "There was no way I shouldn't have caught that ball. On the replays, I looked like C-3PO, the golden droid from *Star Wars*, or, maybe, the Tin Woodsman from *The Wizard of Oz* looking for his oil can. . . . I never made any connection with the ball in flight. Arriving late at the wall, I turned to face the ball and threw myself into a leap that was as poorly timed as I was off target."

Seaver recovered from the initial shock by striking out the next two Orioles batters, Paul Blair and Frank Robinson, before yielding a single to six-foot-four Boog Powell and retiring Brooks Robinson on a fly that Tommie Agee ran down in deep center. On his way into the dugout after the inning, Swoboda was still cursing himself for messing up Buford's homer until Kranepool, the Mets' resident clubhouse cynic, admonished him to "shut the fuck up and get the next one!"

Seaver kept the Orioles at bay in the second and third but then, with two outs in the fourth, suddenly lost it, starting with a single by catcher Elrod Hendricks and a walk to Davey Johnson. Two successive RBI singles by the numbers eight and nine hitters, light-hitting short-stop Mark Belanger and the opposing pitcher, Cuellar, and an RBI double by Buford, and suddenly it was a 4–0 game. If it was anyone other than Seaver, Hodges would have gone to the bullpen at that point.

Instead, he allowed Seaver to pitch out of further damage in the inning and continue on for one more before relieving him with Don Cardwell. In the seventh, the Mets finally broke through for a run, but that was the extent of their offense against Cuellar, a wily thirty-two-year-old lefty. The Birdies, as Frank Robinson had chided, were in position to make a quick kill of the Mets after beating up on their franchise starter, 4–1. But at least one Met—the thirty-six-year-old veteran third baseman Ed Charles, who was considered the spiritual leader in their clubhouse—wasn't disheartened at all. After the game, he happened to run into Orioles pitching coach George Bamberger, an old friend from when they were teammates on the Vancouver Mounties team in the Triple-A Pacific Coast League in 1961, and blurted confidently: "Enjoy it, George, 'cause this is the last game you guys are gonna win."

"I absolutely pitched lousy in the opening game," Seaver said in 2016. "In hindsight, I was nervous and, emotionally, it was very different from my second start in the Series. I wanted to pitch out. I wanted to be mentally tough. I wanted to have the responsibility of doing well and getting us off to a good start, and I didn't control my emotions. Thank God, the next day Koosy handled it much better than I did."

Jerry Koosman had been charting Seaver's pitches from the dugout in game one, and as it appeared more and more there was going to be no Mets "magic" against Cuellar, he felt the terrible burden weighing upon him. "What I felt," he said in a 2019 interview, "was the fear of losing. I didn't want to go back to New York down oh-and-two. So, when I took the mound for game two, I had only one goal, and that was to pitch a perfect game."

And damn if he nearly did, at least for the first six innings. The left-hander retired seventeen of the first eighteen batters he faced and took a 1–1 game into the ninth when the Mets were able to break through on Dave McNally, the Orioles' number one starter. A twenty-game winner from 1968 through 1971, the twenty-six-year-old left-hander had been equally dominant to that point when, unexpectedly, he gave up three straight one-out singles to Charles, Grote, and the go-ahead hit by the slender, unsung second baseman, Al Weis. A .219 lifetime hitter, Weis was another player Hodges had known from the American League; the kind of player who, in his mind, belied his lifetime batting average with a mind-set to be capable of getting big hits at the right time.

Koosman, with a last-out assist from Ron Taylor, who rang up thirteen saves during the season, made the 2–1 Mets advantage stand up, and there would be no Birdies sweep.

"Koosy relieved the pressure on all of us," Seaver said.

On Tuesday, the Series resumed in Flushing for a day game in front of 56,355. Gentry, confirming Hank Aaron's warning to the Orioles' scout he'd encountered at LaGuardia, followed up Koosman's gem by blanking Baltimore on three hits through 6⅔ innings. Nolan Ryan completed the 5–0 shutout, pitching out of another bases-loaded jam in the seventh with the help of a sensational saving catch by Agee in deep right-center. He yielded only one other hit while striking out three over the final 2⅓ frames.

Now it was Seaver's time again for game four. After watching his teammates' heroics the last two games, he could feel the wind at his back.

"I had a whole different feeling from game one," he remembered. "I was still pissed at how I'd pitched. Making that game one start even more humiliating, afterward I was having dinner with Nancy and some friends in the Chesapeake Restaurant in Baltimore, and who do I see across the room? Dedeaux and Buford eating together! On the way out, I yelled to Dedeaux, 'Front-runner!'"

"Tom Seaver could pitch, really pitch—you know, ninety-five on the corner and a slider that looked like that," said Jim Palmer, the loser of game three, in a 2017 interview at the Hall of Fame, "and anybody can have a bad game. Buford was one of our best offensive guys, so the home run he hits in game one? I mean, those things happen. I threw three home runs in the All-Star Game in 1977 and ended up winning two hundred sixty-eight games with the same ERA Seaver has. So, things happen. Bad things happen. But do you think when he went out to pitch game four of the 1969 World Series, he was worried about game one? Hell, no. That was in the rearview mirror."

There was, however, one disconcerting element to what Seaver hoped would be his day of redemption. As it turned out, Wednesday, October 15, 1969, had also been declared Moratorium Day throughout the United States, with organized marches and rallies against the war in Vietnam. On his way to Shea Stadium, Seaver couldn't help but notice groups of antiwar protestors passing out pamphlets. When he got to the clubhouse, Tug McGraw, his fellow marine reservist, was brandishing one and handed it to him, with a grin. "You really say this?" he asked.

The front of the *Mets Fans for Peace* flyer featured prominently a photo of Seaver and a recent short newspaper article from United Press International headlined, "Tom Seaver Says U.S. Should Leave Vietnam." In it, the pitcher is quoted as saying: "If the Mets can win the pennant, then we can get out of Vietnam." Right after the Mets had claimed the National League title, Seaver received a call from someone with the antiwar Moratorium Day Committee, asking him if he would take out an ad saying exactly that. He'd already publicly expressed his criticism about how the war was being conducted on a number of occasions and saw no harm in the quote. In a subsequent interview with a reporter from United Press International that was featured in the October 11 editions of the *New York Times*, Seaver confirmed his intentions of taking out the ad and again was critical of the US involvement in Vietnam: "I think it's perfectly ridiculous what we're doing about the Vietnam situation," he said. "It's absurd. When the World Series is over, I'm going to have a talk with [Massachusetts senator] Ted Kennedy and convey some of my ideas to him."

It had always been extremely rare for professional athletes to make political statements, especially during the turbulent Vietnam War period, but perhaps because of who he was and what he meant to the city at that particular time, Seaver was not criticized by the media for his views. Glancing at the flyer, Seaver frowned. Yes, he'd had harsh words about the US foreign policy in Vietnam, and he thought the United States was conducting the war the wrong way, but he was not about to grab a bullhorn and join a demonstration. Not with all those marines dying over there. The longer he looked at the pamphlet, the angrier he got—especially after realizing the flyer had been put out not by the Moratorium Committee but by a satellite antiwar group called the Chicago Conspiracy, which had been accused of plotting violent demonstrations at the 1968 Democratic convention in Chicago. How dare these people, most of whom had dodged the draft when he had not, use his name and picture without his permission! This was a distraction he and his Mets teammates didn't need, which was why he had earlier refused a request from one of the Moratorium Committee people to wear a black armband on his uniform that day. He tossed aside the flyer and put it out of his mind.

A couple of hours later, Seaver was standing on the mound at Shea Stadium, seemingly oblivious to the din of 57,367 fans chanting "Sea-vuh! Sea-vuh! Sea-vuh!" and staring down once again at the visage of Don Buford, leading off for the Orioles.

When Buford took his first pitch for a strike—almost the exact inside fastball he'd taken over the fence as the first batter of game one—Seaver relaxed. Instinctively, he felt game four was going to be a whole different story. He wound up striking out Buford to start the inning and Boog Powell, looking, to end it. His stuff was on.

Seaver's opponent again was Cuellar, who proved just as frustrating to the Mets as he'd been in game one, his only mistake being a Clendenon home run to deep left field leading off the second. The score remained 1–0 going into the top of the ninth, when Seaver showed his first sign of tiring, yielding successive one-out singles to Frank Robinson and Powell that put runners on the corners for Brooks Robinson.

Prior to the two hits, Seaver had retired nineteen of twenty Orioles batters since the first inning, but now Hodges was at the mound for a conference. He knew his ace was fatigued and had both McGraw and Taylor warming up in the bullpen. But again his gut told him to hold off. This was going to be Tom Seaver's game to win or lose.

At the crack of Brooks's bat, instant fear gripped the Shea crowd. In the official box score, Brooks is credited with a sacrifice fly. In truth, never was a sacrifice fly more misleading. The ball was firmly smacked and looked almost certain to fall in and go all the way to the wall—until here came "Rocky" Swoboda, charging like a wild bull over from right to make a sensational diving, rolling catch, thus atoning for his misplay of Buford's ball in game one.

"It was the least I could do for Tom after screwing up so badly on him in game one," Swoboda said in 2019. "The next day there were all sorts of adjectives in the papers about the catch, including, I think, 'graceful.' I can assure you the words *graceful* and *Swoboda* were never before or after used in the same sentence. But that, I guess, was my one graceful moment."

Seaver went on to retire the lefty-hitting Hendricks on a liner to right to end the inning, but not before Hendricks narrowly missed hitting a go-ahead two-run homer, with a screeching drive toward the right-field corner that, at the last second, curved inches to the right of the foul pole 341 feet away. In their half of the ninth, the Mets threatened to win the game, putting runners at first and third with two out after singles by Cleon Jones and Swoboda off Orioles closer Eddie Watt. But Art Shamsky, pinch-hitting for Ed Charles, grounded out.

It was on to the tenth, where, ordinarily, the manager could be expected to turn the game over to his bullpen. This was what Seaver expected, especially since he'd thrown 135 pitches to that point and barely avoided giving up the go-ahead homer to Hendricks. Except Hodges said nothing to him. No, this was going to be yet another example of Gil asking one of his players to do something they weren't sure they were capable of.

On the other hand, Hodges certainly did not count on Wayne Garrett, who'd replaced Charles at third base, mishandling Davey Johnson's hard-hit leadoff grounder in the tenth for an error. Anticipating a bunt by the next, hitter, Belanger, Seaver fired a high-inside fastball that the shortstop couldn't handle, the ball nicking his bat and popping straight up right to Grote for an out. Orioles manager Earl Weaver, who'd been thrown out of the game in the third inning by home plate umpire Shag Crawford for arguing balls and strikes too strenuously, was notorious for his disdain of sacrificing and giving up an out; no doubt he rued the decision to order it by his stand-in, third-base coach Billy Hunter—especially when the next batter, Clay Dalrymple, pinch-hitting for Watt, singled to center.

At that point, Hodges sent Rube Walker out to the mound for another check on Seaver. "I'm okay, Rube," the pitcher insisted. "I've got a few more pitches in me." Privately, he knew there were very few. Most of his pitches had been up the previous inning, and he could feel himself losing velocity.

With Orioles at first and second with one out, once again Buford was coming to the plate. One could only imagine the mixed emotions Rod Dedeaux, watching in the stands, was feeling at that point. Though he was physically spent, Seaver was not going to let his fellow USC alumnus get the best of him again. He threw a fastball, a tad outside, which Buford hammered into right field. But once again, Swoboda hustled over to haul it in. As he had on Hendricks's long foul in the ninth, Seaver breathed a sigh of relief and pounded his glove in silent thanks. He then struck out Blair to end the inning.

Years later, Seaver was hard-pressed to explain why Hodges had chosen to eschew his usual late-inning move of replacing Swoboda (who'd earned his improbable nickname "Mr. Defense" for his often plodding, roughshod outfield play) with Rod Gaspar for defensive reasons.

"Everything Gil did—and didn't do—just worked," Seaver said with a sigh.

Dick Hall, an intimidating six-foot-six side-arming right-hander who'd had a 1.92 ERA in the regular season, was the new Orioles pitcher in the tenth. and found himself in immediate trouble when Buford lost Grote's leadoff fly ball to left in the sun, allowing it to drop between him and Belanger, who was racing out for it. The official scorer ruled it a double, and the Shea crowd was once more in a frenzy.

Finally, Hodges summoned Gaspar, but as a pinch runner for Grote. With first base open, the Orioles walked Weis intentionally, and as Seaver kneeled in the on-deck circle, he knew it was highly unlikely Hodges would let him hit. Sure enough, the manager motioned him back to the dugout and sent up lefty-hitting J. C. Martin, who'd gotten the game-breaking pinch hit off Atlanta's Phil Niekro in game one of the NLCS.

This time Hodges was not looking for a pinch hit. He assumed the Orioles would seek to counter the lefty-hitting Martin by bringing in the highly effective left-hander Pete Richert (7-4, 2.20 ERA, 12 saves), who was warming up in the bullpen. The reason he'd chosen Martin instead of the right-handed-hitting Duffy Dyer, his other backup catcher, was because, before coming to the Mets, Martin had spent his entire career with the Chicago White Sox, a notoriously weak-hitting team that specialized in "small ball": bunting, hit-and-run plays, and so on. In this situation, Hodges wanted a bunt to sacrifice Gaspar over to third and felt Martin was the man best equipped to execute it.

In a 2019 interview, Martin recalled walking to the plate as Hodges called time out and ran up to him. "We're going to do something a little different here now with Richert," the manager told him. "I want you to get down a bunt, so we'll have two outs to get the runner home from third base. But make sure it's to the right side of the infield where the pitcher, catcher, or first baseman has to field it—and nowhere near Brooks Robinson." (Another likely factor in Hodges's decision was the fact that Richert, being a lefty, would have to glove a bunt to the right side and then wheel around to make the throw to first.) Martin understood. They didn't call Brooks the Human Vacuum Cleaner for nothing, as he was possibly the greatest-fielding third baseman of all time. The perennial All-Star won the Gold Glove Award sixteen years straight, from 1960 through 1975, when he was thirty-eight years old.

On the first pitch, Martin laid down a textbook bunt, about ten to twelve feet in front of home plate, with just enough backspin to slow it down. Richert raced in from the mound, picked up the ball, and as if trying to thread a needle fired a bullet to Davey Johnson, covering first base. But the throw struck Martin—who was running a couple of feet on the fair side of the baseline—on the wrist. The ball ricocheted off him and rolled into short right field as Gaspar gleefully ran all the way home from second with the winning run.

The first person to greet Gaspar was Seaver, the pitcher of record, who led the charge of Mets out of the dugout. The Orioles, with the volatile Weaver still confined to the clubhouse, protested vehemently that Martin had been running too far inside the baseline and should have been called out for interference. (In fact, rule 5:09 of the MLB's *Official Baseball Rules* book states: "A batter is out when in running the last half of the distance from home plate to first base . . . he runs inside [to the left of] the first-base line and in the umpire's judgement, in doing so, interferes with the fielder taking the throw at first base.") Unfortunately for Baltimore, home plate umpire Crawford saw no interference on Martin's part and blew them off. Perhaps if Weaver had not been ejected and was in the dugout to witness the play firsthand, the Orioles would have at least filed a formal protest. But they never did.

Another fluky Mets win, this one decided on a walk-off bunt, in a season that had been replete with games like that. Seaver would say later: "As I watched Gaspar's legs pummeling up and down, kicking up dirt before his front foot stretched out and touched home plate, my whole baseball life flashed before me . . . the grand slam I hit for the Goldpanners, the first game I'd won as a Met, the imperfect game I pitched against the Cubs . . . every minor miracle building to that one magic day. And I felt, in a similar way, so many people in the stands— my father, Rod Dedeaux, Nelson Burbrink [the scout who signed him], Nancy—must have all been reliving some of the same scenes."

In a panel discussion in New York with a few other Mets as part of the golden anniversary celebration of the '69 season, Martin relived his bunt in hilariously self-effacing fashion. "Nobody wants to bunt in the World Series," said the lifetime .222 hitter whose defense kept him in the sport for fourteen seasons. "But Gil said, 'Bunt,' and so I bunted. Years after, I went to so many Old Timers' games in New York because of that one lousy bunt! They'd invite all these players back who'd done something in the World Series and have them play a game. And there would be Mantle and Maris—and *me*! I got to go back to New York more times because of that bunt than I would have if I'd hit a home run."

After the game, the Seaver family—Tom, Nancy, Charlie, and sisters Carol and Katie and their husbands—all went out to dinner at Lum's, Tom and Nancy's favorite Chinese restaurant in Queens, to celebrate what would be his first and only World Series victory. The only family member missing was his brother, Charles, who had a prior engagement at a Moratorium Day rally at Bryant Park in Manhattan. The restaurant owner, George Lum, had set aside a couple of bottles of champagne, and Seaver's proud dad proposed a toast:

"Moments like this," said Charlie, "bring great happiness to our lives."

Naturally, they pressed Tom throughout the dinner to relive the whole game; everything that was happening on the field, in his mind, and in the dugout. At one point, Carol's husband, Bob Baker, pressed him: "Okay, Tom, what will you remember most about this game?"

"The Hendricks foul," Seaver said with a laugh. "I'll remember that for a long time."

Before leaving the clubhouse at Shea, Seaver had made a point of wishing good luck to Koosman, who had the game five—and potential clincher—pitching duties. "I'm counting on you tomorrow, Koosy," Seaver said, "because I don't want to have to go back to Baltimore!"

"There was no way I was gonna lose that game," Koosman said in 2019. "Pearl Bailey assured me of that."

Bailey, the renowned singer-actress performing on Broadway in an all-black revival of *Hello, Dolly!*, was a huge Mets fan who'd been invited to sing the national anthem for game five. As Koosman was getting ready to go out to the field for his pregame bullpen session, Bailey shouted to him from across the clubhouse, "Good luck, Jerry! I know you're gonna win today! I see the number eight!"

She would prove prophetic when Koosman recovered from giving up homers to McNally (his opposing pitcher again) and Frank Robinson in the third inning, and went on to pitch a five-hit, complete game 5–3 Mets victory for the World Series championship. Yes, 5–3—which added up to eight.

The moments after Davey Johnson's final-out fly settled into Cleon Jones's glove in left field were a blur for Seaver, as thousands of fans charged onto the field in raucous celebration. There was precious little time for the spontaneous self-congratulatory hugs before Seaver and his mates realized they were in the midst of an unruly mob and had to frantically fend for their safety by beating a hasty retreat back to the dugout and into the clubhouse. It was a couple of hours later when

Seaver ventured back out onto the ravaged Shea turf that now looked like the pockmarked surface of the moon, to grab a clod of dirt from the mound for himself. "It's just so beautiful what we did . . . so, so beautiful," he told reporters.

On a gorgeous Napa Valley afternoon in late September 2009, Seaver and I were sitting on the bench at the back of his vineyard in Calistoga, talking about wine and baseball, when he began reflecting on the '69 season, trying to put it in context. "When I was a little kid," he said, "my favorite book, which my mom used to read to me, was *The Little Engine That Could,* about the little locomotive that huffs and puffs and keeps repeating, 'I think I can, I think I can,' as it pulls this heavy train over the mountain. That was us."

In the days, weeks, and months after the World Series, the Mets were the toast of New York City—hell, they were the toast of the nation, this little team that could, and did. Everybody wanted them, and they especially wanted Tom and Nancy. Three days after the Series, the whole team appeared on TV's Sunday-night *Ed Sullivan Show.* Not long after, the comedian Phil Foster booked Seaver, Shamsky, Koosman, Clendenon, Jones, Agee, and Kranepool for two weeks to be part of his variety show in Las Vegas. They were paid $10,000 apiece to perform at two shows a night, singing "The Impossible Dream" from the Broadway hit show *Man of La Mancha.* That was in addition to each man's $18,338 World Series winning share, which for many of the Mets was more than their annual salary.

It started out as a lot of fun, but soon friction developed among some of them. It seemed some of the other players, in anticipation of two weeks of "boys' nights out" in Sin City, had not brought their wives. Upon seeing pictures in the newspapers of Tom and Nancy frolicking together in Vegas, the spouses began calling, wanting to know why they were not also invited.

According to local WCBS-TV sportscaster Sal Marchiano, who, as the only New York TV reporter regularly on the scene at Shea Stadium, was close to a number of the Mets players, an incident occurred at one of the Foster shows in which Nancy was clowning around, throwing salt from a shaker on Seaver and the other players. "After the show, Clendenon called Tom aside and told him, 'That behavior was unacceptable,'" said Marchiano. "That was the first time I ever heard anything negative about Tom."

On November 5 Seaver appeared on the weekly TV variety show *Kraft Music Hall*, hosted by country singer Eddy Arnold. With the pop vocal trio the Lettermen providing harmonies, he crooned the Frank Sinatra standard "Nancy (With the Laughing Face)" to his blushing bride in the audience. Whether his teammates liked it or not, the feel-good saga of the underdog '69 Miracle Mets had slowly morphed, post-Series, into the "Tom and Nancy" show.

One week before, the Baseball Writers' Association rewarded Seaver for his 25-7 season with the National League Cy Young Award by a near-unanimous vote of 23-to-1, Phil Niekro receiving the only other first-place vote. At twenty-four, he was the youngest pitcher ever to win the honor. Other awards followed: the S. Rae Hickok Belt for Professional Athlete of the Year, the *Sporting News* Man of the Year, and, in late December, *Sports Illustrated*'s prestigious Sportsman of the Year Award, in which he was featured on the cover.

However, when it came to the National League Most Valuable Player Award, San Francisco Giants first baseman Willie McCovey beat him out, 265 points to 243 points, despite each of them receiving eleven first-place votes. Since the award's inception in 1911, only fourteen pitchers in Major League Baseball had been so honored; the MVP typically went to an everyday player. The six-foot-four McCovey, who could always be counted on for thirty or more home runs a season, swatted 44 and knocked in 126 runs in 1969. In addition, he hit a robust .320, for the only .300 season of his twenty-two-year Hall of Fame career.

Seaver's new marketing agent, Frank Scott, seeking to quickly capitalize on his client's white-hot fame, took out an ad in the *New York Times* that essentially proclaimed "America's couple" to be for hire. "Now available: Tom Seaver, America's top athlete and sports personality, plus Nancy Seaver, Tom's lovely wife, for those situations that call for young Mrs. America or husband-and-wife sales appeal." It was terribly tacky and shocked a lot of Seaver's family and friends—most notably his mother, who was reportedly appalled by the ad and could not understand why her son had felt compelled to tarnish his carefully burnished All-American Boy image by doing such a thing.

It didn't matter. To New Yorkers, Seaver was a deity. An untouchable. The perfect athlete: handsome, articulate, and intelligent, with a beautiful wife whom he clearly loved dearly and to whom he was faithful. Or as sportswriter Robert Lipsyte explained in the *New York Times*: "[Seaver] was somewhat more verbally polished than Jerry Koosman, his pitching partner, and considerably whiter than Donn Clendenon, the batting star of the Series." On December 31 Seaver and Nancy placed another ad in the *Times,* this one saying: "On the eve of 1970, please join us in a prayer for peace."

There would come a time, in the not too distant future, when the toll of celebrity would begin to wear on Seaver, and he would seek to separate himself from the game and his teammates the moment the season was over and go into quiet retreat with Nancy. But in the immediate aftermath of the 1969 season, he was intoxicated by fame. Six years after the assassination of President John F. Kennedy, Camelot was back, at least in New York. Much like Jack and Jackie, he was the king of the city, and Nancy was his queen.

CHAPTER 7

Deaths in the Family

"All glory is fleeting."
—General George Patton

COME THE NEW YEAR, 1970, THE METS CELEBRATIONS HAD fully abated, with New York now in the grips of a new championship season: that of the National Basketball Association Knicks, built around center Willis Reed, guards Walt Frazier and Dick Barnett, and forwards Dave DeBusschere and a future senator from New Jersey and presidential aspirant named Bill Bradley. The Knicks would go on to win their first NBA title and electrify the city in the same way that Seaver and company had a few months earlier, beating the favored Los Angeles Lakers, led by Wilt Chamberlain, in a stirring and dramatic seven-game finals.

In Queens, all had been relatively quiet when on January 14 Johnny Murphy died unexpectedly of a heart attack at Roosevelt Hospital in Manhattan. The Mets' general manager, only sixty-one, had been admitted December 30 after suffering a first, mild heart attack at his home in Bronxville, New York, but doctors had reported he was recovering nicely and expected him to be released in a few days.

No one realized it at the time, but Murphy's death would later have critical consequences for the Mets franchise as a whole and for Seaver in particular.

"I looked at Johnny as a father figure," Seaver said in 2006. "He was the guy who was instrumental in the Mets' getting me in the lottery, and he took care of me in all of my contract negotiations, especially the first one," after his Rookie of the Year season, "in which he came all the way out to California to give me the raise I had asked for. He was a kind and fair man; the guy who put that '69 team together."

"What do we do now?" Mets board chairman M. Donald Grant said to *New York Times* Mets beat reporter Joe Durso. In truth, Grant quickly saw Murphy's death as a way for him to exert increased influence on the baseball operations. That became more evident when, after announcing he would first look to replace the GM from within the organization, he passed over farm director Whitey Herzog, the most logical choice, in favor of Bob Scheffing, who had been serving as a special assignment scout with the club. The outspoken, opinionated Herzog had clashed with Grant on a number of occasions during organization meetings, whereas the genial, mild-mannered Scheffing, a former player and onetime manager of both the Chicago Cubs and the Detroit Tigers, was someone Grant knew he could control. Nevertheless, it took considerable arm-twisting on the chairman's part, along with the promise of an apartment overlooking Little Neck Bay near Shea Stadium, to convince the reluctant Scheffing to leave the comfort of his home and daily golf in Scottsdale, Arizona, and move to New York.

With Murphy's death, Gil Hodges became the most powerful figure in the Mets' high command, the one man whose authority over baseball decisions Grant did not dare challenge. This was confirmed by a story involving Seaver early in 1970 that was later revealed by

Jack Lang, the longtime Mets beat reporter for the *Long Island Press* and later the *Daily News*. Seaver was sitting on the Mets' bench during a game at Shea Stadium when he narrowly missed being struck in the head by a bat that had flown out of a batter's hands at home plate. The TV cameras caught the incident, including Mets trainer Tom McKenna rushing to Seaver's aid, but then the pitcher disappeared from the view of the writers in the press box. Ordinarily, in matters of players being injured during the course of the game, the team's public relations director would call down to the dugout to get an update for the media, but Hodges had a strict rule that no calls were ever to be made to the dugout; instead, he would call the press box when he deemed appropriate. For the rest of the game, the writers, who were on deadline, and the Mets' radio and TV announcers were kept in the dark about Seaver's condition.

It turned out afterward that Seaver had not suffered any injury and had just been shaken up by the flying bat. But the next day, Lang happened to run into Grant in the Shea Stadium press parking lot and explained to him how Hodges's rule had caused a lot of needless anxiety for everyone the night before.

"It seems like everyone is afraid of Gil," Lang said to Grant. "We were all in the dark about Seaver until after the game last night. This can't happen again, Don. Can't you do something about it?"

"I'm sorry, Jack," Grant said. "I'm afraid of Gil too."

Lang persisted.

"But Don," he said. "This was Seaver! He's the *franchise*!"

With that remark, Grant recoiled and gave Lang a stern look.

"Don't you ever call Seaver 'the Franchise,'" he admonished. "Mrs. Payson and I am the franchise."

Maybe in his mind. But if Seaver's Cy Young 1969 season hadn't been enough to earn his niche as the Mets' most precious commodity, his performance on the first Earth Day, April 22, against the San Diego Padres—which would turn out to be the highlight of the Mets' 1970 season—further solidified his place as the most dominant and electrifying pitcher in the game. Being that it was early in the season and the Padres were a second-year expansion team that had lost 110 games the year before, there were only 21,694 (14,197 paid) fans at Shea Stadium on that clear and cool spring afternoon.

And for the first few innings, there was scarcely a hint that number 41 was about to make history. Ken Boswell's RBI double in the first inning provided a 1-0 advantage, but Seaver promptly gave it right back by surrendering a leadoff homer in the second to Brooklyn-born Al Ferrara, who, when he was not playing left field for the Padres, doubled as a concert pianist. The Mets regained the lead in the third on a single by Tommie Agee and a Bud Harrelson triple, and from there, Seaver began his relentless march to nineteen strikeouts, tying the record set by the Cardinals' Steve Carlton against the Mets the previous September. His fanning Ferrara, looking, to end the sixth was the first of ten straight, another record within the record. (The previous record for consecutive strikeouts in a game was eight, set in 1953 by Max Surkont of the Milwaukee Braves.) Ferrara would complete the dual dramas, swinging and missing on a low fastball to end the game as Seaver's nineteenth victim and tenth in a row.

"The right pitch to Ferrara would have been an outside slider, but I decided to challenge him with my best pitch, a fastball," Seaver said afterward. "I went for the strikeout, figuring I might never come this close again."

"Him against me; his best shot against my best shot. He was going for the strikeout, and I was going for the downs," Ferrara joked. "He won."

Satisfying as it may have been to tie the record and set another one of his own, Seaver said he did not feel the same emotion as he did the year before when he came within two outs of a perfect game against the Cubs. "I'm not really blasé. But this doesn't exhilarate me as much as the perfect game would have," he said. "That's the one I wish I had. Plus, this one was against an expansion club, and the Cubs were in first place last year."

Nevertheless, Jim McAndrew, who was charting the game, said it was the most incredible pitching performance he'd ever seen. In all, Seaver threw 136 pitches, 96 for strikes. "Watching him work those first six innings, you could see he had his best stuff, but then those last three innings, when he struck out the side in all of them, he never went beyond four pitches on any of them. I never saw anything like that." For 3⅓ innings, not one Padre hit a fair ball.

Fifty years later, Grote was still kicking himself for preventing Seaver from having a chance at twenty Ks. "Looking back, we had eight putouts in that game; one of them was a ball that Van Kelly popped up to me leading off the sixth inning," Grote told me at the fiftieth anniversary of the '69 season at Shea Stadium. "If I had known Tom was gonna have nineteen strikeouts, I'd never have caught that ball because I know he would have struck Kelly out on the next pitch."

Every season is different, and Seaver could tell early in 1970 that there wasn't the same spirit of plucky togetherness in the Mets' clubhouse as had been the case throughout their miracle run in '69. Reflecting on the '70 season in a 2016 interview, Seaver surmised that some of that may have been due to the absence of the veteran Ed Charles, whom he greatly respected. Charles, one of the spiritual leaders of the team, was released after the '69 World Series and given a position in the team's promotions department—only to leave the organization altogether in a bitter dispute over $5,000 in moving expenses to New York from his home in Kansas City. It was the first sign of erosion of the previous season's good feelings. Besides frequently providing wise counsel based on his nearly twenty years of professional baseball experience, the thirty-six-year-old third baseman would often entertain his teammates by reciting his own poetry. "Charles kept everybody loose," Seaver said. "He played a very important role in that clubhouse. We really missed that in 1970."

In his last trade before he died, Murphy tried to replace Charles at third by sending the Mets' top prospect, center fielder Amos Otis, to the Kansas City Royals, for Joe Foy, who'd averaged thirteen homers in his four seasons in the big leagues. In retrospect, it was the worst trade of Murphy's career and one of the worst in Mets history. In his one season with the Mets, Foy hit just .236 with six homers and was suspected of being under the influence of alcohol and drugs much of the time. He finally wore out his welcome with his bizarre behavior in a doubleheader late in the season, when he walked right in front of Hodges in the dugout, blocking the manager's view during a pitch, and inexplicably began cheering. In the second game, he failed to react when a batted ball rolled right past him at third base into left field. He would play only one more season in the majors, with the Washington Senators, and be out of baseball at the age of twenty-eight. Otis, on the other hand, immediately went on to a highly successful fourteen-year career with the Royals, making the American League All-Star team five times.

The defending champions got off to a sluggish start in 1970 and didn't get over .500 to stay until June 14. They would eventually rally into first place for three weeks from June 24 through July 5 but otherwise spent most of the season in futile pursuit of the front-running Pittsburgh Pirates. For his part, Seaver won his first seven starts and was 7-1 with a 1.96 ERA on May 15, seemingly on track for a second-straight Cy Young Award season.

But the beat writers saw a change in Seaver as well. Unlike his first three years, when he would regularly hold court at his locker, kibitzing with them about everything from baseball in general, to world events, to the *New York Times* crossword puzzle, he suddenly became more distant. Some suggested success had gone to his head, to the point where he considered the media beneath him now.

"Over the winter, he moved from Queens to Greenwich, and he was suddenly driving a Porsche," noted Joe Gergen of *Newsday* in a 2019 interview, "and you did see a difference in him. He was no longer approachable the way he had been. He only went out of his way for the *Times*, the paper he felt could help him most. It wasn't like he was uncooperative; he was still the most insightful player in the room when you were able to get him. He just wasn't nearly as accessible anymore."

Seaver's distance didn't extend to just the writers. His Mets teammates felt it as well. After the experience in Las Vegas with the Phil Foster show, he was now overly protective of his wife. There was also an understandable jealousy on the part of many of the other Mets players because of all the media attention heaped on him and Nancy. He wasn't particularly close to any of them, the notable exceptions being Harrelson and Grote, and the only teammate he and Nancy really socialized with was Nolan Ryan and his wife, Ruth. A longtime close associate of Seaver once told me candidly, "I love Tom, but let's be honest: Tom was an elitist. He thought he was better than everyone else on that team—and he was."

During a stretch of four straight losses, from May 20 through June 5, Seaver became especially short-tempered and even a little hostile with the media in his postgame sessions.

"Tom Seaver is finding out that being the top sports hero in one year demands a heavy penalty the following year," wrote George Vecsey in the *New York Times*. "Everywhere the Mets go, Seaver is the biggest target for autograph seekers, the young and the not-so-young, who think they have the right to the celebrity's time."

"It hasn't affected my life away from the ballpark," Seaver insisted, "but around the ballpark, I find there isn't as much time for playing pepper or just relaxing,"

After losing a 2–0 game to the Montreal Expos on May 30—the second straight shutout defeat he'd suffered at the hands of the National League expansion team—Seaver, who had uncharacteristically walked seven, was openly seething. He got particularly peeved when told that the opposing starter, Carl Morton, whose 18-11 record brought him NL Rookie of the Year honors that season, had suggested to the writers that Seaver may have been trying too hard after losing to them five days earlier.

"Is that what he said?" Seaver snapped. "It just shows how stupid he is."

That prompted Jack Lang to write an eye-opening article, critical of Seaver, in the *Sporting News* under the headline "Tough-luck Setbacks Strip Seaver of Golden Boy Halo."

"Losing is getting to Seaver," Lang wrote. "He is not reacting to adversity as well as he did to success, which is something no one expected of the Mets' man-child. He appeared in his first three years to be impervious to faults, but his fourth season is showing a different side of Tom, a not-so-pleasant side. . . . Following the winter of his great content, writers covering the Mets detected a certain aloofness in Seaver in spring training."

Seaver rebounded from the four straight losses to win nine in a row (with three no-decisions) from June 9 through August 1, and by August 10, with seven weeks left in the season, he was 17-6. His 10–2 complete-game win over Pittsburgh on that date brought the Mets to within two and a half games of the first-place Pirates in the National League East. Up to then, the rest of the Mets' rotation, Jerry Koosman, Gary Gentry, and Nolan Ryan, had all been faltering, either through injury or general ineffectiveness. In the hope of catching the Pirates, Hodges and Rube Walker approached Seaver about pitching every fourth day instead of every fifth day for the rest of the year. He was all for it, if for no other reason than it would give him a better chance to become the first National League pitcher to win thirty games since Dizzy Dean in 1934.

Beginning on August 15, when a cross-up of signs with Grote in the bottom of the ninth against the Braves in Atlanta led to a wild pitch on a strikeout and two runs scoring, Seaver lost his last four starts in August and won only one more game in 1970. Not only did he fail to win 30, he didn't even win 20, finishing at 18-12, though his 2.82 ERA and 283 strikeouts led the league. The Mets, after clawing their way into a tie for first place with the Pirates as late as September 14, lost eight of their next eleven and wound up in third place, six games back.

Hodges conceded later that very probably a sense of complacency afflicted the Mets in 1970 and that they lacked that killer instinct, especially down the stretch. "Some individuals may have been fat cats," he told the *Washington Post*'s Bob Addie. "They weren't as hungry as they were in 1969, when all the pieces fell into place." As for Seaver's late slump, he said, "You can't put it all on Seaver. There were too many other factors. He's a perfectionist who overconcentrated and lost some of his natural command, like a hitter in a slump. He was always trying to be perfect, to be analytical, to be Tom Seaver."

Seaver wasn't necessarily buying that. For whatever reason, perhaps the starts on four days' rest, he said he was gassed. "There was a lot of hangover from the busy winter," he conceded to Joe Durso of the *New York Times*. "It was more overwhelming than I realized. I was really tired at the end."

Early in the season, in an interview with Bill Surface for the *New York Times Magazine,* he vented: "I'm mixing with people any time I go out for a cup of coffee. People who've seen me can associate with me, but I've never seen them before. They act like we're long-lost friends and want me to come and see their little nephew strike out everyone in Brooklyn."

He needed to get away; away from baseball, away from the Mets, away from the fans, the pressure of winning, the media—all of it. So, shortly after the season, he and Nancy embarked on a trip around the country, with Fresno as their final destination. Their first stop was a visit to his brother, Charles, who was now working as an artist and sculptor in remote Ashfield, Massachusetts. Theirs was a mutual admiration society. Charles marveled at how Tom could pitch in front of fifty-five thousand people, and he once made a metal sculpture of a pitcher with Tom's delivery as a testament to his younger brother. Tom, on the other hand, was enraptured with Charles's quiet, artistic brilliance.

"Charles was one of those people who would just *get it*," he said in 2017. "One of the most important aspects of defining pitching for me was how my brother went about his work. I learned so many things from him. I adored him."

In the few days they spent in the quiet of Ashfield, Seaver watched his brother sculpt for hours. Calmly. Easily. With no visible pressure. A total contrast to what he had just put himself through in the 1970 season. Another lesson to take with him. "I need to reevaluate life a little and how I do things," he told Charles.

From Ashfield, it was west to the Baseball Hall of Fame in Cooperstown, New York. Seaver, of course, had no way of knowing he would one day have a permanent residence in the plaque room there, but he'd always been a student of the game who appreciated its history, and this was the first chance he'd ever had to see so much of that history firsthand. As he strolled the museum, taking in the artifacts of all the baseball legends, from Babe Ruth, Ty Cobb, Ted Williams, and Stan Musial, to his pitching idols Christy Mathewson and Walter Johnson, he stopped in front of a glass case with a Mets cap in it—the one he'd worn in his nineteen-strikeout game. "I want my parents, my brother, my sisters, and Rod Dedeaux to see this," he remembered saying to Nancy, "because without them, this wouldn't be here."

The following February, he arrived at spring training in Saint Petersburg with a new attitude, a new understanding of who he was, and a determination not to allow the media to define him. He was also about to become a father. In a 2016 interview, he recounted to me how, in the early morning hours of March 4, he was sound asleep in his room at the Saint Petersburg Hilton when he got a call from Nancy in Greenwich. She had gone into labor, and he needed to get home pronto to assume his duties as her maternity coach. He caught the first plane home, landing in the midst of a blizzard at Newark Airport, and made it to the hospital. Nancy was lying in the bed, covered with sweat. As he gently wiped away the beads of perspiration on her face, she looked at him and blurted out: "That's it. I quit."

"Nancy," Seaver said, sternly, "there are a lot of things you can do right now, but quitting is not one of them. You have to have this baby!"

That calmed her down, and a short time later, Tom and Nancy welcomed Sarah Lynn Seaver into the world.

Seaver remained with Nancy and his new daughter for five days before returning to spring training and the business of getting ready for the new season. Rather than make any wholesale changes after the disappointing 1970 campaign, Scheffing had merely fine-tuned the Mets' roster, acquiring past-his-prime thirty-two-year-old Bob Aspromonte from the Atlanta Braves as a third-base replacement for Joe Foy, and trading Ron Swoboda, one of the heroes of the '69 team, to the Expos to make room for Ken Singleton, a promising rookie power hitter, in right field.

Before making his fourth straight opening-day start, a visibly more relaxed Seaver told reporters: "I have only one goal this season, and that's consistency. I'm not going to allow myself to press over every start like I did last year. I'm not going to try to be perfect with every pitch. I just want to be consistent."

He more than fulfilled that goal, compiling what he would later maintain was his greatest and most consistent season, starting out with four wins and one no-decision in April in which he allowed a total of just six earned runs in 39⅓ innings. On June 29 he hurled a 3–0 shutout over the Phillies, striking out thirteen, to run his record to 10-3, lower his ERA to 2.03, and earn his fifth straight selection to the National League All-Star team.

The '71 Mets, on the other hand, were anything but consistent. They were 32-20 after Seaver pitched them into a tie for first place in the National League East with a 4–2 victory over the Padres on June 9. But that was the last time they would be in first place. In July the team completely collapsed, going 9-20, to fall out of the race and into fourth place, 11½ games behind first-place Pittsburgh, which was on its way to a world championship.

July was also Seaver's worst month in '71, as he won only one of his six starts. But he pitched poorly in only one of them, and, come August, he got back on a roll, giving up a total of six earned runs over fifty-three innings in six starts, including a club record thirty-one consecutive scoreless innings. Most memorable were the two stirring pitching duels he had with the Padres' number one starter, Dave Roberts. In San Diego on August 11 the two pitched scoreless ball for ten innings before Hodges removed Seaver from the game for a pinch hitter; he'd given up only three hits and struck out fourteen to that point. But the Mets wound up losing, 1–0, in twelve innings, with Roberts going all the way.

"I'm glad Seaver didn't get the loss," Roberts told reporters, "because he pitched too well to lose. His record shows he's gone out there every fourth or fifth day and pitched well. That's as much as you can ask of anyone." The two met again on August 21 at Shea, and this time Seaver won, 2–1, when Cleon Jones touched Roberts for a game-winning, walk-off solo home run with two outs in the bottom of the ninth.

On September 26 Seaver pitched one of the best games of his career, a one-hit 3–1 win over the Pirates in which he struck out ten, walked only one, and retired the first eighteen batters in succession before issuing a leadoff walk to second baseman Dave Cash and a single to right fielder Vic Davalillo to start the seventh inning; Cash scored Pittsburgh's lone run on a sacrifice fly. Another failed effort for perfection. Six days later, he earned his twentieth victory, another complete game, 6–1 over the Cardinals, striking out thirteen. He finished the '71 season with a 20-10 record and a major-league-leading 1.76 ERA. He also led the league with 289 strikeouts, which broke his own National League record from the season before for most strikeouts in a season by a right-hander, while walking only 61. Amazingly, however, he was beaten rather handily for the NL Cy Young Award, 97 points to 61, by the Cubs' Ferguson Jenkins, who led the league with 24 wins and 30 complete games.

"I don't know about the Cy Young Award; I just know I felt 1971 was my best season," Seaver said in an interview with MLB.com's Jack O'Connell in December 2009. "Why? The main job of a starting pitcher is to give your team a chance to win. So, what does it say if over a period of thirty-five starts your ERA is 1.76? It says that you have given your team a chance to win every time you went out there. Good pitching raises the level of play. Look at the ratio between strikeouts and bases on balls. That's the phenomenal thing about that year to me. I didn't concern myself with run support. I was supposed to pitch a shutout. If I gave up a run, I was supposed to pitch a one-run game. That's the way I looked at it."

The Mets' disappointing 83-79 third-place finish in 1971, in which they ranked eighth in the twelve-team National League in runs, underscored the need for GM Scheffing to bolster the offense at the December baseball winter meetings in Phoenix—particularly at third base, where Bob Aspromonte (.225, five homers) had proven to be as big a failure as Foy the year before.

By the time the meetings were about to conclude, a flurry of fifteen trades had been completed, not one of them involving the Mets. A group of Mets beat writers confronted M. Donald Grant in the lobby of the Arizona Biltmore Country Club and pleaded for him to make a deal.

Seaver's 1956 North Fresno Rotary Little League team. Seaver is second from left in the first row, Clyde Corsby is fourth from left in the first row, Russ Scheidt is second from left in the second row, and Jeff Ring is fifth from left in the second row. All three would remain close friends of Seaver's.

Tom Seaver and Nolan Ryan (left) at Mets spring training in St. Petersburg in 1968. Both would go on to the Hall of Fame with a combined 635 major-league victories.

Mets manager Gil Hodges with his "young stud" 1969 starting pitchers: Jerry Koosman, Seaver, and Ryan.

WALTER KELLEHER/NEW YORK DAILY NEWS

The patented "drop-and-drive" Seaver delivery: one of the pitches he threw in his near-perfect game against the Cubs on July 9, 1969, which was broken up by Chicago's Jimmy Qualls with one out in the ninth inning.

NEW YORK DAILY NEWS ARCHIVE

Seaver and his favorite Mets battery mate, Jerry Grote, who caught almost of all of his biggest games, including Game 4 of the 1969 World Series and the near-perfect game against the Cubs earlier that year.

Seaver enjoys a celebratory beer with his best pal, Bud Harrelson (far left), and Seaver's wife, Nancy, after the Mets' 1969 World Series championship.

Seaver and his Mets teammates during their regrettable Las Vegas stage act after the 1969 championship season. Left to right: Art Shamsky, Tommie Agee, Seaver, Donn Clendenon, Ed Kranepool, Jerry Koosman, and Cleon Jones.

Seaver receiving his 1969 Cy Young Award from Jack Lang, secretary-treasurer of the Baseball Writers' Association of America.

ED CLARITY/NEW YORK DAILY NEWS

Seaver with Mets owner Mrs. Joan Payson, teammate Art Shamsky, and Mets general manager Johnny Murphy at a reception a few weeks after their 1969 World Series championship.

VINCENT RIEHL/NEW YORK DAILY NEWS

"We're No. 1!" Seaver and Mets manager Yogi Berra celebrate the Mets winning the National League pennant in 1973.

In happier times: Seaver and Mets chairman M. Donald Grant exchange greetings at Seaver's locker in 1973, four years before their bitter falling out in 1977.

The famous *New York Daily News* back page that drew the battle lines between Seaver and Mets chairman M. Donald Grant, ultimately leading to Seaver's June 15, 1977, trade to the Cincinnati Reds.

Seaver with Carlton Fisk, his White Sox batterymate who caught his 300th win.

Tom and his father, Charlie, embrace after Seaver's 300th victory at Yankee Stadium, August 4, 1985.

Tom and his brother, Charles, in conversation at Charles's apartment. On the table is the metal sculpture of a pitcher in his motion, which Charles made for Tom. Tom said it was one of his most prized possessions and placed it in the garden in front of his home in Calistoga after Charles died.

The "Fresno Gang" was all there for a celebratory barbeque at the Seaver house in Greenwich three days before Seaver's induction at the Hall of Fame. In the second row, second from left is Jeff Ring, third from left Clyde Corsby, and far right Don Reinero, who coordinated the trip. In the back row, Seaver (center) is flanked by his Fresno City College coach Len Bourdet on his right and Larry Woods on his left.

The Seaver family on Tom's Hall of Fame induction day, August 2, 1992. From left to right: daughter Sarah, Nancy, Tom, and daughter Annie.

Tom making his Hall of Fame induction speech.

Seaver and his "best bud," Cincinnati Reds catcher and fellow Hall of Famer Johnny Bench, at the induction.

Tom and his longtime pal and Mets teammate Rusty Staub talking wine and baseball in the Hall of Fame plaque room the night before Tom's induction.

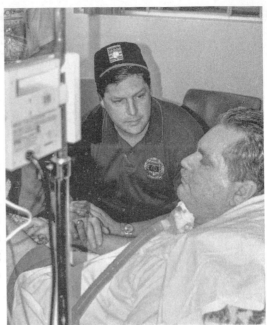

Seaver at the bedside of his lifelong friend Don Reinero, who, on September 27, 1994, suffered permanent brain damage after being struck by a drunken driver while bicycling in the foothills of Fresno.

On the day of Charlie Seaver's memorial service, Tom paid tribute to his dad with a "Scotch and Soda" toast—which not only was Charlie and his mom's favorite drink but also the title of their favorite song, by the Kingston Trio.

Seaver throws out the ceremonial last pitch to fellow Mets Hall of Famer Mike Piazza at the last game at Shea Stadium, September 28, 2008.

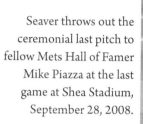

The Seaver house atop Diamond Mountain in Calistoga, California, which overlooks his vineyard.

The "Lord of the Grapes" Tom Seaver, strolling his GTS vineyard in Calistoga with his trusty companions, the "Rowdy Boys."

"We're trying," a visibly exasperated Grant said, shrugging, "but it takes two."

Five days after the meetings concluded, on December 10, Grant and Scheffing announced the completion of a five-player trade with the California Angels in which they'd acquired twenty-nine-year-old Jim Fregosi, a six-time All-Star shortstop, in exchange for Nolan Ryan and three minor league prospects: outfielder Leroy Stanton, catcher Frank Estrada, and pitcher Don Rose. The plan was to move their new acquisition to third base, where no fewer than *forty-five* players had tried their hand during the franchise's ten-year existence.

In their desperation to appease the fans by landing a name player in Fregosi, the Mets' high command had finally decided it could wait no longer for Seaver's pal and rotation stablemate, the hard-throwing Ryan, to reach his vast potential. When Whitey Herzog, the former Mets farm director who'd developed Ryan, heard about the deal, he was flabbergasted. "They gave up Nolan plus three *other* players for Fregosi?" exclaimed Herzog, who, after being passed up by Grant for both the Mets' manager and GM jobs, left the team at the end of the '71 season to take the Texas Rangers' managing job. "I wouldn't have traded Stanton straight up for Fregosi!"

It was a pointed dig at his former boss that proved prophetic when Fregosi showed up overweight and out of shape at Mets spring training in 1972 and was yet another bust at third base with his poorest season: .232, 5 HR, 32 RBI in just 101 games. (Actually, after a career season in 1970 [.278, 22 HR, 82 RBI], Fregosi hit just .233 with five homers and 33 RBI in 107 games in '71, indicating his skills were already declining.) After an even less productive first half in '73, he was sold by the Mets to Texas in July. By contrast, as Seaver predicted, Ryan, who'd never won more than 10 games for the Mets, came into his own in the laid-back baseball environment of Southern California. He won 19 for the Angels in 1972, leading the American League in strikeouts, and went on to become one of the greatest pitchers of all time, with 324 wins, a record 7 no-hitters, and 5,714 career strikeouts.

At the time of the four-for-one swap, Seaver expressed regret at the departure of his close friend but was also philosophical. "I think all things considered, now that it's been done, it could help Nolan as well as the Mets," he told the *Times*'s Joe Durso. "I hate to see him go because we're such good friends, but New York's a tough town to pitch in because of all the pressure, and he'll be able to concentrate better there. When the season ended, he knew there was a possibility he might be traded, and I wrote him a long letter and told him not to feel badly because he'd finished badly." Heading into July, Ryan appeared to be coming into his own: 8-4 with a sterling 2.05 earned run average. But he lost ten out of twelve decisions the rest of the way to end 1971 with a 10-14 register and a 3.97 ERA. "He did some good things last season," Seaver continued, "but you have to finish what you start, and he just sort of fell short of that the second half."

"We had him for three years, and although he's a helluva prospect, he hasn't done it for us," was Scheffing's explanation. "How long can you wait? I don't rate him in the same category as Seaver, Koosman, or Gary Gentry."

In a 2006 interview, Seaver elaborated to me on why the trade, bad as it was for the Mets, was the best thing that ever happened to Ryan. "Nolan was a country boy from a tiny little town in Texas, and I think he and Ruth were a little intimidated by New York. I think privately he was hoping the Mets would trade him."

But forty-eight years later, during the golden anniversary celebration of the Mets' '69 season, Ryan still expressed some regrets about his time with Seaver being cut so short. He often said that he was most impressed with Seaver having a college education. "I would have liked to have had the opportunity to pitch an extended time with Tom," he told *Newsday's* Steve Marcus. "I give Tom a lot of credit for having an impact on my career. He was the first guy that I was around who truly focused on his career and had goals and set out to achieve those goals. His work ethic and just being around and observing him had a very positive influence on me."

Partly because of that college education, Seaver was active early on in the Players Association. He was a fierce advocate for players' rights and took seriously his role as the Mets' union representative—which is where he found himself at the end of March 1972 after major-league players voted 683-to-10 to go on strike in another dispute over the owners' contribution to their benefit plan. The strike would last for thirteen days and force the cancellation of eighty-six regular season games. While Gil Hodges, his coaches, and some of the Mets players remained in Florida waiting for the strike to be resolved, Seaver returned to New York to take part in the labor negotiations. He'd been playing with Sarah at home in Greenwich on Easter Sunday, April 2, when he got a call from Bud Harrelson.

"What's up, roomie?" Seaver asked.

"Have you heard the news?"

"What news?"

"Gil died."

"What?" Seaver exclaimed. "What happened? How?"

For the next couple of minutes, Seaver just listened in stunned disbelief as Harrelson recounted what details he knew about the sudden death of their manager, Gil Hodges, at age forty-seven, in West Palm Beach, Florida. Hodges had just completed a long afternoon of twenty-seven holes of golf with his coaches Rube Walker, Joe Pignatano, and Eddie Yost, and was walking from the golf clubhouse back to the nearby Ramada Inn where they were staying, when he collapsed from a heart attack in the parking lot.

Upon hanging up with Harrelson, Seaver sat at his desk, staring out the window, his mind a scramble of thoughts about the man he'd considered the second-most important person in his life after Nancy. He thought about the lessons Hodges had taught him: about family, preparedness, and self-discipline; those private talks only they could have as one marine to another. He remembered how Hodges had trusted him through those nearly 150 pitches of game four of the '69 World Series, and how the next day they were giddily dousing each other with champagne. He closed his eyes, the image of Hodges with that toothy grin of joyous celebration, flashing before him. How could this good man, this model of integrity, who stared down death for two weeks at the battle for the Japanese island of Okinawa and who on a hot Sunday morning in May 1953 had a whole Catholic parish in Brooklyn praying for him to get out of a terrible slump that had begun with a hitless 1952 World Series, be gone so soon? With so much more yet to be accomplished?

At that moment, Seaver slumped over his desk and began sobbing uncontrollably.

CHAPTER 8

It Ain't Over 'Til It's Over

THE NEWS OF GIL HODGES'S SUDDEN DEATH HAD BARELY MADE it out to the wire services when M. Donald Grant summoned Yogi Berra, a Mets coach since 1965, to his Hobe Sound home near Palm Beach that Easter Sunday night to offer him the job as the new Mets manager. Since the players' strike was still unresolved, with the final two spring training exhibition games canceled, the start of the regular season was now certain to be delayed. There seemed no good reason why Grant could not have waited until after Hodges's funeral before deciding on his successor.

Even more insensitive was Grant's decision to hold a press conference at four o'clock the following Thursday in the Mets' Shea Stadium clubhouse—at the same time that Hodges was being laid to rest in a Brooklyn cemetery—to officially announce Berra as the fourth manager in team history. And if that wasn't enough of a planned distraction from Hodges's funeral, Grant followed up the Berra hiring to announce a trade in which the Mets had acquired Rusty Staub, the popular, red-headed lefty slugger, from the Montreal Expos in exchange for three of their top young players: outfielder Ken Singleton, first baseman Mike Jorgensen, and shortstop Tim Foli. Gil was gone, and it was back to business.

Thursday, April 6, was originally supposed to have been the Mets' home opener, but even before it was canceled by the strike, Seaver told reporters, "There's no way I am pitching Thursday. I doubt there is a man on this team that would play."

The day before Hodges's funeral, his body lay in state in Our Lady Help of Christians Church in Brooklyn, from one in the afternoon until ten at night, and more than thirty thousand mourners filed past his casket. Another ten thousand lined the streets and sidewalks outside the church the morning of the funeral. Besides Grant, Joan Payson, and the Mets players, dignitaries in attendance included New York City mayor John Lindsay; Baseball Commissioner Bowie Kuhn; the American and National League presidents, Joe Cronin and Chub Feeney, respectively; and many of Hodges's teammates from his sixteen seasons wearing the uniform of the Brooklyn, then Los Angeles, Dodgers: Jackie Robinson, Don Newcombe, Carl Furillo, Pee Wee Reese, Joe Black, and Sandy Koufax. .

Years later, Seaver reflected on his close relationship with Hodges, as well as how his relationship with Grant began to deteriorate after the patrician board chairman so indelicately handled the managerial transition. Even before Hodges's death, Seaver felt Grant's resentment, especially the fact that he lived in Greenwich and had friends in the same circle. He thought Grant regarded him as just another piece of Mets property.

"I thought it was awful how they held the press conference for Yogi on the day we were burying Gil," Seaver said. "Where was the respect? But that was Grant.

"Gil was the one guy Grant didn't dare look down on because he was baseball and Dodgers royalty. I think back now on Gil and how we were all scared to death of him. I know I was. But I was also a very proud marine, and he knew it. One time he called me into his office. I was sure he was unhappy about something I'd done, but as I'm standing there in front of his desk, he said: 'Do you ever look at your wife when the game is being played?' I said: 'Yes sir, especially when I'm on deck to bat. I'll look up in the stands to where she's sitting. She's an inspiration to me.'"

That was it. Hodges thanked Seaver and dismissed him to the clubhouse. But the next day, he summoned him once again into his office.

"This time," Seaver related, "Gil pulls out a photograph from his desk and slips it over to me. It's a picture of him, rounding first base after he'd hit a home run. As he told the story, he'd been in a terrible slump, and his wife, Joan, had said to him before he left for the ballpark, 'Hit a homer for me today.' In the picture, you can see he's blowing a kiss to her. I mean. that was such a beautiful story. It gives me goose bumps to this day just remembering it."

Besides Joan, who campaigned faithfully over the next forty-eight years for his election to the Hall of Fame, Hodges left behind a son, Gil Jr., then a player in the Mets minor league system, and three daughters.

The players strike lasted another week after Hodges's funeral. Finally, on April 15, Berra got to make his debut as Mets manager, and with Seaver pitching the first six innings and Tug McGraw the last three, New York shut out the world champion Pirates, 4–0, before an opening-day Shea Stadium crowd of only 15,893. The fans had voiced their displeasure over the players' strike in letters to the editors of the New York newspapers and calls to local radio shows.

The newest Met, Rusty Staub, went 1-for-3 with a walk as the new cleanup hitter. It had been a hefty price for the Mets to pay in young talent for the twenty-eight-year-old outfielder, beloved in Montreal, where the fans referred to him fondly as "Le Grand Orange." But New York had released veteran Donn Clendenon shortly after the 1971 season and once again had a dire need for a big bat in the middle of their lineup. Staub, a National League All-Star the last five seasons in a row, had hit .311 with 19 home runs and 97 RBI for the Expos in 1971. It was the third time he'd surpassed .300 since 1967.

"Getting traded to the Mets was the only time I was caught with my pants down because I didn't realize it was going to happen," Staub said in a 2017 interview. "I wasn't ready for it. I'd been a big personality in Montreal, and I loved that city. But at least I knew I was no longer gonna have to face Seaver, Koosman, and Matlack. That was a lot of 'oh-fors' for me." Jon Matlack, an impressive twenty-two-year-old left-hander from West Chester, Pennsylvania, had seen action in just seven games in 1971 and would win the National League Rookie of the Year Award in '72. As Staub found out quickly, the Mets were a pitching-centric team, and though he and Seaver would later become best of friends, bonding over their shared passion for wine, there was a period of adjustment at first. "Tommy didn't like hitters," Staub said. "I got that right away. For the most part, he hung with the pitchers on the road. We didn't socialize much. It was only after we'd been teammates and he became so interested in wine and the making of it that we became really close friends. I helped introduce him to a lot of people in the wine business."

Much as their hearts were heavy at the loss of their respected manager, the Mets got off fast in '72 under Berra, their 8-2 record on April 28 marking the best start in their history. Seaver won seven of his first eight starts. On May 11, in the first game of a doubleheader, he beat the Dodgers, 2–1, with ninth-inning relief help from Danny Frisella, who had blossomed into a solid member of the bullpen, leading the team in saves in 1971.

After the second game, a 6–4 loss, Mrs. Joan Payson announced that she was giving herself and all of New York a special present by bringing Willie Mays back home from the Giants in a trade for pitcher Charlie Williams and $100,000. A lifelong Giants fan, Joan Payson idolized Mays, and her admiration for the Say Hey Kid was shared by M. Donald Grant, who'd been on the Giants' board of directors until owner Horace Stoneham abandoned New York for San Francisco following the 1957 season. As for the Mets' players, no one was more pleased by this development than Seaver, who'd gotten to know Mays well from being National League All-Star teammates the past five years.

The forty-one-year-old Mays, who was hitting only .184 for the Giants at the time of the trade, seemed instantly rejuvenated by his return to New York. In his first game for the Mets, May 14 at Shea, he came to bat in the fifth inning with the score tied 4–4 and hit a home run that proved to be the 5–4 margin of victory. He finished May with nine hits in twenty-four at-bats for the Mets, including two homers and four RBI. After the game on May 30, in which he'd gone 1-for-3 with two walks and a run scored, his new teammates began shouting at him, "Player of the Month! Player of the Month!" This was Seaver's cue to give the old man some of his own patented needling.

"You can't be Player of the Month, Willie," Seaver said. "No one over forty is eligible!"

"What you mean?" Mays shrieked. "You don't know how old I am!"

"Nobody else does, either," Seaver shot back. "But that's okay, Willie. We honor your Social Security checks here."

The turmoil of spring, between the strike and Hodges's untimely death, soon abated. With the help of Seaver, Staub, and the new Mets pitching prodigy, Jon Matlack, on May 1 Berra guided them into first place, where they remained through much of June. Seaver, despite experiencing pain in his shoulder in spring training—which he later attributed to having thrown too hard too soon—was 9-3 with a 2.90 ERA after beating the Cincinnati Reds, 2–1, on June 18. He did it pretty much singlehandedly, too, launching a tie-breaking homer in the seventh inning. However, Staub, batting .301 at the time, had to leave the game after five innings, complaining of a spasm in his right hand. It had been hurting ever since George Stone of the Atlanta Braves hit him with a pitch on June 3. After a lengthy stint on the disabled list, it was later determined that the outfielder had suffered a fracture of his hamate bone, which required surgery and limited him to just sixty-six games in '72—a devastating blow to an already offensively challenged Mets team.

The Mets had just fallen out of first place when they faced the Padres in a July 4 doubleheader at Shea. Seaver pitched the first game and was protecting a 2–0 lead in the third after San Diego starter Clay Kirby suddenly lost his control with two outs, giving up a single to Bud Harrelson followed by four consecutive walks. Those were the only runs Seaver was to get in the game, but he didn't need any more as he once again found himself flirting with history, carrying a no-hitter into the ninth inning. As in the Jimmy Qualls game in '69, he retired the first batter of the ninth, Dave Roberts, on an infield ground out, only to surrender a broken-bat single lined to center by outfielder Leron Lee, spoiling yet another bid for his first no-hitter.

In the clubhouse afterward, Seaver said that, at least initially, he wasn't nearly as disappointed as he'd been in the Qualls game. "I knew to get it I was going to have to retire Nate Colbert," the Padres' danger-ous cleanup hitter, kneeling in the on-deck circle. "When Lee got the hit, the important thing now was 'I've got to win the game,' and to do that, I had to get my head back in the ballgame and get that big guy up next out."

He did, inducing a grounder to shortstop for a game-ending 6–4–3 double play, "and only then was when I was really disappointed," he said. Nancy had brought sixteen-month-old Sarah into the clubhouse, and as Seaver talked to the reporters, his daughter kept running up to him and interrupting his responses. "I'm glad she was here," he said. "Rube Walker says she's my good luck charm. She sure was today."

Between the loss of Staub's big bat, and off years incurred by other key players from the '69 miracle season—Tommie Agee, Jerry Koos-man, and Gary Gentry—the Mets gradually fell out of the '72 race, finishing third, 13½ games behind the swaggering Pirates, who all but left the rest of the NL East in the dust. Only Seaver (21-12) and Mat-lack (15-10) contributed standout seasons, but for the Mets' ace, it was not at all satisfying. Seaver was frustrated by what he perceived to be a loss of movement on his fastball, which he felt may have accounted for his recording forty fewer strikeouts than the year before, as well as the highest ERA (2.92) of his first six years in the majors. "This season was harder than any I've ever had," he said after shutting out the Pirates, 1–0, striking out thirteen, for his twentieth win on September 29.

The writers agreed with him but for not for the same reason. That same day, Jim O'Brien wrote in the *New York Post*: "Seaver could sue the Mets for nonsupport and win the case without a jury." In fact, the 3.06 runs per game the Mets scored for Seaver in 1972 were the second-lowest support of any National League pitcher with thirty or more starts.

More subtle, for Seaver and all the Mets, was the uneasy adjustment from Hodges to Berra. Compared with Hodges's stern demeanor and his uncompromising rules, the easygoing Yogi ran a loose ship—which reportedly was the reason why the Yankees had fired him as their manager after just one pennant-winning season. When the Yankees quickly replaced Berra with Johnny Keane, the manager of the Cardinals who had just beaten them in the World Series, it was viewed as a particularly heartless move on their part—but became a public relations coup for the Mets when they snapped Berra up as a player/coach for '65.

Much as the Mets' players may have liked Yogi personally—who didn't?—the more they watched him, the more they felt his managerial acumen left something to be desired. It didn't help Yogi when, twice within a one-week period in July 1973, he brought in a relief pitcher and then attempted to replace him with another pitcher before he'd faced a batter—an alarming lack of knowledge of the rules, which the press was quick to criticize.

Seaver never said much publicly about Berra. Following Gil Hodges would have been a hard act for anyone. He personally liked and respected Berra as a great ballplayer and devoted husband and family man. At the same time, friends said, he thought Yogi was a terrible manager. This was perhaps personified by an August 10, 1973, incident in San Francisco in which the Mets had a comfortable lead over Giants ace Juan Marichal, but Seaver was struggling in the middle innings, prompting a visit to the mound by Rube Walker. Reportedly, Seaver told the pitching coach there was no way he was coming out of the game and added: "And tell that to Yogi. I don't want to see him out here."

"Tom would never publicly call Yogi out if he disagreed with a decision he'd made," said a longtime close Seaver associate. "He had too much respect for him. But privately, he thought Yogi was overmatched as a manager, especially in the 1973 season."

The '73 season again began promisingly, with the Mets winning their first four games and Seaver outpitching the Phillies' 1972 Cy Young Award winner, Steve Carlton, 3–0, on opening day. He struck out eight over 7⅓ innings, and Tug McGraw completed the shutout. By the end of July, Seaver was 12-5 with a 1.96 ERA but, in a repeat of the previous season, had pretty much been a one-man show. Plagued by long-term injuries to many of their key players—Grote (broken wrist), Harrelson (broken left hand), Jones (elbow contusion), to name just three—the Mets fell into last place on June 29 and remained there for the next two months.

Going into play on Monday, August 27, the Mets were twelve games below .500, at 58-70, having just lost two heartbreakers in a row to the Giants at home: on Saturday, San Francisco touched Seaver for a run in the first and made it hold up the rest of the way, handing the Mets' hard-luck hurler a 1–0 loss. The following afternoon, veteran starter Ray Sadecki, in his fourth year in Flushing, fell behind early, 5–0, and although the Mets fought back beginning in the seventh, they came up one run short.

None of this boded well for Berra. Nevertheless, he maintained a sense of calm in the face of fan and media criticism and a halfhearted vote of confidence from Grant, who said he had no intention of letting his manager go "unless the public demands it." The best thing he had going for him was that none of the other National League East teams had played well, either. Only the Cardinals were over .500, and by just one game. So the cellar-dwelling Mets, despite their woeful record, were a mere six and a half games back.

It was that reality which Berra kept pointing to, noting how every team in the division had enjoyed a hot streak at some point except the Mets. Perhaps they were due. After one particularly tough loss in early September, Berra was holding court with the writers in his Shea Stadium office, being peppered with questions about his club's apparent dire fate. At one point, he smiled, shrugged, and said: "It ain't over 'til it's over."

"Who knew such an offhanded remark would become forever synonymous with Yogi?" Seaver said with a laugh in 2016. "But he was right, wasn't he? We got our guys back and, for the last five weeks, were the best team in baseball."

That they were. The Mets went on a 24-9 tear the rest of the way. Most instrumental in the surge was the irrepressible McGraw, who had struggled mightily through the first four months, blowing numerous save opportunities and prompting Berra to temporarily replace him as the team closer. The Tugger was 0-5 with a 5.31 ERA on August 22 when, almost miraculously, he rediscovered his form. He never could explain exactly what he did other than getting his bread-and-butter screwball to start behaving again. He was nearly unhittable from then on, giving up only four runs in his last nineteen relief appearances and racking up twenty-five saves for the season.

After one game in early September, Grant decided to come down to the Mets' clubhouse to deliver a rally speech. The stuffed-shirt Grant, whom the players mostly resented, was out of his element as any kind of an inspirational speaker, and as he was exiting the clubhouse after addressing the team, from the back of the room, McGraw suddenly shouted out: "Ya gotta believe!" Thinking he was being mocked (which he probably was), Grant whirled around and confronted McGraw, who explained he was only reiterating what a couple of nuns had said to him at church the previous Sunday. "You've got to believe."

"God bless Tug," Seaver said. "Nothing and nobody ever bothered him. Everybody laughed when Grant left, but whether we realized it or not, we had ourselves another rallying cry."

The Mets' late run to the National League East division title in '73 was similar to their '69 championship in that it was improbable (although for a different reason), and it was pitching driven. From August 15 on, Matlack, Jerry Koosman, and twenty-seven-year-old left-hander George Stone—the same George Stone who had drilled Staub on the wrist the year before, only to be acquired by the Mets in a trade from the Braves over the winter—were a combined 21-2.

Seaver won just four of seven decisions over that span, but once again he was hung with yet another 1–0 defeat, this time to St. Louis in ten innings, for the second time in five days. However, number 41 was on the mound on September 21, the night the Mets manhandled first-place Pittsburgh 10–2 in front of 51,381 Shea Stadium faithful to squeak past the Pirates and into first place by a half game. Their record: a perfectly symmetrical 77-77. Three days earlier, they'd gone into the ninth inning trailing the Pirates 4–1 and rallied for five runs and a 6–5 victory. "That was the night we began to believe in ourselves," Seaver said.

Going into the final frantic weekend of the season, the Mets, who had a four-game series in Chicago against the Cubs, clung to a half-game lead over Pittsburgh and 1½ over St. Louis. But after being rained out on Friday, they were forced to play back-to-back double-headers, Saturday and Sunday. Then it rained on Saturday, washing out the first doubleheader. Meanwhile, the Pirates lost Friday and Saturday, leaving the Cardinals the Mets' lone challengers. When the Cardinals won their Sunday game and the Mets lost the first game of their doubleheader with the Cubs, it all came down to Seaver needing to preserve their one-game advantage over St. Louis. In his previous start against the Expos five days earlier, Seaver had lasted only two innings for his shortest outing of the season, walking five.

Against the Cubs, with the division title on the line, Seaver struggled again. He didn't have his good stuff, especially his fastball, and was racked for eleven hits and four runs in six-plus innings. He departed after giving up a two-run homer to his old Alaska Goldpanners teammate Rick Monday in the seventh. But by then, the Mets had provided him with a 6–4 lead, and McGraw came on to pitch a brilliant three innings of four-strikeout shutout relief. In victory, Seaver admitted the season had begun to take its toll on him. Of his start against the Expos, he complained that "the ball felt like a shot put."

At least he was able to briefly forget his arm and body fatigue amid the jubilant cries of "Ya gotta believe!" by McGraw and the rest of his mates in the visiting clubhouse celebration afterward. Naturally, the majority of media questions were framed around the comparisons to '69. But as Seaver insisted, the only thing improbable about this title was that the Mets had been in last place right up until September. Their final record, 82-79, .509, was the lowest winning percentage to ever win a championship of any kind in baseball. "This was *not* unexpected," Seaver insisted, "at least not to us. In '69 we were young and didn't understand. This is nothing like that. This time we knew what we had to do and went out and did it."

A sad footnote to the Mets' otherwise inspiring finish to the NL East title was Willie Mays's retirement announcement on September 25 at Shea Stadium The forty-two-year-old Mays had been troubled by injuries throughout the '73 season and played his last regular-season game in Montreal September 9, going 0-for-2 with two walks to leave his average at .211 with six homers and 25 RBI in 66 games. "When you're forty-two years old and hitting .213, it's no fun," Mays told the writers. Then, before a crowd of 53,603, Mays, pointing to the Mets' dugout, said: "I see these kids over there fighting for a pennant and to me it says one thing: 'Willie, it's time to say goodbye to America.'"

Despite his struggling finish and failure to win 20 games (19-10) for the first time in three years, Seaver led the National League in ERA (2.08), complete games (18), and strikeouts (251), and was an overwhelming winner over the Dodgers' workhorse reliever Mike Marshall for his second Cy Young Award. Earlier in the season, he had waxed philosophically, albeit with a trace of anger in his voice, about his approach to baseball and pitching with *Newsday* reporter Howard Schneider.

"People who say baseball isn't relevant—that it's just a game of grown men in funny hats—they don't understand," he said. "They don't have a sense of the preparation, of the mental attitude involved. When you get right down to it, what has been my life but baseball? It gave me self-respect. It gave me pride. It gave me a place to get rid of my energies. It gave me a *purpose.*"

With four days of rest between the end of the '73 season and the start of the National League Championship Series on Saturday, October 6, Seaver felt renewed when Berra gave him the ball for game one against Sparky Anderson's Cincinnati Reds in Riverfront Stadium. Oddsmakers had declared the Reds, boasting the best record in baseball (99-63) and a lineup of three future Hall of Famers—Johnny Bench, Joe Morgan, and Tony Perez—plus Pete Rose, as 8-5 favorites..

And he was indeed again the Seaver of April through mid-August, his pitches crisp and his fastball registering regularly in the midnineties. Unfortunately, the Mets' hitters similarly reverted to their anemic presurge form, managing a meager three hits against right-hander Jack Billingham, one of them Seaver's own RBI double in the second. Tom Terrific was pitching a 1–0 shutout with twelve strikeouts when Rose poked a game-tying one-out homer in the eighth. Bench then won it with another one-out homer in the bottom of the ninth. So, abruptly and seemingly without notice, the Reds had struck down the "Franchise" and taken a 1–0 lead in the best-of-five NLCS.

"Mets Tom Was Truly Terrific, but Billingham, Reds Better, 2–1," read the headline in one of the Cincinnati papers the next day. In all, the game took exactly two hours to complete, two hours of sheer frustration on Seaver's part, with the Mets' hitters leaving him so little margin for error. He knew he'd pitched well enough to win while also acknowledging that he'd tired after seven innings and that the game-losing fastball to Bench "had nothing on it."

"You feel like your team's going to open it up. You keep waiting and waiting," he said.

An ebullient Anderson could hardly contain himself at starting out the NLCS by beating the best pitcher in baseball, saying, "If we had lost today, it wouldn't have been the end of the world for us. But we got one, and Seaver's out of the way."

Quite possibly, the Reds' skipper felt the slaying of Seaver in game one had provided sufficient momentum for his club to make it a short series. If he did so, it was at the peril of overlooking the fact that the two Mets lefties to follow, Matlack and Koosman, had pitched far better than Seaver in September. In game two, Matlack evened things by shutting out Cincinnati on two hits, 5–0, and the next day at Shea, the Mets won again, 9–2, behind a nine-strikeout complete game by Koosman.

In the fifth inning of that game, however, there'd been a wild benches-clearing melee that got started when Harrelson took umbrage at Pete Rose's hard slide into second base trying to break up an inning-ending double play and came up swinging. After order was restored and Rose took his position in left field, irate Mets fans proceeded to bombard him with debris, including a whiskey bottle thrown from the upper deck that landed a few feet away from him.

This prompted Anderson to pull his entire team off the field and presented National League president Chub Feeney with a real dilemma: How to calm down the fans and resume the game? He turned to the two New York icons, Berra and Mays, and asked them to go out to left field to plead with the fans to cease and desist. Seeing Willie and Yogi Berra starting to walk out, Seaver, on his own, quickly joined them, along with Cleon Jones. The four of them succeeded in convincing the fans the game had to go on, without incident, if the Mets, who were already leading, 9–2, were to complete their victory.

Suddenly it was advantage Mets at home, with Stone, who had finished the regular season with eight straight wins to go 12-3, set to take the mound in game four. But the six-foot-three left-hander's effort to close out the series was stymied by another Mets hitting outage. A quartet of Reds pitchers combined to hold them to just three hits over twelve innings, and, much to the chagrin of Mets fans, Rose homered to break up a 1–1 deadlock in the twelfth and force a fifth and deciding game.

Anderson was certainly happy about that, but it also meant Seaver was no longer "out of the way." He was not nearly as sharp as he'd been in game one, but he gutted it out for 8⅓ innings, uncharacteristically walking five while limiting the Reds to just one run. This time the Mets provided him sufficient support, with two runs in the first and another four in the sixth, including a pinch-hit infield RBI single by the aged, retiring Mays. It took McGraw to close it out, retiring the final two Reds batters after Seaver had walked two straight to load the bases in the ninth.

"I was tired, sure," Seaver said. "But I had a lot of good stuff."

He then referred to a key play by his battery mate, Grote, in the first inning, when Seaver was battling his control. After issuing a one-out walk to Morgan and a single to third baseman Dan Driessen, he allowed both runners to advance on a wild pitch to Perez, but was then able to strike out the dangerous Reds first baseman on what was actually a foul tip. "Jerry not only called a great game, he made a play on Perez in the first inning that might have changed the whole ballgame," Seaver said. "That strikeout was actually a foul tick, and, thank God, Jerry held on to it. In a game like this, it's so important not to give up the first run. My whole thought process today was 'Don't make the fellas play catch-up ball.'"

Because it was a clincher, he added, "it was the most satisfying postseason win of my career."

The swashbuckling Oakland Athletics—they of the colorful Kelly green and Fort Knox gold on wedding-gown-white uniforms and flowing mustaches, along with their flamboyant owner, Charles O. Finley, the P. T. Barnum of baseball, who paraded around the stadium and even into the press dining hall on a mule during all the postseason games in Oakland—were the defending world champions and brimming with confidence for a lot of reasons before game one of the 1973 World Series. The biggest one was they knew they weren't going to have to face Seaver until game three.

Holding court with a herd of reporters before game one at

Oakland-Alameda County Coliseum, A's slugger Reggie Jackson was expounding on the veteran, pressure-tested makeup of his team when someone asked him if Oakland may have gotten an added advantage when Seaver had to pitch game five of the NLCS. "All I know is, there isn't a person in the world who hasn't heard about Tom Seaver," said Reggie, whose .293 BA and league-leading totals in runs (99), home runs (32) and runs batted in (117), would earn him the 1973 American League MVP Award. "He's so good blind people come out to hear him pitch."

By the time Seaver got the ball, the Series had moved to New York, tied at one game apiece. After Matlack had come up a hard-luck 2–1 loser in game one, the Mets prevailed, 10–7, in game two, thanks to a pair of critical errors in the twelfth inning by A's reserve second baseman Mike Andrews. (Because of the errors, Andrews became a cause célèbre in the World Series when Finley abruptly "fired" him and ordered him sent home, drawing the wrath of the rest of the Athletics players. Before the game was even over, Finley had ordered an impromptu medical exam for Andrews and then forced the second baseman to sign a document stating he had a "chronic" shoulder problem. Baseball Commissioner Bowie Kuhn was quick to intercede, sternly ordering Finley to reinstate Andrews, who later received a standing ovation at Shea Stadium when he came to bat as a pinch hitter in the eighth inning of game four.)

It had been six days now since Seaver won the NLCS clincher against the Reds, and he felt invigorated by the chilly forty-five-degree night air and the overcapacity 54,917 fans at Shea Stadium. It was also heartening for him when the Mets actually scored two quick runs in the first inning off Oakland's ace, Catfish Hunter, 21-5, 3.34 ERA, on a leadoff homer by Wayne Garrett, consecutive singles by second baseman Felix Millan and Rusty Staub, and a wild pitch with Cleon Jones at bat. But then Hunter regrouped to escape further damage, and not another Met would cross home plate all night.

Seaver kept the A's at bay for the first five innings, fanning five in a row in the first two innings and then striking out the side in the fifth, before yielding a pair of doubles to third baseman Sal Bando and catcher Gene Tenace in the sixth that cut the Mets' lead to 2–1. It remained that way until the eighth, when he felt himself tiring. He gave up a leadoff single to Oakland's speedy shortstop, Bert Campaneris, who quickly turned it into the tying run by stealing second and scoring on a single by left fielder Joe Rudi. When Seaver made Tenace his twelfth strikeout victim to end the eighth, he knew he was spent and informed Berra as much before it was his turn to bat in the bottom of the inning. Much as he could feel satisfied with the way he'd pitched, it could not overcome the helplessness he felt when the A's rallied to win the game against Mets reliever Harry Parker in the eleventh.

"I had good stuff up until the sixth, when my arm started to tighten up," Seaver said. "I don't like a lot of early strikeouts. It takes something out of you, and you don't realize it—especially on a cold night like this one was."

What consoled him, though, was the way the Mets shook off the tough loss and took the next two games at Shea, 6–1 and 2–0, behind Matlack and Koosman. The Series was going back to Oakland with the Mets up 3–2 and squarely in the driver's seat. The only question was, how was Berra going to handle it?

He had two choices for game six. He could go with the rested George Stone, the Mets' hottest starter down the stretch. Or he could elect to go for the quick kill by pitching Seaver on just three days' rest instead of four.

"I really thought I was going to get the start," Stone said in a 2019 interview. "I'd been the hot pitcher, and I felt I deserved a shot."

He wasn't the only one. Both Ed Kranepool and Cleon Jones went to Berra lobbying for Stone because the A's were primarily fastball hitters. "Stone was a guy who changed speeds and was a 'location' guy who could keep the A's batters off balance," said Kranepool in a 2019 interview. "If we lost with him, we still had Seaver on full rest for game seven."

But Berra wasn't wavering. As soon as the Mets arrived at Oakland-Alameda County Stadium on Friday for the off-day workout, he announced that Seaver was pitching game six and, if necessary, Matlack would pitch game seven.

Things began ominously in the bottom of the first when Jackson scorched a two-out line-drive double into left-center field to score Rudi all the way from first base. Two innings later, Reggie struck again with another RBI double—this one to right-center—that scored Bando from first. That proved to be the only damage off Seaver in seven innings. But it was more than enough because Hunter, his opponent again, baffled the Mets into the eighth inning, when they finally broke through against him with their only run of the game. Jackson, who'd struck out three times against Seaver in game three, would say later that Seaver didn't have either the velocity or the big curve he'd had in New York, adding, "It was obvious from watching the man's face, his shoulder was killing him."

Afterward, Berra was steadfast about his decision, citing that but for the two pitches to Jackson, Seaver had more than pitched well enough to win, if only the Mets had scored him some runs. "Some guys want the man to pitch a shutout every time he goes out there. I wish every pitcher I sent out there gave up only two runs," he said.

Seaver, after brushing off questions about his shoulder, agreed.

"I don't think the three days' rest hurt me any more than my shoulder was hurting me," he said. "I gave up two runs in seven innings, and I lost. What am I supposed to do?"

Through the annals of time, hardly anyone remembers that Matlack came up short in game seven, battered for a pair of two-run homers in the fourth inning, as the A's went on to the second of three straight world championships. Instead, the debate raged on, to Berra's dying day, as to why he didn't make the safer choice of pitching Stone in game six and have Seaver fully rested, with Matlack in reserve, for game seven, if necessary.

"People told me Tom had wanted the ball so he could close out the Series because he didn't get to do it in '69," Stone said. "I don't know if he went to Yogi or went over his head. It's just what I heard."

Kranepool, however, refutes that notion. "I know Tom wouldn't have done that," he said. "He was still in line for a game seven. As far as I know, the decision was Yogi's alone—he always insisted it was. It just turned out to be a bad one. George Stone was bypassed. Why? You come to your own conclusion. We should have won that World Series."

In his 1990 autobiography *No More Mr. Nice Guy: A Life of Hardball*, A's manager Dick Williams was still second-guessing Berra's strategy. "The Mets having put our backs to the railing could afford to blow off game six," Williams wrote. "That would give their ace, Tom Seaver, an extra day of rest if there was a game seven, and he'd probably be damn near unhittable. Imagine my surprise, and my team's surprise, when Yogi decided to go with Seaver for game six. It was as if he'd decided to either win the Series right there with a pitcher working on just three days' rest, or not win at all. Yogi played right into our hands."

In all our conversations, Seaver always maintained that it had been

Berra's decision for him to start game six; that he was never consulted about it but had no problem with it. At the time, he was at least content with the knowledge that he'd pitched a good game in his only start, and the Mets' losing the World Series certainly could not be blamed on him. In another month, he would turn twenty-nine, just entering the prime of his career. There would be other World Series starts, other glorious October moments for him.

Except there never were.

CHAPTER 9

A Bitter Queens Farewell

SOMETHING WAS DESPERATELY WRONG.

Whatever thoughts Seaver and the Mets might have entertained about their season-ending surge carrying over into 1974 were quickly dispelled. On opening day against the Phillies at Philadelphia's Veterans Stadium, Seaver again matched up against fellow future Hall of Famer Steve Carlton. Twice he was provided leads, and twice he failed to hold them.

He came up a 5–4 loser and did not notch his first victory until his fifth start of the season, a 2–1, four-hit shutout over the Giants on April 26. In his next start, May 1, he limited the Dodgers to just three hits and one run in twelve innings, striking out sixteen, but got a no-decision when the Mets' bullpen lost the game in the fourteenth inning. Seaver wasn't sure what that hard-luck outing had taken out of him. He knew only that he didn't feel right six days later when he gave up ten hits, including an eighth-inning, game-winning three-run homer to Gary Matthews in a 4–3 loss to the Giants. Afterward, he uncharacteristically refused to talk to reporters.

"I don't think I was ever more frustrated and scared than I was in 1974," Seaver said to me in 2016. "I kept feeling this off-and-on stabbing pain in my buttock from what I thought was my sciatic nerve, but the doctors and trainers could not figure out what was causing it. So, I kept pitching with it, even though it was screwing up my mechanics, and I was probably risking injury to my arm. It was messing up my mind, too. I'd try to challenge hitters, and I had no fastball. I knew I was trying to throw too hard, but I couldn't help myself. I started overstriding to try to get more on my fastball, and that led to my landing on my left heel instead of the ball of my foot. It got to a point where I started thinking about what I was gonna do if I couldn't pitch anymore."

When he and the Mets lost to the Dodgers, 7–1, on June 16, Seaver's record dropped to 3-6, and his ERA ballooned to an unseemly (for him, anyway) 3.80. He was giving up one more earned run per game than he had in his first seven seasons.

The defeat dropped them into last place in the National League East. By then, it was apparent this was going to be a lost season for the Mets. They never got any better, winding up fifth, 71-91, for their first losing record since 1968. The disheartening season could reasonably be attributed to their franchise pitcher having the worst year of his career—as well as the front office's own complacency in not making a single move over the '73–'74 winter to improve the team.

It was of no consolation to Seaver that, during spring training, he'd signed the largest one-year contract ever given to any pitcher in baseball to that point: $173,000. If anything, Seaver said, that put added pressure on him to straighten himself out. The beat writers, for their part, were sympathetic to his struggles, treading delicately with him as he sought to outwardly distract from the obvious. After one early loss in which he was pounded for twelve hits and six runs in five innings by the Pirates, he responded to a writer's question about his decreased velocity by rummaging through his locker and muttering, "Where are you, fastball? Are you in here somewhere?"

When he was able to craft a four-hit, eleven-strikeout shutout over the Cubs in the first game of a September 13 doubleheader to run his record to a respectable 11-8, he felt that maybe whatever had been causing this seasonlong pain in his left leg had somehow corrected itself. But in his next start, six days later against the Expos in Montreal, there it was again, and after Seaver gave up three singles and a walk in the sixth inning, Berra removed him.

"I need a rest. I can't keep going on like this," Seaver told the media. It was agreed to give him a week before his next start, but the extra rest was to no avail. He pitched shutout ball for the first four innings of his September 25 start in Philadelphia until, facing the Phillies' Jay Johnstone leading off the fifth, he once again felt this stinging pain in the same place. He could barely withstand it, and when he served up a three-run homer to pinch hitter Tommy Hutton three batters later, Seaver stalked off the mound in disgust.

"That's it. I just can't do it. I've got to shut it down," Seaver told Mets physician James Parkes. It was a telling statement of resignation from a man who'd never before been on the disabled list.

Parkes, who had been baffled by the constantly recurring pain in Seaver's left leg, got on the phone to Mets board chairman M. Donald Grant in New York to explain the situation. "It seems like it's the sciatic nerve again," he told Grant, "but we can't seem to figure out why."

"Look," said Grant, "we can't go on prescribing ten days of rest for him. I know this osteopath who has done wonders for me. He lives in Westchester. Would you mind if I had him take a look at Tom?"

"Not at all," said Parkes. "Will you call him?"

The osteopath, Dr. Kenneth Riland, was actually quite renowned in the New York area. One of his notable patients was former New York governor Nelson Rockefeller. After receiving Grant's call, he agreed to see Seaver three days later—a Saturday—at his home, no less.

"Dr. Riland took one look at me and determined my pelvis had become turned and twisted, causing the muscles above the left hip to push the sciatic nerve against the hip bone," Seaver told me in a 2016 interview. "He was able to 'adjust' my back with massage and other treatments right there."

The following Monday, Riland saw Seaver for a checkup in his office. Patting the hip, he said confidently, "Good. You're good to pitch."

"That's really great, Doc," Seaver said. "When?"

"Now," said Dr. Riland. "You can pitch now if you want to."

The Mets' season was scheduled to end two days later at Shea Stadium, and Seaver wasn't sure if it was worth it to make another start in a meaningless game. Grant, however, felt otherwise.

"Why don't you pitch tomorrow night?" he said. "I think it's vital to your own peace of mind that you not go through the entire winter uncertain about your situation."

Tuesday night, October 1, Seaver pitched for the first time all season without any pain. He didn't just pitch. He pitched dominantly. His fastball restored, he struck out 14 Phillies that night. It didn't matter that he lost, 2–1. What mattered was that he knew he was fine again physically and would no longer have to concern himself with finding a new occupation. Plus, the 14 strikeouts had brought his season's total to 201, giving him seven straight seasons of 200 strikeouts, one shy of the major-league record held by baseball immortals Walter Johnson and Rube Waddell. Only Grant would know how much that meant to Seaver. What Dr. Riland may have considered to be a routine procedure, for Seaver had been a miracle. A year later, after he tied Waddell and Johnson for the consecutive season 200-strikeout record, he presented Grant with a baseball on which he inscribed: "To D. Grant. I give you 1/8. Tom Seaver."

That was about the last friendly gesture the two ever enjoyed with each other.

On the final day of the '74 season, Bob Scheffing announced his resignation as Mets general manager. He'd been on the job for five years, but with Grant micromanaging his every move, he'd done little to substantially improve the team. To replace Scheffing, Grant chose to stay within the organization and, in Joe McDonald, promoted the consummate organization man to GM. The Brooklyn-born McDonald had been with the Mets since their 1962 inception, starting out as a statistician for the broadcasters and working his way up through the player development department.

One of McDonald's first orders of business was the matter of Seaver's 1975 contract. Salary arbitration and free agency were still a couple of years away, and baseball was still operating according to the feudal system in which players were paid what the owners wanted to pay them. Thus, after his 11-11 season, in which his ERA went up more than a run per game (2.08 to 3.20) from 1973, Seaver resigned to taking his first pay cut after raises in each of the previous seven seasons. Remarkably, he made it easy for McDonald by saying he deserved it, although the cut was substantial—just over 20 percent, from that record $173,000 for '74 to $136,000.

"I wasn't disturbed that I got cut after just one bad year," Seaver insisted. "The ball club's been very good and honest with me and I with them. They paid me a good amount of money last year, and I didn't pitch up to that amount."

Ironically, three weeks prior to Seaver's contract resolution, he had already been supplanted as the highest-paid pitcher in the game, when his '73 World Series rival, Oakland's Catfish Hunter, signed a five-year $3.1 million contract with the New York Yankees after a baseball arbitrator ruled that A's owner Charlie Finley had breached Hunter's contract by failing to pay $50,000 into his annuity fund, making him a free agent.

"My primary motive in pitching this year is not to outdo Catfish Hunter," Seaver said. "I'm all for him. Any time you have somebody who gets money like that, he raises the salaries for everyone."

"It was amazing," said McDonald. "In all my contract negotiations this winter, no Mets player mentioned Hunter. I brought it up to Tom and Joe Torre, and they both said it was a unique situation." Shortly after succeeding Scheffing, McDonald had traded for the thirty-four-year-old Torre, a nine-time All-Star, to play third base. Although Torre arrived in the majors as a catcher in 1960, his bat was so potent that he gradually began spending more and more time at first base and then at the hot corner. In 1971 his extraordinary numbers (.363 batting average, 230 hits, 24 home runs, 137 runs batted in) as the St. Louis Cardinals' starting third baseman won Torre the National League MVP Award. He'd slipped since then but was still a threat, averaging .286 over the next three seasons. Finally, it appeared that, for the first time in franchise history, third base wouldn't be a drain on the lineup.

With his contract resolved, Seaver looked forward to spring training and what he hoped would be a pain-free '75 season, enabling him to recoup that lost salary. First, however, there was a Mets three-week goodwill trip to Japan shortly after the World Series. The pitcher wanted no part of it but was ultimately forced to go. Nancy, pregnant with their second daughter, Annie, was reluctant to travel overseas, and Tom didn't want to leave her. Several other Mets regulars, including Harrelson, Grote, McGraw, and Cleon Jones, also begged off the trip, but the Japanese promoters were insistent on Seaver, since he was the team's star attraction. Ultimately, he and Nancy went, but after Seaver pitched briefly in five games, the two returned home.

Having benefitted from Dr. Riland's realignment procedure, Seaver spent most of the winter watching films of himself pitching prior to the '74 season, if nothing else to reassure himself of his old form. Then, in the early weeks of '75 spring training, something else happened that promised to improve his performance dramatically: he developed a changeup.

According to Jon Matlack, the new pitch had evolved by trial and error as he and Seaver were playing catch in the outfield.

"I had the good fortune of lockering next to Tom on one side and Jerry Koosman on the other side," Matlack said in a 2019 interview. "I learned so much about pitching from both of them. I'm not sure exactly when it was, but Tom kept telling me, 'We need another pitch, something slower.' We just couldn't seem to come up with the right grip. But then one day when we were playing catch, he said, 'Check this grip out and watch this.' He'd made a circle with his index finger and his thumb and put his other three fingers on the ball. He'd always admired Andy Messersmith, who could throw a ball that looked like a hundred miles per hour but took forever to get to the plate. That was it. His body showed fastball, but there was a difference of speed of about eight miles per hour."

Seaver celebrated that day, although there was still a lot of refining to do with his new pitch.

"I don't know how much he used it in '75," Matlack continued, "but it was good enough to make the hitters aware of it; putting it in the back of their minds that he just might mix one of them in. Of course, later on in his career, it became his signature pitch."

If, in Seaver's opinion, 1971 had been his greatest season, 1975 was positively his most satisfying. He was, in a word, magnificent: from opening day, when he outdueled Carlton, 2–1, striking out nine Phillies; to the month of June, when he gave up a total of just six earned runs in six starts; to September 25, when another unsung rookie backup outfielder for the Chicago Cubs, this one named Joe "Tarzan" Wallis, broke up yet another bid for his first no-hitter with a two-out single in the ninth inning. "All the doubts I let creep into my head in 1974 were erased," he said. "It all came together again. I was whole."

Along the way to leading the National League in wins (22-9) and strikeouts (243), there were a couple of milestones too. In the second inning at Shea Stadium on July 24, he made Dan Driessen of the Reds his two thousandth career strikeout victim, and on September 1, before 52,410, he struck out Pirates catcher Manny Sanguillen, a .328 hitter in '75, in the seventh inning, giving him two hundred for the eighth straight season.

All he had done, however, was not nearly enough to offset another subpar (82-80) Mets season. On August 6 Yogi Berra was fired. Seaver reserved comment, preferring to let others, such as Joe Torre, to express the obligatory condolences. But it was no secret he had never been enthralled with Berra as a manager. He made that point publicly for the first time after his April 13 start, when he seethed openly at being pinch-hit for in the seventh inning, trailing the Pirates by only one run. After the game, even the writers were taken aback when Seaver lashed out at Berra.

"I wasn't outstanding, but I was getting them out," Seaver said. "I just couldn't believe it when he took me out. I won't say anything without being negative about what was an obvious decision to me. There are times he's working on a hunch, and I haven't the slightest idea. The strength of this team . . . one of the strengths of this team is the starting pitching."

In November the Baseball Writers' Association voted Seaver his third Cy Young Award, 98 points to 80, over Randy Jones of the Padres, the National League's only other twenty-game winner in '75. "I thought it would be a lot closer," Seaver said. "I'm sure it was a big disappointment for Randy. I've gone through the same thing. I felt I pitched well enough to win it in '71, but they gave it to Ferguson Jenkins. If Jones had won, I wouldn't have felt as badly as I did in '71."

A month before the Cy Young was announced, Joan Payson died in New York Hospital–Cornell Medical Center from complications of a stroke. The Mets' founder and principal owner was seventy-two, and, under terms of her will, controlling interest in the team went to her husband, Charles Shipman Payson, who had no interest in baseball. He, in turn, passed control to Mrs. Payson's daughter, Lorinda de Roulet, who, by her own admission, was a fan of baseball but knew little about it. With no one above him now to offset his authority, the ultimate power of the Mets had fallen solely to the imperial chairman, M. Donald Grant.

Meanwhile, storm clouds were forming over baseball that would soon change the game profoundly. In his continuing quest to nullify the reserve clause in the standard players' contracts, which effectively bound them to the clubs in perpetuity, Executive Director Marvin Miller of the Players Association convinced two stars, Dodgers pitcher Andy Messersmith and Expos pitcher Dave McNally, to test the clause by refusing to sign new contracts after the 1974 season. Their contracts were subsequently renewed automatically for one year by their clubs. But since they hadn't signed anything during the '75 season, Miller contended they were now free agents. As expected, the owners disagreed vehemently, and the case went to baseball's arbitrator, Peter Seitz, who, on December 23, 1975, ruled in favor of Messersmith and McNally—a landmark decision that rocked the foundation of baseball and gave birth to free agency.

The Seitz decision led to an immediate escalation of the labor talks between Miller and the owners on a new basic agreement that was now going to have to resolve the thorny issue of how free agency was to be implemented. While the owners appealed the Seitz decision to the courts, negotiations were stalemated, resulting in the 1976 spring training camps remaining closed. Since most of the Mets had already reported to Saint Petersburg, Seaver initially organized informal workouts at Eckerd College, just as he'd done in the 1969 spring training work stoppage. However, as the Mets' player rep and a member of Miller's advisory board, he realized quickly this was weakening the players' bargaining position with the owners and abandoned the workouts. On March 19 an agreement was finally reached between the owners and the players, but Seaver, knowing free agency was now coming, had made up his mind he didn't want to leave the Mets and sought to sign a multiyear contract to ensure that. He proposed a three-year $825,000 deal to McDonald and Grant, and was both surprised and dismayed when they indicated no interest in doing that.

"I gave them a contract proposal that I thought was fair, and I had to go back to them five days later when they didn't even bother to respond," Seaver told the New York writers. "This was the way they were treating me after nine good years with the club? Why couldn't they at least have the courtesy to give me a yes or no answer? They were trying to intimidate me if I didn't sign."

The Mets' indifference so infuriated him, Seaver finally took it upon himself to confront McDonald face-to-face at the Mets' spring training offices.

"You know what he told me?" Seaver recounted in disbelief to the Met beat writers. "He said: 'No one is beyond being traded here. I have one deal I can make right now.' I was so incensed I said, 'Then pick up the fucking phone and make it!' He never moved, but I realized right then everything I had ever done for the Mets—everything I had meant to the team—could go out the window on one damn phone call."

Actually, unbeknownst to him, it almost did.

On March 28, when the Mets were playing the Dodgers in Vero Beach, Florida, McDonald met with LaRue Harcourt, the agent for Dodgers pitcher Don Sutton, like Seaver a future Hall of Famer and fellow member of the exclusive 300-win club. The purpose of the meeting was to satisfy Sutton's demands in order for him to approve a proposed trade to the Mets for Seaver. Since it never came to pass, details of the trade are a bit sketchy—one report had it straight up Seaver for Sutton, another had the Mets getting two other top prospects from the Dodgers, outfielder Pedro Guerrero and pitcher Rick Sutcliffe, both of whom would go on to become impact players for many years. According to Sutton, the deal was close enough that he was prepared to open the 1976 season with the Mets.

"I was called into the Dodgers' office and asked what I wanted to approve the trade," Sutton related to me in 2018. "I told them that when I retired, I wanted a job as a Mets broadcaster, and they agreed to that. As far as I was concerned, that was it. I was going to New York."

Word of the possible swap began leaking out, stirring up such a furor in New York, the Mets backed off. Still unresolved, however, was Seaver's contract situation, although now Grant knew what a public relations disaster it would be for the Mets to part ways—either by trade or free agency—with their franchise pitcher. Superseding McDonald, on April 7 he met personally with Seaver in Fort Lauderdale, Florida, where the Mets were finishing up spring training with a three-game series against the Yankees. The two worked out the most lucrative contract in Mets history: three years, with a base pay of $225,000, plus numerous bonuses and incentives for games won beyond nineteen, and earned run average.

Still, the contract represented about $150,000 less guaranteed money than what Seaver had sought initially—not to mention the great unknown of how it would compare to those contracts signed by players after free agency. And the whole acrimonious process—the initial indifference, the trade threats—with McDonald and Grant left a bad taste in Seaver's mouth. For the first time in his career, he was learning the hard truth about how the Mets' management really felt about him now that Mrs. Payson was gone.

"There are two things Grant said to me that I'll never forget, but illustrate the kind of person he was and the total 'plantation' mentality he had," Seaver told me in a November 2007 interview. "During the labor negotiations, he came to me in the clubhouse once and actually said, 'What are you, a Communist?' And then there was that time when he said to me, 'Who do you think you are joining the Greenwich Country Club?' It was incomprehensible to him if you didn't understand his feelings about your station in life."

Grant's attitude toward players become more evident to Seaver in the way the chairman treated Rusty Staub, whose own contract was up after 1975 and who, like Seaver, was seeking a substantial raise and a multiyear contract with free agency looming at the end of '76. Next to Seaver, Staub, who led the team with 105 RBI in 1975, was the most popular Met, and it was assumed Grant would want to do everything he could to keep him. Instead, he made no secret of his dismay over Staub's contract demands and began leaking stories to the press that, besides wanting an exorbitant raise, Rusty, who had a fear of flying, wanted assurances that the runways were of a specific length when the team took charter flights. They never came close to a contract and on December 12, 1975, Grant traded Staub to the Tigers for thirty-five-year-old left-handed pitcher Mickey Lolich.

Much as he believed in the importance of starting pitching and welcomed to the rotation a proven vet like Lolich, who'd won more than two hundred games for the Tigers from 1963 through 1975, the abrupt trading of Staub, it seemed to Seaver, was an ominous sign that Grant, irrespective of free agency, was going to tighten the organization's purse strings. Staub wound up driving in 302 runs for the Tigers over the next three years, while Lolich, who hated pitching in New York, won just eight games for the Mets in '76 and then retired in order to get out of the final year of his contract. It was with that backdrop of unrest that the Mets slogged through a depressing 1976 season in which they were fifteen games out of first place on June 25 and never contended. Only a 20-9 September, when the games meant nothing, was enough to save the job of overmatched new manager Joe Frazier, whom Grant had promoted from their Triple-A minor-league club rather than pay for an established skipper.

Seaver's 14-11 record in '76 belied his overall performance, in which he again led the National League in strikeouts. In his eleven losses, the Mets scored a total of fifteen runs. As a result of such egregious nonsupport, he was able to collect very little of his anticipated bonus money.

"There are only two columns over which I have no control," Seaver said. "One is games started and the other is games won. Whatever the figures show in the other columns"— strikeouts, ERA, and so on—"I am responsible for. I can control them. That's why I'm not frustrated. I guess my reaction to all that has happened this season is a sign of maturity. There's a certain amount of frustration; I won't deny that. But not the frustration I might have felt a few years ago."

On November 4, 1976, at New York's posh Plaza Hotel, baseball held what it called the first reentry draft, in which the twenty-four clubs, drafting in the reverse order of the previous season's standings, selected the negotiation rights to twenty-four newly minted "premium" free-agent players. It was the first step of a salary revolution in baseball, with one record-setting multiyear contract after another coming down just in time for the Christmas holidays. And there were certainly plenty of marquee players in this first free-agent class: All-Star sluggers Reggie Jackson, Gary Matthews, Don Baylor, Bobby Grich, and Sal Bando, as well as hurlers Don Gullett, the ace starter of the defending world champion Reds, and Rollie Fingers, who'd been the closer for the three-time world champion A's.

But by the time spring training '77 came around, Grant had signed none of them, making only a token (largely deferred money) offer to the left fielder Matthews, who instead reaped a five-year, $1.2 million deal from the Braves. The windfall of free agency—Gullett signed a six-year, $2 million deal with the Yankees, and Nolan Ryan, even though he was not a free agent, got a three-year, $600,000 extension from the Angels—was not lost on Seaver. Nor was it lost on Dave Kingman, the Mets' lone pure power hitter, who'd hit seventy-three homers for them the previous two seasons and who was engaged in a contract squabble with Grant. Kingman was eligible to become a free agent after the '77 season and let it be known he wanted the same $2.7 million over five years that the Yankees had given Jackson. Grant adamantly refused, and Kingman, without any leverage yet, was eventually forced to accept a one-year deal for $95,000.

"All this club needs is one more power hitter to be a contender," an angry Seaver told the Mets beat reporters on his first day at spring training, "and we've done nothing. We traded our center fielder last year." In that deal, McDonald had sent Del Unser to the Expos in July '76 along with "Miracle Mets" fixture Wayne Garrett. "How can a team that depends so much on pitching trade its center fielder without a replacement?" he asked. "Gary Matthews goes from the Giants to the Braves. How can you not even try? Who knows how long this pitching staff can keep holding up?" And when he saw the kind of money Gullett got from the Yankees, despite having never won more than 18 games or struck out more than 183 batters in a season, Seaver realized he should have waited until free agency before signing a long-term deal.

But as he insisted to the reporters, he'd been coerced into signing the previous spring by Grant, who was attempting to establish a new Mets salary structure. "I was made a complete example of," Seaver complained. "I was pictured as the ingrate, after nine years with the club, and I was to be punished. And even now, a year later, I still resent the way they did it."

Citing the fact that, across baseball, eleven starting pitchers had signed new multiyear deals for $1 million or more, Seaver insisted it was only right that the Mets should renegotiate his contract and pay him commensurate with what the other starting pitchers were getting in baseball's new world order. "I have no loss of feelings for the owners, Mrs. de Roulet and the others," he said, "but I think it was mishandled by Grant and McDonald. Things between us are different now. The relationships have changed."

The battle lines were drawn. Grant felt Seaver was being greedy and should honor his contract. To reinforce his hard-line stance, Grant enlisted the support of the *Daily News*'s Dick Young, the most powerful sports columnist in New York. Beginning in April, Young began referring to Seaver as an "ingrate" and a "troublemaker" in his columns, while implying that Seaver's periodic barbs at Grant were leaving the board chairman no choice but to consider trading him.

"Tom Tewific is a pouting, griping, morale-breaking clubhouse lawyer poisoning the team," Young wrote shortly after Seaver pitched the fifth one-hitter of his Mets career, 6–0, against Chicago, on April 17.

Dick Young had first joined the *Daily News* as a teenage messenger boy in 1937 and a few years later had worked himself up to become the *News*'s Brooklyn Dodgers beat reporter. With his staccato, populist style of writing and relentless reporting, Young quickly gained wide appeal as a "must read" for the *News*'s largely blue-collar 2.8 million readers. A prototypical Young lead was his characterization of a particularly ugly 17–6 Dodgers loss to the Giants, in which they'd been the victims of six home runs: "This game doesn't belong in the sports section. It belongs on Page 3 with all the other axe murders."

In the early 1950s, Young separated himself further from other baseball beat writers by becoming the first reporter from a morning paper to go down into the clubhouse to interview players for his game stories. "Dick Young was like our commissioner," said the *New York*

Times's Pulitzer Prize–winning columnist Dave Anderson, who was a rookie Dodgers beat writer for the *Brooklyn Eagle* in 1953. "He outworked all the a.m. writers by going down in the clubhouse, and then he beat the afternoon-paper writers at their own game by coming up with quotes they didn't have. My graduate school was Dick Young. I learned how to cover the team, while the other guys just covered the games."

After Dodgers owner Walter O'Malley took the team west to Los Angeles following the 1957 season, Young moved up to columnist at the *News*, while covering the Mets extensively after their formation in 1962. But now, much older than most of the players, he didn't enjoy the same daily camaraderie he'd had with the Dodgers when he traveled with the team, seeing all and hearing all. He gradually evolved from being perceived as a "players' guy" to a "management guy," and, especially after his close friend Gil Hodges died, Young began forming a closer friendship with Grant.

But in his role as Grant's hatchet man on Seaver, Young was already tarnished by a conflict of interest: his son-in-law, Thornton Geary, was the Mets' vice president of communications—a fact all the other papers in New York were quick to seize upon during those turbulent weeks of 1977.

"That was probably the toughest year of my life," Geary told me in 2007. "There were writers, particularly at the *Post*, who wanted to get Dick, and I was a consistent pawn. I admit, I wouldn't have gotten through the door with Grant had it not been for Dick, but I was good at my job. What was especially disheartening for me was I had a really great relationship with Tom before everything blew up like it did, and I never got that back."

Typically for him, Young defiantly sloughed off the conflict of interest charges being leveled against him, writing: "My son-in-law does work for the Mets. He has a master's degree, and he is probably, if anything, being underpaid. I warned him about taking a job there. I told him people working in the front offices of baseball are the most underpaid people in the world."

Besides Geary, the other person squarely in the middle of the Grant-Young-Seaver feud was the *Daily News*'s Mets beat man, Jack Lang. Lang and Young were best friends. The day Lang's newspaper, the *Long Island Press*, folded in 1977, Young hired him immediately to be the *News*'s Mets beat writer. Beginning in Seaver's rookie 1967 season, Lang had taken it upon himself to forge a trusting relationship with Seaver, who, after the '69 season, made a point of being cooperative with the writers but also keeping them at a distance. The lone exceptions were Lang and Joe Durso of the *Times*. So it was quite a tightrope Lang was walking, somehow maintaining Seaver's confidence as the team's biggest star went over Grant's head to begin negotiating a new contract with Lorinda de Roulet, while Young continued to blast away at him in the same newspaper. At one point, a meeting was held among Young, Lang, and all the editors at the *Daily News* to strategize how to continue handling a story that had quickly spiraled out of control.

"Don't worry about what I'm writing," Young told Lang. "You just cover Seaver and the club the way you always do. Feel free to take his side in this. It'll make good copy, us taking different sides."

On June 1, the day after Grant replaced Joe Frazier as Mets manager with Joe Torre, despite his having no experience whatsoever, Young wrote a column under the headline "Joe Knows the Score, Nobody Wants Seaver," in which he quoted Grant as saying, "Seaver has destroyed his market and become a headache." Young then added in his own words: "In discussing Tom Seaver, we must never mix up the two Tom Seavers. As great as a talent as is Tom Seaver, he has become an irreparably damaging and destructive force on the Mets."

Despite Young's continuing salvos, a few days before the trading deadline on Wednesday, June 15, Seaver quietly worked out a new two-year contract extension with Mrs. de Roulet and Joe McDonald in which he was to be paid $300,000 for 1978 and $400,000 for 1979. Still, before the deal could be announced, he and Grant continued exchanging verbal brickbats right up to the deadline. With a big, bold headline, "Seaver vs. Grant" in capital letters, the back page of the June 15 editions of the *Daily News* featured a story by Lang in which Seaver continued to vent about his treatment from Grant and the chairman's refusal to sign any free agents. And right alongside it ran a column by Young in which Grant urged the pitcher to see the light.

It was then that Young wrote the thirty-three words that effectively drove Tom Seaver out of town:

"Nolan Ryan is getting more now than Seaver, and that galls Tom because Nancy Seaver and Ruth Ryan are very friendly, and Tom Seaver has long treated Nolan Ryan like a little brother."

Seaver and a bunch of reporters were sitting poolside at the Marriott Hotel in Atlanta, where the Mets were staying, when Dick Schaap, his former book collaborator who was now working for NBC Sports, approached him and asked him if he'd read Young's column.

"What now?" Seaver asked.

Informed of Young's insinuation that Nancy was jealous of Ruth Ryan because Nolan had signed a much bigger contract than his, Seaver silently contemplated it for a moment. Suddenly he burst from his chair and marched briskly around the pool to his hotel room, where he called his agent in New York to have the column read to him. After hanging up, he then got on the house phone to Arthur Richman, the Mets' public relations director.

"Get me out of here! Do you hear me?" he screamed to Richman. "Tell Mrs. de Roulet to tell Joe McDonald that everything I said last night is forgotten. This attack on my family is something I will not take!"

The shaken Richman called the Mets' office at Shea Stadium and got Mrs. de Roulet's daughter, Whitney, on the phone. She'd been in a board meeting in which her mother was going over the terms of Seaver's new contract with the other Mets directors. Under orders from Grant, McDonald had been exploring various potential trades for Seaver leading up to the deadline and had in fact a four-for-one deal with Cincinnati: in exchange for Seaver, New York would receive two promising minor-league outfielders, Steve Henderson and Dan Norman, capable young infielder Doug Flynn, and right-handed starter Pat Zachry, the 1976 NL Rookie of the Year who was mired in a sophomore slump at the time (3-7, 5.04 ERA).

"It was a deal I certainly never wanted to make," McDonald said in a 2019 interview, "but Seaver was adamant. The die was cast. The board of directors still had to vote to approve it, which they did, I think, unanimously. I can't say for sure because I was not invited to the meeting. Everybody, especially Grant, knew how I felt."

Immediately after hanging up with Richman, Seaver packed his bags, took a taxi to the airport, and flew home to New York. In what was dubbed the "Midnight Massacre," Richman informed the writers of the Seaver trade after the game as they were about to file out of the clubhouse to the press box. On the team's late-night charter flight back to New York, he announced two other trades, the bigger one sending Grant's other malcontent Dave Kingman, then leading the club in home runs, to the Padres for backup infielder Bobby Valentine and a minor league pitcher. In one night, the Mets had traded away the most popular player in their history and their all-time career home run leader as of 1977—all because they'd incurred the ire of M. Donald Grant for wanting salaries comparable with those of other major-league players who'd reaped the benefits of the new free agency. With a 26-35, .426 record, the club was entombed in last place, 14 games behind division leaders the Chicago Cubs.

The next morning, Seaver arrived with Nancy at the Mets' clubhouse at Shea to clean out his locker. At first, as he sat at the picnic table in the middle of the room, he bantered lightly with the reporters, trying to maintain his composure. He was doing well until someone asked him if he had a parting word for the Mets' fans. It was as if he'd just given up a three-run game-winning homer. His head slumped, and both his and Nancy's eyes began watering. After a moment, he began to answer hesitatingly.

"The question of the fans in New York . . . I know they appreciated watching me . . . As far as the fans go, I've given them a great number of thrills, and they've been equally returned . . ."

"The ovation I got the other night . . ." (In a June 7 game against his soon-to-be new employer, Cincinnati, he'd passed Sandy Koufax's career strikeout total of 2,396 Ks.)

At that, Seaver stopped and began tapping his heart.

"C'mon, George!" he implored, invoking his given first name, before choking up.

Unable to continue, he turned to Joe Durso and reached out to borrow his notebook and pen, then began writing the rest of what he wanted to say.

As Durso read from the notebook, "The ovation the other night after passing Sandy Koufax will be one of the most memorable and warm moments of my life," Seaver listened wordlessly.

It was over. There was nothing more to say. The writers stood there in silence as Seaver got up from the bench, put his arm around Nancy, and slowly exited the clubhouse.

CHAPTER 10

Cincinnati

NOT JUST METS FANS, BUT ALL OF NEW YORK WAS CONSUMED with rage.

The man who'd deservedly earned the nickname the Franchise as the most important and revered Met in team history was now quite rudely an ex-Met. Backlash against M. Donald Grant and Dick Young was fast and furious.

The next day in the *New York Post* under a banner headline, "Dick Young Drove Seaver Out of Town," baseball columnist Maury Allen wrote: "It is Young who forced the deal, who urged Grant on, who participated strongly in the unmaking of Tom Seaver as a Met. . . . He made an offer Grant couldn't refuse. He offered him his son-in-law, Thornton Geary. Grant accepted the young man, put him to work in the radio-TV department of the Mets, and Young has been a Grant apologist ever since."

In the *New York Times*, Red Smith, the dean of America's sports columnists, skewered Grant for his failure to understand the essence of Seaver: "For a decade, Tom Seaver has been one of the finest pitchers in the game. More than that, he is his own man, thoughtful, perceptive, and unafraid to speak his mind. Because of this, M. Donald Grant and his sycophants put Seaver away as a troublemaker. They mistake dignity for arrogance."

But perhaps no media outlet was harsher in its criticism of Young and Grant for having alienated Seaver than Young's own paper, the *Daily News*. The day after the trade, both of its signature general columnists, Jimmy Breslin and Pete Hamill, lamented Seaver's departure and came down hard on the principals who engineered it. Breslin paid a visit to Grant's Manhattan apartment at the Mayfair House on East Sixty-Fifth Street for the purpose of getting the Mets chairman's side of it, but he very skillfully portrayed him as the patrician "plantation lord" Seaver had accused him of being:

[Grant] was going on the way of the businessman. The businessman in charge. You always hear them squealing about the morality of a contract when an individual with one life to live decides he is going to put the arm on the organization for more money. So, when Seaver asked, M. Donald Grant of Park Ave. and Hobe Sound, Fl. was hurt. Grant then sat down and decided to trade Seaver. Oh yes, he owned Seaver. He could trade Seaver to another owner and get bodies in return. This is almost as much fun trading baseball players you own as it is to sit with a breeding chart in front of you and plan marriages for the horses you own. Always the ways of the rich in the sports world retain some of the better aspects of slavery. . . . For a sparkling physical possession of this city, Grant, who comes to us out of the late Joan Payson's purse, accepted three plow boys and a fry cook.

But Hamill aimed the thrust of his anger squarely at Young:

And so the long good-bye is finally over, and Tom Seaver is gone. For the years he worked among us, he was an ornament of New York. He leaves behind a diminished city. . . . There is, of course, no way to discuss the departure of Seaver without discussing the role of Dick Young. Nothing is more squalid than a quarrel between writers, and I have too much respect for Young's talent than to want to pick a fight with him. Attacking Dick Young does not make me a better person. But for almost two years, Young has been functioning as a hit man for Mets management, and in that role he has helped drive a great ballplayer out of town, helped demoralize younger men, and, worst of all, has demeaned his own talents. Now Seaver is gone. It is hoped Young can now go back to doing his job. The fans can look back at the shambles of Grant's Tomb, and maybe all of us can remember that great late summer drive in 1969 when Seaver was pitching so strongly down the stretch, and New York felt light and happy and invincible. I only wish all of us with those memories could get to Tom Seaver and find some way to say we're sorry.

In his own defense, Young was characteristically uncompromising about his criticism of Seaver. While Breslin's and Hamill's columns appeared in the front of the *Daily News's* June 16 editions, Young wrote, from his customary place on the top of the second page of the sports section: "It is too bad for the fans that Seaver forced the issue and compelled the Mets to trade him. There have been some player-managers in big-league history. He wanted to be the first player–general manager. He wanted to run the ball club. No club can permit that without risking anarchy in its ranks. . . . The fans will be angry, but it will pass. It always does."

Except in this case, it never did. To his dying day, November 28, 1998, Grant was forever villainized as the man who traded Tom Seaver. "I cannot even go into my own seat in my own stadium. I have become lower than the lowliest bum on the street," he told the *New York Times* bitterly a few months before being fired as Mets chairman in 1978. Young, too, felt the forever wrath of Mets fans. On the occasion of his induction into the writers' wing of the Baseball Hall of Fame as the 1978 winner of the J. G. Taylor Spink Award, he was booed lustily by the crowd gathered at Cooperstown. As far as anyone could remember, it was the first and only time a writer was ever booed at the Hall of Fame inductions. Forcing a smile, Young began his speech: "Ladies and gentlemen and members of the Tom Seaver fan club . . ."

All of the fan and media vitriol directed at Grant and Young was of no consolation to Seaver. Despite Nancy's contention that he turned the page the moment they walked out the clubhouse door on June 16, he would never forgive the Mets for what they did to him. It would be a long time before he could ever think in a good way of the only organization he had ever known. At the same time, however, he would forever savor the love he got from the fans—and all that he and his Mets teammates accomplished in turning a franchise that had been a laughingstock before he got there into the toast of New York in 1969.

He was leaving a Shea Stadium environment that had become toxic and going to the talent-rich defending two-time world champion Cincinnati Reds. He could at least thank Grant for that. There couldn't be a better place, or a better bunch of highly accomplished teammates—including Johnny Bench, Joe Morgan, Pete Rose, George Foster, and Ken Griffey Sr.—for him to begin the second phase of his career.

"We talked about it the night it happened, and he accepted the trade," Nancy said in 2016. "I was hurt because Tom was hurt. He'd invested a lot of his passion and hard work into that team. But they could never take anything away from him. His record would stand, and then we started looking objectively about the Reds. He could get more runs. He was getting older as a player, and this could be a good thing. You hate to leave your surroundings, but we knew we were never going to sell our house in Greenwich. You can't let it be a knife in your heart. You accept it as a new challenge and start making your choices and your transition and not be emotional about it."

Two days after the trade, Reds manager Sparky Anderson, who would one day also be elected to the Hall of Fame, was holding court with a cadre of baseball writers in the lobby of the Reds' hotel in Montreal. "People think of Tom Seaver mainly in terms of releasing the baseball," Anderson said. "But he has so much he can give the kids I have on my staff, so much pitching knowledge and class as a person. It's like Vince Lombardi said: without class, all the ability in the world will not make you a champ. With Seaver joining those other guys I have in my clubhouse, I feel now exactly how I'm gonna feel when I walk into Yankee Stadium, July 19, as manager of the National League All-Star Game."

When Seaver walked into the visitors' clubhouse in Montreal that night, he knew immediately there would be no problem blending in with his new team replete with superstars and two world championships under their belts.

"Okay, boys, heads up. Tom Terrific is here!" shouted Johnny Bench. "We've got to win, win, win now. We're going to be all right."

Joe Morgan, who'd won the National League Most Valuable Player award in 1975 and 1976, said in a 2017 interview at the Hall of Fame that Seaver's sudden arrival initially meant a bit of an adjustment for him. "You have to understand this guy had been my fiercest competitor, and I didn't like him. But all of a sudden, he's in the locker room, and we start talking, and I said, 'Hmmm, he's okay, you know.' He had this big personality, and you're either going to gravitate to him or run away from him. Our guys gravitated to him, and I think they were better players for it."

The Reds were in second place, 33-27, six and a half games behind the Dodgers at the time of the trade, and they never got any closer— although that was hardly any fault of Seaver, who went 14-3 with a 2.34 ERA the rest of the season, for an overall record of 21-6, along with a league-leading seven shutouts. In his first start for the Reds, June 18, he shut out the Expos, 6–0, on three hits. Making his Reds debut even more impressive, he was 2-for-4 at bat, helping his own cause with a two-run single in the eighth inning.

"That was the first time I ever had my name on a uniform since Fresno High," he said, in reference to the Reds' road jerseys. "At the start, I was pretty emotional. But after two innings, I felt I was part of the game and part of the people I'm playing with now. It was a beautiful experience."

"We didn't need any more bats on this team, but it looks like we got another one," quipped Anderson. "I learned a lesson today. The true professional is not bothered by anything."

A month later, Seaver found himself back in New York at Yankee Stadium as a member of the National League All-Star team. The day before the game, he downplayed his return. "This is not a homecoming as far as I'm concerned," he insisted. "Yankee Stadium doesn't mean a thing to me."

But as he would find out, the New York fans felt differently. As he stepped forward from his National League teammates on the third-base line for his pregame introduction, the Yankee Stadium crowd of

56,683 stood and applauded . . . and applauded, for a full minute, as Seaver turned to the outfield and waved his Reds cap, and then his arms, in appreciation.

"I didn't think it was going to be this big," he confessed later. "But those people obviously had something to say."

Conspicuous in a front-row box seat to the left of the American League dugout was M. Donald Grant, sitting stoically, drinking an occasional beer while never removing his gray suit jacket. Asked if he saw Grant, Seaver replied: "Yeah, I saw him."

"Did he wave to you?" another reporter pressed.

"Not that I noticed."

It would be another month for the "real" homecoming, in which Grant was notable by his absence. The day after he'd been traded, Seaver checked the Reds' schedule and circled the dates August 19, 20, and 21: a four-game weekend series against the Mets at Shea Stadium. Following the All-Star Game, he went on a roll with five wins and two no-decisions from July 9 through August 16, setting up a face-off against his former mates in the Sunday game. Shea was packed, though not to capacity—a reflection of just how Mets fans had turned off to a Seaver-less team marooned in last place with a record of 49-73, .402, twenty-seven games behind the division-leading Phillies. Nevertheless, the second-largest crowd of the season, 46,265, made it clear from the outset they were there for one reason only and it was not to root, root, root for the home team. The instant he stepped out of the Reds' dugout to take a turn in the cage for pregame batting practice, still wearing number 41 on his back, the fans began shouting "Sea-ver! Sea-ver! Sea-ver!" There were more, much louder cheers when Mets public address announcer Jack Franchetti, reciting the starting lineups, reached Seaver's name in the Reds' batting order. The cheers then quickly dissolved into thunderous boos when Franchetti began: "And now for the Mets . . ."

Adding to the emotion of the day for Seaver was the turn of fate that Jerry Koosman, his longtime rotation stablemate with the Mets, was his opponent. Joe Durso, in the *New York Times*, labeled it "the battle of the brothers."

"There was a carnival atmosphere that whole weekend," Seaver recalled. "It was the start of a road trip for the Reds, but we were still essentially home in Greenwich, so Nancy came to the game. To be honest, I didn't know what to feel. I almost wished we didn't have to face the Mets in New York again that season. As much as I looked forward to seeing Buddy, Grote, Kooz, and Skip Lockwood [who'd succeeded Tug McGraw, now with Philadelphia, as the Mets' closer], I dreaded having to pitch to them. It was hard enough pitching to Buddy in batting practice when I was with the Mets. I always worried I'd hit him with a pitch and hurt him."

Whatever nerves he may have felt dissolved quickly when, after being handed a 1–0 lead in the top of the first inning, he faced down Harrelson, the second Mets batter in the bottom of the inning, and struck him out looking. It was only the second time all that season he had double-digit strikeouts in a game. And much to the delight of the Shea crowd, he outpitched Koosman, limiting New York to six hits in a 5–1 complete-game victory.

"It was awfully nice to come home," Seaver said afterward, "but this was no fun. It was just too emotional. I was aware they were there at bat, but I tried to just block it out of my mind."

"I think the best man came out on top," said Koosman, who was laboring through a horrific year in which he seesawed from twenty-one-game winner in '76 to twenty-game loser, worst in the National League. "I really don't think I can put myself in Tom's class."

By then, it had pretty much become a lost season for the defending champions. Even after sweeping the four-game series at Shea, the Reds were still marooned in second place, nine and a half games behind the Dodgers, and without Seaver winning fourteen of his last sixteen starts, they'd have likely finished an even more distant fourth in the West. It was, however, a season of personal satisfaction for Seaver, who on September 15 beat the Dodgers, 3–2, for the two hundredth win of his career while throwing 150 pitches.

The Dodgers' two runs in that game came on a fluky home run by Seaver's old Alaska Goldpanners teammate Rick Monday, whose two-out, fourth-inning drive down the left-field line bounced off the glove of Bob Bailey, normally a third baseman playing out of position, into the seats. For his career, Monday had the highest batting average (.349) and most homers (eleven) of any batter against Seaver. In a 2020 interview with the Athletic sports-news website, Monday said his uncommon success against Seaver might be perceived as sweet revenge from an incident between the two at the 1968 All-Star Game in Houston.

Before the game, Monday, who was then with the Oakland Athletics as part of the American League squad, was standing in the lobby of the All-Star headquarters hotel with his mother, Nelda, when they spotted Seaver. It was actually Nelda who recognized Seaver from watching him and her son playing in Alaska years earlier, and suggested they go over and say hello. According to Monday, during their conversation, Seaver said if the occasion arose where the two should face each other in the game that day, "I'm gonna give you something to hit. It'll be as hard as I can throw it, six hundred miles per hour, but it'll be a fastball. That's your one chance."

But when Monday did happen to come to bat against Seaver, the first pitch he got was not the hard heat Seaver had promised but rather a *curveball*, and he wound up grounding out. "I was screaming at him all the way running down the line to first base, yelling, 'You're gonna pay for that!'" Monday said, "while Seaver had to put his glove over his face because he was laughing so hard as he covered first base."

So, when Bailey misplayed that fly ball into a homer, Monday said he got special pleasure watching Seaver seething on the mound. "As I told him at the time back in '68: 'You didn't just lie to me, you lied to my *mother*!" Monday laughed.

Ten days after beating the Dodgers, Seaver shut out the Braves, 4–0, to become a twenty-game winner for the fifth time. As turbulent and upsetting as the 1977 season had been for him, at least there was a satisfying ending. The Mets were in his past, and although his maiden voyage with the Big Red Machine had not been quite what he'd expected, none of that could be helped. All he could do now was to look ahead.

"If I stay healthy the next five years, I can win three hundred," he told the media after the twentieth-win game. "My health is important to me, and my legs and arm have to stay strong."

Sarah Seaver was seven years old when, in June 1978, Nancy informed her they would be spending the summer in Cincinnati. As she quickly discovered much to her delight, her dad's new team was a very family-oriented organization with a number of events such as photo day and dads-versus-kids baseball games at Riverfront Stadium. Making it even more like one big summer vacation, Seaver rented a condo on the other side of the highway from King's Island amusement park.

"My dad was very much a part of my childhood, even though he pitched in different places and was on the road half the summer," Sarah said in a 2019 interview. "We did all sorts of things together as a family, and he would not tolerate my sister and I acting like children of a superstar athlete. People would ask me, 'What's it like to have Tom Seaver as a father?' and I would always say, 'He's just my dad.' He was always extremely supportive of anything I did."

Not long after Nancy and the girls arrived in Cincy that June, Tom took Sarah aside and taught her how to keep score at the games. "It was something to keep me interested in the game," she explained. "To keep me from being bored."

As it so happened, her very first scoring assignment was a night game on Friday, June 16: Seaver and the Reds versus the St. Louis Cardinals. They were seated in the family section behind the visitors' dugout on the third-base side of Riverfront Stadium, Sarah with her scorecard and pencil, next to her mom. As the game progressed— neither team scoring until the Reds broke through with three runs off Cardinals starter John Denny in the fifth inning—Sarah remembered it as being fairly routine. After dutifully recording each at-bat, she'd show her scorecard to Nancy for assurance she'd gotten it right. There was a little confusion for her in the Cardinals' second, when Keith Hernandez drew a one-out walk from Seaver, stole second, and continued on to third on a throwing error by Reds backup catcher Don Werner. It was the nineteenth consecutive day Werner had been behind the plate in place of Bench, who was sidelined by a back injury. After another walk to third baseman Ken Reitz, Seaver pitched out of the jam by getting his onetime Mets teammate Mike Phillips to ground out to second. From that point on, he retired the next eighteen batters in a row.

"I remember late in the game my mom began tensing up," Sarah said. "I'd show her my scorecard, and she barely looked at it, especially after my dad walked the first batter in the ninth." Pinch hitter Jerry Mumphrey flung aside his bat and jogged to first base.

How many times had Nancy been here? Three times Seaver had taken no-hitters into the ninth inning only to be deprived. Nancy could feel her heart pounding when Lou Brock flied out to left field and Garry Templeton, coming off a .322 season, grounded harmlessly to Gold Glove shortstop Dave Concepcion, who threw to Joe Morgan at second for the force-out. Had anyone else been at-bat, the veteran second baseman might have tried turning two, but, given the left-handed-hitting Templeton's blazing speed, he wisely held on to the ball. Staring straight ahead at Seaver on the mound, Nancy forgot momentarily that Sarah was keeping score. Two outs, man on first.

"I tried getting my mom's attention, but she was so tensed up," recalled Sarah, "and then she started crying. I said, 'What's going on, Mom?' I had no idea other than we were winning."

On a 1-and-2 pitch, with the entire stadium on its feet, center fielder George Hendrick bounced a one-hopper to first baseman Dan Driessen, who easily gloved the ball, took four steps to his left, and stomped on the bag. Seaver was right there to accept his handshake while the rest of the Reds hustled over to mob their ebullient star pitcher and move as one toward the dugout. Before descending the steps, number 41 waved his cap above his head in acknowledgment of the roar from the crowd of 38,216.

It was not one of Seaver's more dominating performances—he walked three and struck out only three—but there were only two close calls, both involving Keith Hernandez: In the fourth, the St. Louis first baseman rapped a hard hopper between first and second that Morgan, dashing to his left, was able to snare and throw to first for the out. And in the seventh, Hernandez hit another hard smash up the middle that deflected off Seaver's glove right to Dave Concepcion at short for a 1–6–3 putout.

"The thing was, Tom had *nothing* that day," recalled Hernandez. "I kept looking for the power, the fastballs, the hard breaking balls, and it just wasn't there. All he threw were slow curves, off-speed pitches, and changeups, all away, all night long. He caught us all by surprise. I kidded him about it years later. I told him, 'You had nothing in that no-hitter,' and he'd laugh and say, 'No shit!' But that was what separated him from all the other pitchers. He had the physical tools *and* the intelligence."

"I had my good sinker most of the way, and my fastball came along later," Seaver told reporters afterward. The next day, reflecting on having finally achieved his first no-hitter, he remarked that it didn't compare to winning a World Series. "A no-hitter is momentary," he said. "You enjoy the moment, that's all."

But years later, he never let Johnny Bench forget that he pitched his one and only no-hitter without him. "Oh, yeah," said Bench, "he loved telling me, 'What did you ever do for me?'—always citing that damn no-hitter."

For the Cincinnati Reds, Seaver's no-hitter and Pete Rose's forty-four-game hitting streak from June 14 to August 1, tying Wee Willie Keeler's National League record, set in 1897, were about the only highlights in another otherwise disheartening season. Both Bench and Morgan were hurt much of the year, and the club fell out of first place on June 11 and never got back there, finishing second again to the Dodgers, who, in a repeat of 1977, lost the World Series to the resurgent New York Yankees. At the end of the year, Rose, the born-and-bred Cincinnati icon, took advantage of free agency and signed with the Phillies. Little by little, through age and the economics of free agency, the Big Red Machine was beginning to break apart. After the 1976 season, first baseman Tony Perez had been traded, and now Rose, too, was gone, while Bench and Morgan were showing signs of wearing down. Also, the Reds' pitching, never their strongest suit, had deteriorated after '76. Besides losing Gullett to free agency, three of their other '76 starters, Pat Zachry, Gary Nolan, and Jack Billingham, were all traded in '77.

Seaver's unexceptional 16-14 won-loss record in '78 was belied by his 2.87 ERA and more indicative of the same lack of run support he'd become used to with the Mets. In the month of July, Seaver lost four straight starts, in three of which he gave up a total of four earned runs. He never said anything, but Bench could sense his frustration. In a July 23 game against Montreal, Seaver had a 4–0 lead when, in the sixth inning, he suddenly couldn't get anybody out. A single, a triple, and successive doubles by the Expos' Larry Parrish and Warren Cromartie, and the score was tied.

Bench decided the situation required some levity. Trudging out to the mound, he calmly handed Seaver the ball and asked nonchalantly: "Are you even trying?"

"Screw you!" Seaver shouted as Bench began walking back to the plate, both of them convulsed with laughter. Seaver didn't give up any more runs, and the Reds went on to win the game in fourteen innings, though way too late for their long-suffering starter to earn a win.

One bright spot in the '78 Reds season was the emergence of twenty-five-year-old right-hander Tom Hume in the starting rotation. A native of Cincinnati who was originally drafted out of high school by the Reds as a third baseman in 1972, Hume had impressed Anderson by winning three starts after a September call-up from the minors in '77 and then earned a regular spot in the rotation in spring training. Hume's instant attachment to Seaver was precisely what Sparky had talked about when he predicted how much influence Seaver would have "on the kids I have on my staff."

"In 1978 Tom took me under his wing, and I became his student," Hume said appreciatively in a 2019 interview. "I still wonder every day, 'Why me?' but God meant it to be. He taught me so much, not just about pitching but about life. I grew up in a rather sheltered world in small-town Cincinnati, and Tom taught me culture—when we'd go on the road, he'd take me to museums—and educated me about so many things: history, art, literature, world events. In the clubhouse, we'd play cribbage and bridge. He told me how he'd learned bridge from his dad and how it helped make you concentrate.

"After games I pitched, especially in games I didn't do well, he'd say to me: 'What were you trying to do out there?' and then he'd tell me what I needed to do. With Tom, he was always pitching three pitches ahead in his mind, where I was a guy who wanted to get hitters out on the first pitch. He was both a student of the game and a teacher of the game and taught me everything I knew about pitching. That ten-strikeout game he had against the Mets the first time he faced them in '77? He put on a clinic that day."

In November '78, the Reds shocked all of baseball by dismissing the popular Sparky Anderson after nine years that brought Cincinnati five division titles, four National League pennants, and two world championships. He never did get a satisfactory answer from upper management for his firing after two straight second-place finishes, and Seaver said later that, after Gil Hodges, Sparky was the best manager he ever played for. But under Anderson's successor, the genial, low-key Irishman John McNamara, the Reds returned to the top of the National League West in 1979. Seaver, 16-6 despite missing a month with a pulled buttock muscle, was a major factor in that. In the National League Championship Series, which the Reds lost to the Pirates in three straight, they scored a paltry five runs total. Seaver pitched masterfully in game one, limiting Pittsburgh to five hits and two runs over eight innings. But he came away with a no-decision after being pinch-hit for in the eighth inning and replaced by Hume, who, had been converted from a starter to the Reds' closer that year. Though he again led the league in shutouts, with five, Seaver's career-low 131 strikeouts in 215 innings (after 226 the year before) in '79 raised questions as to whether he was evolving from a power pitcher to relying more on finesse.

"I'm certainly not the power pitcher I used to be," Seaver acknowledged to *Cincinnati Post* baseball writer Earl Lawson, "but I'm still a pitcher. I've always been a pitcher. That doesn't mean I don't have the fastball when I need it. The fastball is still my best pitch. It means the percentages of fastballs to breaking balls have changed somewhat."

Above all, he insisted, the decrease in strikeouts had nothing to do with any arm issues.

"I've never had a sore arm in my career. Most of my injuries have been in the lower part of my body. That's because I keep the strain off my arm and put it in my legs and buttocks. The smallest muscles in your body are in your arm, so you have to put that strain somewhere else."

Six months later, however, Seaver would reveal that he had not been entirely truthful. He had, in fact, felt pain in his shoulder periodically through the '79 season, which was the reason he began relying less on his fastball and mixing in more and more breaking pitches. He attributed it to normal muscle strain and said it was never enough to warrant any rest. But in the spring of 1980, the pain grew more persistent, and Seaver was feeling his thirty-five years. By June 20, he was 5-7 with a 4.61 ERA and had gone five straight starts without pitching past the sixth inning. On June 30 against the Giants in San Francisco, he reached his point of exasperation, yielding a three-run homer and a two-run homer in the first three innings. The homers were the fifteenth and sixteenth he'd given up in a season that wasn't even half over.

Coming into the dugout after the fourth inning, he said disgustedly to Reds pitching coach Bill Fischer: "That's it. I can't continue to pitch like this. There's something that's keeping me from doing what I want to do. It manifests itself with pain. It's difficult and depressing after having pitched thirteen years and never had any arm trouble."

It was decided to fly Seaver home to Cincinnati for conventional X-rays and an arthrogram (an imaging procedure incorporating dye to detect joint problems) of his shoulder under the supervision of team physician Dr. George Ballou. On July 2 Reds general manager Dick Wagner reported the good news that there were no structural issues with Seaver's shoulder, merely tendon inflammation, or tendinitis. He was placed on medication and—for the first time in his fourteen-year career, remarkably enough—the disabled list.

"I'm not going to rush this thing," Seaver told the Reds' beat writers. "The sixteen homers is most indicative of my problem, because my arm keeps getting weaker, and my fastball keeps getting weaker. I'm not in it to take a cortisone shot and be a hero and get back to pitching right away. However long this thing takes—if it takes two weeks, if it takes a month, if it takes the season—whatever it's going to take, that's how long it's going to take."

As it was, Seaver sat out all of July and returned to the mound

August 4 against the Padres, with vintage Tom Terrific results: six innings pitched, four hits, one unearned run, one walk, and five strikeouts. Rest had cured the tendinitis, although for the first time, he admitted, he couldn't help thinking that it might be a harbinger of more serious problems with the shoulder. Still, with each succeeding start, he felt stronger and stronger, finishing with six consecutive victories in which his ERA was 1.64, including two complete games and a shutout in September. That brought his season record to a respectable 10-8 and 3.64 ERA.

Before heading home to Greenwich, Seaver had a sit-down with Fischer and Dr. Ballou to discuss his off-season regimen. In the past he'd stayed in shape over the winter by playing a lot of squash and tennis, to condition his legs. "Not good enough anymore for a pitcher who's gonna be thirty-six," the pitching coach said. "You've got to throw the ball a few times a week during the winter to keep your arm loose. You can do it in your basement."

Beginning in December, Seaver set up a foam rubber strike zone on the far wall of his basement and, after measuring off exactly sixty feet, six inches, fired thirty baseballs through an open doorway at it. On days he didn't throw, he put in an hour on a stationary bike. As he told the *New York Times*'s Dave Anderson: "The last two years I've had trouble early with my calves that led to a hip problem two years ago and tendinitis in my shoulder this year. But with all this work I'm doing now, I'm hoping the stretching and strengthening will keep my muscles and tendons loose." He then joked, "I need only twelve strikeouts for three thousand. I figure I ought to be able to get them by August."

In many ways, the 1981 season was the most satisfying of Seaver's career, and also the most discomfiting. The off-season exercise program paid huge dividends. His legs were stronger than ever, his shoulder was pain free and loose, and by June 11, he was 7-1 with a 2.06 ERA. Even in his only bad start—April 18 against the Cardinals, when he was knocked out after only five innings—he made history by fanning his old nemesis Keith Hernandez in the fourth to become the fifth member of baseball's exclusive three thousand strikeout club, behind Walter Johnson, Gaylord Perry, Bob Gibson, and his friend Nolan Ryan. (A couple of days later, Steve Carlton would become the sixth.)

He'd regained it all, everything but the strikeouts. And then, on June 12, the 1981 season came to an abrupt halt when the players went on strike after failing to reach agreement with the owners on the final tenet of the labor deal they'd been negotiating since the previous May: compensation to teams losing free agents. The strike, which lasted fifty days, was finally settled when the owners and players agreed on a plan in which a team losing a free agent would be indirectly compensated by choosing from a pool of hundreds of players left off the other clubs' twenty-six-man protected lists. Seaver, a member of the players' negotiating committee, was delighted they were finally able to settle this thorny issue so that he could get back to pitching. He had no way of knowing the so-called free-agent compensation draft would come back to once more drastically disrupt his life.

At the conclusion of the strike, Baseball Commissioner Bowie Kuhn, declaring he wanted to give every team a fresh start, announced a new "split season" format for determining the postseason playoffs. The four teams in first place in their divisions at the time of the strike were all guaranteed spots in the postseason and would be joined by those teams finishing first in their division in the second (poststrike) half. For the Reds, who came in second to the Dodgers by a half game in the National League West in the first half, and second to the Astros by one game in the second half, this was the unkindest solution of all—especially since their overall 66-47 record turned out to be best in baseball. "There's no sense in getting upset about matters over which you have no control," John McNamara said resignedly.

But when it came time for the '81 postseason awards in November, Seaver lost the National League Cy Young Award by 3 points to the Dodgers' rookie Mexican strikeout phenomenon, Fernando Valenzuela, then McNamara and the rest of the Reds could no longer contain their outrage. Piece together the two halves of the strange season, and Seaver had the most wins and highest winning percentage in the league: 14-2, .875, along with a sparkling 2.54 ERA. First the Reds had been screwed as a team by Kuhn's cockamamie split-season idea, and now the spiritual leader of their pitching staff had been beaten out for a fourth Cy Young Award when the two baseball writers from San Diego (where Valenzuela was even more popular than in LA) left him off their three-man ballots. Valenzuela, just twenty years old, had become an instant international celebrity—"Fernandomania," it was called—after starting the season with eight straight complete-game victories in which he yielded a total of four earned runs. He wound up leading the NL in strikeouts and innings pitched, but slumped precipitously (5-7, 3.67 ERA) in the second half for a 13-7 ledger overall while Seaver had kept on winning.

Perhaps nobody felt as badly as Hume, after reflecting on an April 23 game in Houston in which he'd relieved Seaver with two on in the eighth inning and the Reds leading 4–1. "I gave up a three-run homer to Cesar Cedeño," he said. "That should've been Tom's fifteenth win."

Seaver, vacationing in Paris with Nancy when the Cy Young vote was announced, was not immediately available for comment; and it was surely no consolation for him when, a week later, he was named

United Press International's Comeback Player of the Year. Rather, it was left for McNamara and Bill Fischer to air their frustrations.

"Taking nothing away from Fernando Valenzuela, Tom Seaver deserved this award," the Reds' manager said bluntly. "There wasn't any doubt in my mind. This was a season full of mistakes—the strike, the split season—and this was yet another mistake."

"I really thought Tom would win it," said Fischer. "I'm very disappointed. This is my third big disappointment of this season. The strike was the first and then not making the playoffs. Now this. Tom may never get another whack at it. With his age now, it's going to be tough."

Fischer's lament turned out to be prophetic. During spring training of '82, a lingering respiratory infection prevented Seaver from making his first start of the season until mid-April. When he finally did join the Reds' rotation, his weakened arm strength was evident. He won only one of his nine starts in April and May, and by midsummer, when he felt he was at last starting to get it together again, the soreness in his shoulder resurfaced. On August 15 against the Astros, he gave up successive doubles to the first two batters of the game, Dickie Thon and Terry Puhl, and walked Ray Knight before taking himself out without retiring a batter. He was done for the year. The first losing season (5-13) of his career had been a bitter pill that left him wondering where he was going to go from here and what, if anything, he had left.

"I don't know where I am right now," he told the Cinci writers. "I came out of spring training with a virus and tried to pitch too soon. All I know is, it hurts when I throw. This year everything has been wrong."

It was indeed the end of an era in Cincinnati. Joe Morgan had left as a free agent for Houston after the 1979 season, while George Foster and Ken Griffey were traded after the 1981 season because Reds ownership couldn't afford to keep them as free agents. As for Johnny Bench, a broken ankle in May 1981 ended his days behind the plate. Plagued by more nagging injuries in '82, he hobbled through the worst season of his career, playing mostly third base. And one year after compiling the best record in baseball, the Reds lost the most games (101) in their history to finish last in the National League West.

In five and a half seasons with the Reds, Seaver was 75-46, with a 3.18 ERA, 42 complete games, and 12 shutouts in 158 starts. Even though he hadn't been able to get back to the World Series, he'd loved his time in Cincinnati, particularly his camaraderie with Bench, who'd become his best friend in baseball. But there was nothing to be gained by being part of a rebuilding process, and his girls were growing up.

It was time for Tom Seaver to go home.

CHAPTER 11

Soxed

DURING TOM SEAVER'S TIME AS AN EXPATRIATE NEW YORK MET, his former organization had undergone major changes, most notably a turnover of ownership.

In 1980 book publishing magnate Nelson Doubleday and New York City real estate developer Fred Wilpon purchased the team from the estate of Joan Payson for $21.1 million. M. Donald Grant had already been fired as team chairman two years earlier, and one of the first orders of business for the new owners was to fire Joe McDonald as head of baseball operations and replace him with J. Frank Cashen, a onetime Baltimore sportswriter who was working as an administrator in the Office of the Commissioner of Baseball. A roundish man with a cherubic Irish face and a signature bowtie, Cashen had been a top executive with the Baltimore Orioles from 1965 to 1975, a period that produced four trips to the World Series and two world championships.

After one year in his new job, Cashen fired Joe Torre as Mets manager and, reaching back to his Baltimore roots, replaced him with George Bamberger, the respected pitching coach of the great Orioles staffs of the sixties and seventies. At the same time, his player development people were mining the amateur draft for future stars such as outfielders Darryl Strawberry, Lenny Dykstra, and Kevin Mitchell, Cashen executed a couple of trades indirectly related to Seaver, designed to improve the team immediately. In February 1982 he acquired Seaver's Reds teammate George Foster, the 1977 National League Most Valuable Player, and, to keep him from becoming a free agent, signed him to a five-year, $10 million contract extension. A year later, in the final concession that the Mets had gotten nowhere near equal value for Seaver in 1977, Cashen brought slugger Dave Kingman back to the team in a February 28, 1981, trade with the Cubs for outfielder Steve Henderson. It was Henderson who had been the key player for the Mets in the "Midnight Massacre" Seaver trade with the Reds, touted as a "five-tool" power-and-speed supertalent. But in his four seasons with the Mets, Henderson was a major disappointment, battling injuries and never driving in more than sixty-five runs. None of these transactions would bear fruit immediately, however, and New York finished 1982 at the bottom of the NL East for its the sixth sub-.500 season in a row. One person not enthralled with Cashen's acquisition of Kingman to play first base was Rusty Staub, the beloved red-headed Met slugger. In December 1980, Staub had passed up remaining in the American League as a designated hitter to re-sign with the Mets as a free agent with the promise from Cashen that he would be the first baseman. Instead, he spent the final five years of his career with the Mets relegated mostly to pinch hitting duties, and after falling 284 hits shy of 3,000, he ruefully blamed Cashen's breach of promise about playing every day at first base for depriving him of the Hall of Fame.

As Seaver pondered his future after his own exasperating '82 season, the thirty-eight-year-old was fully aware that, at $750,000, he'd become an expensive ornament for the rebuilding Reds. He had also been closely monitoring the seemingly positive developments in Queens and wondering if the new sheriff in town there might want to bring him back as well. Cashen did. He was not convinced Seaver's career was over, and, in anticipation of yet another popular score with Mets fans, approached Reds president Bob Howsam at the December baseball winter meetings in Honolulu.

It was a very easy negotiation. Cashen told Howsam he'd be interested in taking Seaver's contract off his hands, and Howsam readily agreed to a deal in which the Reds got back Charlie Puleo, a twenty-seven-year-old second-line starting pitcher who'd been 9-9 with a 4.47 ERA for the Mets in '82, plus a couple of minor leaguers. The Seaver-Mets reunion was on.

"We'd really enjoyed our time in Cincinnati," said Nancy in 2017 in Calistoga, "but we were really pleased with the trade. There was nothing more to be accomplished for Tom in Cincinnati. They weren't the same team of stars that he'd originally joined, and this was sort of going home for him. It was gratifying that we could now . . . live in our real home and spend the last part of his career in New York."

On April 5, 1983, a sun-splashed but chilly opening day at Shea, she was back in her familiar seat a few rows behind the Mets' dugout, fashionably clad in a brown tweed turtleneck sweater and a matching wide-brimmed hat, with Sarah and Anne sitting next to her. Also in attendance were Seaver's parents, Charlie and Betty, his brother, Charles, and sisters Carol and Katie, in what was truly both a Seaver-Mets and Seaver-family reunion. As on opening day in 1973, 1974, and 1975, he would be facing Steve Carlton and the Philadelphia Phillies.

Unknown to anyone, before the game there was some question whether Seaver would be able to make his start. Or at least that's what Ed Lynch thought. Lynch was a twenty-seven-year-old middle reliever and spot starter on the '83 Mets who grew up in New York and had idolized Seaver in his youth.

"You have to understand," Lynch said in a 2020 interview, "Tom had a huge ego, and he was not the friendliest guy, especially with the younger players on that team who didn't know him. He could 'big-time' players and writers he didn't know as well as anyone I've ever known. But I didn't care. He was my hero, and I sought him out. But before that first game, Bamberger came to me and said, 'Tom's still nursing that hamstring that bothered him all spring, and if he can't go, you're going to start today.' I thought, 'Oh my God! There's no way!'

"Can you imagine? We got forty-six thousand people there, Steve Carlton's pitching against us, and I'm all of a sudden going to be walking to the mound instead of Tom Seaver? So, we're down in the bullpen, Tom and I warming up at the same time, and all of a sudden Tom keels over after a pitch, grabbing his hamstring! I about shit in my pants, and then he gets up laughing."

At about that same time, Mets PA announcer Jack Franchetti was completing his recitation of the Mets' starting lineup, "batting ninth and warming up in the bullpen, number forty-one!"—leaving out Seaver's name—as the crowd of 46,687 erupted in a thunderous roar that shook the stadium. It had been Cashen's idea for Franchetti to announce just Seaver's uniform number. "I believe in understatement," the general manager said. "Didn't have to mention his name. Number forty-one was all that was necessary."

"It was about the loudest crowd roar I think I ever heard," said Jay Horwitz, the Mets' longtime public relations director.

Horwitz, who had been hired in 1980, did not know Seaver when he first approached him at '83 spring training. "He was sitting in the whirlpool in the trainer's room when I introduced myself to him,"

Horwitz recalled in a 2020 interview, "and he said, 'Come closer, Jay, I can't hear you.' So, I moved closer to the whirlpool, and all of a sudden he pulled out the hose and stuffed it down my pants! Our relationship got better after that."

Backup catcher Ron Hodges, who spent his entire twelve-year career with the Mets and was one of only four players remaining from 1977 (the others being Kingman, Stearns, and pitcher Craig Swan), could see from their first game together in spring training that Seaver was a vastly different pitcher. "He was mixing in a lot of sliders, curves, and changeups," Hodges explained, "but number one"—his fastball—"was still his bread-and-butter pitch. He just wasn't going to it as often."

According to Hodges, Seaver requested that he be his catcher for opening day, and that continued for most of the season, as did his inclusion in Seaver's bridge games on Mets charter flights. Finishing up his pregame warmup throws, Seaver was asked by Mets reserve catcher Ronn Reynolds, who got into twenty-four games that season, if he wanted to take the ball with him.

"Why?" Seaver asked.

"Well," said Reynolds, "there's a handicapped kid sitting in the front row in the right-field seats who'd asked me for a ball before. I thought maybe you might want to give him one."

Without comment, Seaver exited the bullpen and, upon seeing the kid hanging over the railing, handed him the baseball.

"That showed me so much. I had tears in my eyes," Reynolds said later.

As number 41 took the long, slow "return of the hero" walk from the bullpen toward the Mets' dugout, past the right-field and first-base stands, he was greeted by waves of cheers from the crowd. Seaver acknowledged them by alternately doffing his cap, putting it back on his head, and doffing it again. Later, he would say, "I knew it was going to be emotional. I just didn't think it would be *this* emotional. I had to block it all out because I was pitching. If I wasn't, I would have cried. I know my mom did."

"I have to admit when he walked in from the bullpen, I had goose bumps," said Cashen.

Upon taking the mound, following the opening-day pregame festivities in which New York governor Mario Cuomo and New York City mayor Ed Koch combined to toss the ceremonial first pitches, Seaver remembered Betty Seaver's cautionary words to him before he left home that morning: "Take your time. Don't rush and don't fall off the mound. Don't swear and don't spit."

Most appropriately, the first Philly batter was his old Reds teammate Pete Rose. Seaver remembered that in one of his last outings as a Met in '77, against the Reds, he'd struck out Rose three times. More than likely, Charlie Hustle, second only to Ty Cobb in career base hits and destined to surpass him in 1985, remembered too. Seaver immediately got him in an 0-2 hole with a called strike and then a swinging strike on what Rose would later say "was a fastball from ten years ago." Four pitches later, Rose struck out—on a slider—igniting the crowd once again.

"He's not the blower he was when he was here the first time," Rose commented afterward, "but he made some great pitches—about what you would expect of a Hall of Fame pitcher."

Joe Morgan, Seaver's other ex-Reds mate, followed Rose by drawing a walk and was nearly picked off when Seaver's wide throw to first eluded the defensively challenged Kingman. Morgan raced to second on the error but was left stranded when Seaver retired Gary Matthews on a groundout and Mike Schmidt on a fly to left.

Morgan turned out to be the only Philly to reach scoring position against Seaver. He retired eleven straight batters from the first to the fifth, when Tony Perez, yet another former Red, led off with a single. But he advanced no farther, as Seaver got the next two batters on flyouts and struck out center fielder Bob Dernier to end the inning. He then began the sixth by striking out Carlton and Rose before Morgan singled to left and was thrown out trying to stretch it into a double. After the Carlton strikeout, though, Seaver had felt a twinge in his thigh—probably the result of the cool weather—and Bamberger took note.

The Franchise had made one grand return—"Same Ol' Seaver" was the *Daily News*'s next-day back-page headline. Six efficient shutout innings, five strikeouts, and just one walk—albeit with another air of dismaying familiarity about it: the Mets scored no runs for him. There was an almost-as-loud chorus of boos when Bamberger sent up infielder Wally Backman to pinch-hit for Seaver in the bottom of the sixth. The Mets won, 2–0, by scoring a pair of runs off Carlton in the seventh, with Doug Sisk, the team's top right-hander in the bullpen, picking up the victory.

"All that mattered was that we won," said Seaver. "It was a perfect opening day."

If only the rest of the 1983 Mets season would be nearly as perfect. The club got off to a 4-10 start, and things never got much better. At the June 15 trading deadline, Cashen pulled off another trade that would pay huge dividends for the Mets in the years to come: acquiring All-Star first baseman Keith Hernandez from the Cardinals. And on May 4 twenty-one-year-old outfielder Darryl Strawberry joined the team and went on to have a stellar Rookie of the Year season with 26 homers, 74 RBI, and 19 stolen bases. But Kingman (.198, 29 RBI) had a horrible year, and Foster hit a career-low .241, and the Mets reeled to another ninety-four-loss, last-place season. Bamberger resigned as manager on June 2 to be replaced by coach Frank Howard after Cashen was unsuccessful in luring legendary Orioles manager Earl Weaver out of retirement.

Through all of this, Seaver pitched creditably but could not avoid a second straight losing record, 9-14, largely the residue of nonsupport. In one stretch of twelve starts, the Mets scored a total of twenty-two runs for him. However, he never missed a start, and his 3.55 ERA, 230 innings, 135 strikeouts, and 1.242 WHIP all led the pitching staff substantially.

One Mets pitcher who was especially impressed with how the old man went about his business and persevered was twenty-three-year-old Ron Darling, a former number one draft pick of the Texas Rangers whom Cashen had acquired the previous year. Darling had been one of the top collegiate pitchers in the country at Yale University, and at first, when called up to the Mets in September, he found Seaver to be arrogant and distant. But as a fellow student of pitching and one college-educated player to another, he gradually came to appreciate Seaver's intellect and approach to pitching.

"You had to really admire his mental toughness, which, in my mind, was much the same as Bobby Fischer, the chess champion," Darling said. "You know most pitchers are playing checkers, but Tom was playing a high, high end of chess. He just had the aptitude to be able to decipher how to cut up a lineup. Yes, he did have the stuff, did have the power, but it's not only that. It's the precision. With Tom, he had the power and the precision, and then he had the mental aptitude to do things very few people could do on the mound."

"There's only about six inches of a bat that has decent enough wood to hit the ball anyplace," Seaver told Bill Surface of the *New York Times*

Magazine at the start of the season, "and that's exactly where I'm *not* going to pitch. I release the ball at a certain point in my movement so I can pitch downstairs—trying to tick the edge of the plate around the hitter's knees. All I want is the red seams over the plate. But I have to be flexible enough to alter my game plan."

The failure of the Mets to make any progress in his third year as general manager was particularly hard on Cashen. At season's end, he fired Howard as manager and replaced him with forty-one-year-old Davey Johnson, skipper of the Mets' Triple-A Tidewater Tides. Johnson had been the second baseman on those powerhouse Orioles teams of the sixties and seventies, and then in 1973 enjoyed a career season for the Atlanta Braves: .270 BA, 43 HR, 97 RBI. That he lacked the usual prerequisite of major-league managerial experience would quickly be proven immaterial.

With that decision settled, Cashen took a trip to Ireland, unaware that one of the other decisions he made just before departing would come back to haunt him.

On the morning of January 17, 1984, I was at my desk in the sports department of the *New York Daily News* when I took a phone call from an old friend, Art Berke. A native of Chicago, Berke worked in the public relations office at the ABC network, where one of his primary duties was the unenviable task of handling PR for the insufferable egomaniac Howard Cosell. Before landing at ABC, Berke had worked in the Baseball Commissioner's Office from 1975 through 1980 and still had a lot of friends and contacts there.

"Are you writing a story about the draft Friday?" Berke asked.

He was referring to the free-agent compensation draft that Major

League Baseball would be conducting in two days. This "draft" was the primary tenet of the settlement of the 1981 baseball strike—the avenue for indirectly compensating teams that had lost premium (type A) free agents, by having each select a player out of a pool of hundreds from the other twenty-nine clubs. At the end of the season, each team was required to submit to the Commissioner's Office a list of twenty-six players from its entire organization to be protected from the draft. Teams that had opted not to sign any type-A free agents were exempt from having to place any players in the pool. By virtue of having lost their top relief pitcher, Dennis Lamp, to the Toronto Blue Jays, the Chicago White Sox were awarded the first pick in the '84 compensation draft.

Berke explained he'd been talking to a friend in the Commissioner's Office who was privy to the protected lists and who, in turn, passed on the info to him, knowing he was a lifelong White Sox fan with particular interest in the draft.

"You're not going to believe this," Berke said excitedly, "but guess who the Mets left unprotected!"

"I give up, who?"

"Tom Seaver."

I paused in thought for a moment, trying to comprehend what he had just told me.

But there was more.

"Not only that, but the White Sox are taking him!" Berke exclaimed. "I talked to one of their guys in the front office just now, and he confirmed they're taking Seaver Friday. They couldn't believe he was available."

After hanging up with Art, I pondered how to handle this news, which would become about the biggest story I would ever break in my forty years at the *Daily News*. The first thing I needed to do was to get confirmation from the Mets. I called Jay Horwitz.

"Jay, I need to talk to Frank. It's very important."

"Uh, he's in a luncheon right now," Horwitz said.

"Well, you're going to have to get him out of that luncheon and have him call me, ASAP."

"What is this about, Bill?" Horwitz asked. "I can't call Frank out of a luncheon unless I know what this is all about."

"All right, Jay," I said. "I'll tell you, but I swear if this gets out to anyone else, I will personally drive out to Shea Stadium and freaking kill you. Do you understand?"

I told him what Berke had just relayed to me.

"Okay, okay, I'll get him," Horwitz stammered. Five minutes later, my phone rang, and it was Frank Cashen.

"Frank," I said, "I'm sorry to have interrupted your lunch, but I've come across a story that I need your confirmation on."

"What story?" Cashen asked.

"I understand you've left Seaver off your protected list for Friday's draft."

After a long pause, he said, "I've known you too long, Billy, so I'm not gonna lie to you.

"We did leave him off our list. He's a thirty-nine-year-old pitcher out of all the hundreds of players in that pool. We didn't think anyone would take him. Plus, everyone knows, he's our guy."

"That may be true, Frank," I said, "but I hate to tell you, the White Sox *are* going to take him. I have that on good authority."

Again a long pause.

"I don't know what to say," Cashen said. "I guess you have to write your story, and if you're right, I'll just have to deal with it."

I had my confirmation, but before I could write the story, I felt I owed it to Seaver to inform him so that he wouldn't be blindsided the next day. It was a risky call. I didn't know him that well, since I had covered mostly the Yankees for the *News* and didn't spend much time around the Mets. When I called his home in Greenwich, he answered the phone himself.

"Tom," I said, "this is Bill Madden with the *News*."

"How ya doin', Bill," Seaver replied. "What's up?"

"I'm afraid I may be the bearer of some bad news, Tom," I said.

"Uh-oh. What bad news?"

"Well, apparently the Mets have left you off their protected list for the free-agent compensation draft on Friday."

"What?" Seaver said. "I don't understand."

"I guess they figured they were safe; that no one would take you because you're their guy, their franchise player," I said. "But I've been told the White Sox *are* gonna take you with the first pick. You're going to have to leave the Mets again."

Once again, there was a momentary silence on the other end of the phone.

"We'll see about that," Seaver said finally. "Thanks for giving me the heads-up, Bill. I've got a lot of thinking to do now."

What happened next could never happen today in the age of Twitter and the internet: We sat on the story all day long and held it out of all editions until the last one, which didn't go off the presses until one thirty in the morning. The whole time, I held my breath in fear that it was going to leak out somehow. Amazingly, neither Cashen nor Seaver called anyone, except perhaps each other. The next day, under the *Daily News's* back-page headline "Mets Leaving Tom Exposed to White Sox," the following was reported under my byline:

"Tom Seaver, who only a year ago thought he had come home to stay, may be leaving again. In a daring gamble that may well blow up in their faces before the week is out, the Mets have elected to leave the thirty-nine-year-old pitcher unprotected in the free-agent compensation pool, the *Daily News* has learned."

On Friday, the deed was done. The White Sox announced they had selected Seaver. I called Sox general manager Roland Hemond, who was positively euphoric.

"When I saw Tom Seaver's name on the list" of unprotected players, he said, "I jumped right out of my chair. In our opinion, he was clearly the best player available. We took him not only because our scouts assured us he was still a first-rate pitcher but because he's the sort of class person we want on our ball club. If we had had Tom Seaver last year, we'd be celebrating a world championship now instead of just a division championship. I can understand how people in New York might think we wronged the Mets, but this was a business decision. It was our thinking if we didn't take Seaver, the A's, who had the next pick in the draft, certainly would have, and they're in our division."

None of this, of course, was of any solace to Cashen or Seaver, who, the next day, found themselves sitting together uncomfortably for one of the most embarrassing press conferences in Mets history. To his credit, Cashen took the fall for the organization.

"If we felt there was even a slight chance Tom would have been taken, I would never have brought this embarrassment to the owners of this ball club," the general manager said. "We looked at Chicago's club and the fact that they won their division by twenty games, and we figured they might be more apt to go for a prospect—which is why we protected as many of our young players as we could."

During Seaver's combined tenure with the Mets, in which he set likely

unbreakable team records for wins (198), complete games (171), shutouts (44), starts (395), innings pitched (3,045⅔), strikeouts (2,541),
and ERA (2.57), Seaver had made 105 regular season starts in which
he pitched nine innings or more and allowed one run or less. His record
in those starts was 90-3 with twelve no-decisions. In the twelve no-
decisions, he allowed only 56 hits and 5 earned runs in 117 innings for a
0.38 ERA. Seemingly, Seaver was at a loss for runs throughout his Mets
career. He pitched fifteen 1–0 games for the Mets, in which he was 6-9,
and an amazing thirty-eight 2–1 complete games, in which he was 23-15.
Overall, of all the pitchers with five hundred or more starts since 1900,
Seaver's teams' collective 3.94 run support is the third lowest behind fellow Hall of Famers Nolan Ryan (3.80) and Gaylord Perry (3.92).

As Cashen spoke, Seaver sat stone-faced.

After the GM had concluded his mea culpa, the man at the center
of this curious baseball drama finally made his thoughts known.

"It's an unfortunate situation," Seaver understated. "I've gotten a
little more upset as things have gone along. I'm not here to blast anybody, though. They had their meetings, and they had to do what they
thought was best. I don't agree with what they did. They made a mistake, that's for sure. I just don't understand their thinking behind it."

At one point, Seaver was asked about the whole concept of the free-
agent compensation draft that the players' union, for which he was the
Mets' player rep, had agreed to in order to end the 1981 walkout.

"I felt at the time it was a farce and a joke and that somebody would
get hurt by it," Seaver said.

"I just never thought it would be me."

The free-agent compensation pool was abolished after its fourth
year in 1985 and replaced with a new system in which amateur draft
picks became the compensation to teams losing free agents.

By sheer happenstance, the day after the press conference, Seaver had to attend a promotional engagement at a trade show in Chicago. When Sox GM Roland Hemond learned of this, he called Seaver in his room at the Hyatt Regency and asked if the club's owners, Jerry Reinsdorf and Eddie Einhorn, could come over and meet with him. Seaver agreed—reluctantly—and gave Hemond his room number.

"Eddie and I went up to the room while Roland stayed in the lobby," Reinsdorf said. "But when we knocked on the door, Seaver opened it and said, 'How do I know you guys are who you say you are?' He made us show him our driver's licenses before he let us in the room!"

"For all I knew they were holdovers from the Capone gang," Seaver joked later.

From there, the meeting went downhill quickly.

"We could see he was still pretty hot," Reinsdorf said. "He kept saying, 'I don't know how the Mets could do this to me'; that this was an act of complete disloyalty on their part. He said how he'd taken less money to go back to them. He was very, very, very, very angry. And I kept saying to him, 'Don't be angry at us. Be angry at the Mets if you want to be angry at anybody. I mean, if you were us, and somebody told you that you could have Tom Seaver, what would you do?' That seemed to calm him down a little. He didn't make any threats or talk about a contract extension at that point. He just basically said, 'I don't know if I'm going to report. I don't know if I'm going to do this.'"

Reinsdorf and Einhorn gave Seaver a few days to think about his options and then called him to arrange another meeting in New York, where they would discuss a contract extension. They met at the Palace Hotel, near St. Patrick's Cathedral, but, again, it did not go well at first.

"We got into some pretty intensive negotiations," Reinsdorf recalled in a 2019 interview at the Hall of Fame in Cooperstown, "and at one point, there were some pretty strong words. He wasn't happy with our initial offer and blurted out, 'Do you realize I have a 273-170 lifetime record, which means if I go 0-and-20 in each of the next five years, I'll still be over .500?'"

Looking back, Reinsdorf said, he just should have let Seaver vent. But he couldn't resist making a flippant remark.

"I said, 'Yeah, but you didn't win any of those two hundred seventy-three games for us!"

An enraged Seaver bolted out of his chair and charged across the room with his fist raised, before Einhorn jumped in front of him and restrained him. Once Seaver calmed down, the sides were finally able to agree on a two-year contract extension at $1.13 million each through 1986. The White Sox had been reluctant to go to a second year for '86, but as Reinsdorf related, "Tom said to me, 'If I can't pitch in 1986 at a level that I think is appropriate, I'll quit. You don't have to worry about paying me for not performing.' And I took his word for it. I believed he had integrity, and that's how the deal got done. Actually, most of the negotiations were between Eddie and Tom's lawyer, because after Tom threatened to belt me, we didn't think it was very productive for me to hang around Tom too much."

Now that he was officially with his third major-league organization, Seaver set his sights on what he needed to accomplish in Chicago. He was going from a bad team to a division leader that in 1983 boasted the best record in baseball—99-63, .611, leaving its closest challenger in the AL West, the Kansas City Royals, twenty games back—so there would be no excuse for not getting back on the winning track. In stark contrast to the Mets, Chicago's lineup was stocked with big bats: Ron Kittle clubbed 35 homers in '83; Greg Luzinski, 32; Carlton Fisk, 26; and budding superstar Harold Baines, 20. Combined, the four of them drove in 380 runs.

In Fisk, the nine-time All-Star catcher who'd finished third in the American League Most Valuable Player voting the year before, Seaver couldn't have dreamed of a better guide for helping him navigate a whole new league of opposing batters. Of utmost importance to Seaver, though, was three hundred wins, which would certify his place in the Hall of Fame.

But as he was soon to discover, the biggest challenge in his new surroundings was figuring out just what planet his new manager, Tony LaRussa, was on. Throughout his career, Seaver had been used to old-school managers—Gil Hodges, Sparky Anderson, John McNamara—who may not have been great strategists as much as they were one-on-one motivators. He admired and respected them all.

The thirty-nine-year-old LaRussa, who after a brief major-league career as an infielder earned a law degree from Florida State University, was a different cat. Entering his sixth full season as White Sox manager, LaRussa had already earned a reputation around the league as a new-age innovator and stickler for detail. Much to Seaver's utter dismay, he found out just how detail-obsessed his new manager was in his very first start for the White Sox, on April 8, at Comiskey Park against the Tigers, when LaRussa took him out of the game with one out and runners at first and third in the fifth inning. Granted, he hadn't been pitching particularly well to that point, but he was down only 3–2. Seaver was not accustomed to exiting games before he had a chance to be credited with a win, and his managers always had accorded him the option of pitching out of his own jams. But LaRussa didn't even consult with him. He merely asked for the ball and signaled to the bullpen for left-hander Juan Agosto.

At this point, Seaver picks up the story because he loved retelling it: "I go into the dugout, and I'm steaming at LaRussa. And then Agosto walks the first batter he faces and gives up a bases-clearing double to Barbaro Garbey. Now the game is completely out of hand. I went back into the clubhouse, changed into my street clothes, and left the ballpark in disgust. Yes, disgust! LaRussa took the ball from me and gives it to Juan effing Disgusto. My first freakin' start for him!"

The next day, Seaver was still seething when he joined the other pitchers shagging flies in the outfield during a workout at Milwaukee's County Stadium. Only he was deliberately making no effort to shag them, instead remaining stationary as balls fell out of the sky all around him like hand grenades. All the while, he was staring straight ahead at LaRussa standing on the top step of the dugout.

"Oh, yeah, I was still pissed," Seaver said. "I stood out there and didn't pick up one damn ball. There's baseballs all over the place. It was like an orange orchard. Fruit everywhere. This was as subtle as I could get: 'You know, Tony, we've got an issue here, and you're going to have to talk to me about this.'"

White Sox pitching coach Dave Duncan, standing next to LaRussa, said to him, "You know what he's doing, don't you?"

"No, what?" replied LaRussa. "He just wants to be alone."

"No, no," said Duncan, a former serviceable catcher who became one of the most highly regarded pitching coaches in the game. "He wants you to come out there."

So, LaRussa took a slow walk to the outfield for what he now realized was going to be a very testy confrontation with his clearly disgruntled veteran pitcher.

"It seems you have a problem," he said to Seaver.

"I'll say! How in the hell could you take me out of that game yesterday?"

"Well," said LaRussa, "I thought you'd had a tough five innings, weather-wise and such, and I was looking for the right time to get you out. First and third. One out. It was a bunt situation. I liked Agosto in that situation. Left-handed pitcher who's a cat off the mound."

That was all Seaver needed to hear. Now LaRussa was telling him he took him out of the game because he thought Agosto would be better at fielding a bunt!

"Look," said Seaver, "I'm not gonna second-guess you on this, but I'm just asking you: Do you know how many fucking games I've won in the big leagues? Two-hundred and seventy-three! And I'm a hundred games over .500! I didn't get there not being able to field my position!"

"Well, you know, lefty going to the third-base side . . ."

"I'm just telling you that I can field my position, and I know where to make a pitch to where I know the batter is going to bunt the ball. You could have asked me how I felt."

LaRussa was properly chastened.

"I told him, 'I know I'm learning,'" LaRussa said in 2017. "I had learned from Paul Richards you never ask a pitcher because they all want to be heroes." (Richards, a successful White Sox manager in the 1950s, and later an executive for several clubs, came out of retirement at the age of sixty-eight to helm the Sox again for the 1976 season.) "So, we established that between us. From that day on, he's the only pitcher I would ever ask."

To prove his point, LaRussa then related a story about another game later in the '84 season. Seaver was leading by a run late in the game when, with two out, there were suddenly runners at second and third and a dangerous left-handed hitter, coming to bat.

"I had a left-handed reliever warming up," LaRussa said, "but I'm thinking, 'No, I'll go and ask Tom.' I go out to the mound, and he says, 'Don't worry, I got this guy.' So I turn around and start heading back to the dugout, and Tom says, 'But just so you know, I'm gonna fall behind in the count on purpose, make my pitch, and he'll pop up to the left side.'"

Shaking his head, LaRussa walked back to the dugout and watched Seaver fall behind 3-1 in the count.

"I could see the hitter on his front foot looking for the fastball," LaRussa said, "and instead Tom throws him a changeup, which he pops up to the third baseman. When he came off the field, he winked at me. That was Tom."

Another time, Seaver was watching with bemusement as the ever-experimental LaRussa had his pitchers doing drills for defending against the running game, working on a play that he called the fake pitchout. After a couple of minutes, Seaver asked: "Why are we making this so complicated? Suppose I think I can just strike the batter out on a pitch, you know, instead of trying to throw out one of the base runners?"

"I got kind of flustered trying to explain it to Tom, and I could see this light in his eye," recalled LaRussa, "and I realized he was just messing with me. I remember that was exactly the day he started calling me 'McGraw'"—in reference to the famously strategic Hall of Fame manager John McGraw, nicknamed "Little Napoleon," who piloted the New York Giants to ten pennants and three World Series titles from

1902 to 1932 and is second on the all-time wins list.. "From then on," said LaRussa, "if he thought I was getting too strategic, he'd yell, 'Hey, McGraw, just let us play!' "

What had started off as a very tenuous relationship between Seaver and LaRussa gradually evolved into one of mutual respect. On May 9, thanks to LaRussa, Seaver entered the record books by being the winning pitcher of record in two games on the same day, against the Milwaukee Brewers.

The Brewers–White Sox game the night before had been suspended after seventeen innings with the score knotted at 3. Play resumed the following afternoon. Milwaukee plated three runs in the top of the twenty-first, only to have Chicago counter with three of its own. By the time the twenty-fifth inning came lumbering around, LaRussa had gone through seven pitchers. He asked Seaver, penciled in to start the regularly scheduled night game, if he was up to pitching an inning or two.

"We need to win this game first," the manager said, "and we'll worry about your game later." Seaver agreed and, fortunately, had faced only three batters when Harold Baines won the game for the White Sox with a home run in the bottom of the twenty-fifth. Having notched one fast and easy win with his first relief appearance since 1976, Seaver pitched another 8⅓ innings to win the second game as well, 5–4.

At the end of the '84 season, in which he was 15-11 with four shutouts, ten complete games, and a 3.95 ERA, Seaver told the Chicago writers: "I'm not a pitcher who can throw the ball by you anymore, but I think I'm a better pitcher than ever before. I enjoy pitching more because I know more about it than twelve years ago when I was throwing harder."

"I realized quickly Tom was a scientist," said LaRussa. "I'll never forget a conversation we had early on, when he was talking about the game having twenty-seven outs but asking me if all twenty-seven outs were the same. I knew he was going to make a point, and I was trying to give him a good answer before he says: 'No, they aren't. There are key outs in every game. For example: you're winning the game, 5–1, it's the seventh inning, and you got runners on second and third with two outs. Guy gets a base hit, it's 5–3. And they've got seven outs to go. Right there. That's the game. If you'd gotten that guy out, you've got a four-run lead going into the last two innings.'

"In other words, what he was saying was, you need to understand the importance of those outs. You need to concentrate and cut all the other garbage out of your mind. It's the same thing for a manager and the defense. Don't be there thinking where you're gonna eat that night. This is one of those outs. Bear down and do everything you have to, to get it. Great tip. I used it forever."

One White Sox player for whom Seaver developed an immediate affection was the rookie shortstop Ozzie Guillen, who, in following All-Star shortstops Chico Carrasquel, Luis Aparicio, and Dave Concepcion from Venezuela to the big leagues, would go on to win American League Rookie of the Year honors in '85. Seaver loved the kid's brashness and his passion for the game. One of Seaver's favorite stories involved a game in 1985 when he was having a particularly hard time with the signs from White Sox backup catcher Marc "Boot" Hill. According to Seaver, Hill was talking to all the batters "about where they were going to be buying pizza after the game and all that other stuff." Finally, he'd had enough and called Hill to the mound.

"Dammit, Booter," he said, "we're not being paid by the hour here. Put some fucking numbers down!"

Equally frustrated at being repeatedly shaken off, Hill replied: "If you're so goddamn good, maybe you just don't need any signs today."

"Okay, fine," Seaver said. "If that's the way you want it, we won't have any signs the rest of the game. You gotta catch 'em."

Hill went back behind the plate, and Seaver resumed pitching—without any signs. Meanwhile, Guillen, playing shortstop, was dumbfounded. He always looked at the catcher's signs to know what pitch was coming so he would know where he should play the hitter. After a couple of pitches, Guillen called time out and ran to the mound.

"What the fuck is going on?" he screamed. "You not getting any signs!"

"We're not using signs today, Ozzie," Seaver said matter-of-factly.

"Whaddaya mean you not using any signs?" Guillen said in consternation. "How I supposed to know where to play the hitters?"

"Don't worry, Ozzie," Seaver said calmly. "I'll tell you where to play them."

Trotting back to his position, Guillen, shook his head, turned, and shouted to Seaver: "You crazy, mon!"

"That," said Seaver, completing the story with a loud guffaw, "was a whole different issue."

In the dugout later, Dave Duncan also asked Seaver what the hell was going on. When Seaver explained the dispute with Hill, Duncan shook his head. "Just don't tell LaRussa," Seaver said. "He'll never understand. He's so goddamn anal."

Seaver turned out to be LaRussa's most dependable starter in '84, a disappointing season in which the Sox finished fifth, fourteen games under .500. Both men knew privately knew that, barring injury, he'd get those remaining twelve wins for three hundred in 1985. Of course, neither of them could have known it would happen back in New York and, of all places, at Yankee Stadium, on August 4. Whenever he talked about it in the years after, Seaver always said he was most proud of win number three hundred being a complete game.

"There's a picture in my mind which I'll never forget about that game," said LaRussa. "It's the eighth inning, two out, runners at first and third, and Seaver's facing down Dave Winfield at the plate, representing the tying run. You could just see the exhaustion and fatigue in Seaver's face. You know, it's like a movie. And then he strikes Winfield out, and it's as if the world is lifted from his shoulders. That was *the most important of those twenty-seven outs*, right there! Still gives me chills."

After the game, Seaver reiterated what he'd said after the '84 season. He wasn't done yet. It was on to 301, and who knew how many more? But after being back home, taking in all the adulation of the New York fans and surrounded by his family, he admitted to a reporter that he wished he could have finished his career there.

"Chicago's not a home for me," he said. "I feel at home with the people I work with there. It's as good a bunch of guys as I've ever been with, and the city's fine. But as far as living there, I feel like a visitor."

Four days later, Sarah Seaver and Carlton Fisk's daughter Carly attended a Bruce Springsteen concert at Soldier Field in Chicago. Springsteen was unaware they were in the audience, but he dedicated his current hit "Glory Days" to Seaver for having won his three hundredth game.

"I was both shocked and thrilled," Sarah said, "although I much would have preferred if he'd pulled me up onto the stage to dance."

Seaver would finish the '85 season by winning four of his last five starts to bring his record to 16-11 and a sense of fulfillment. When the '86 season began, however, the longing to be home started to consume him.

On April 29, 1986, Seaver had just returned to Chicago from a road trip in Detroit when he got word that his mother, Betty, had died in Fresno after a long battle with cancer. Since the season began, he'd been making periodic trips to the West Coast to visit her. She'd always been his biggest supporter, his protector, and his moral compass. Her loss, which devastated him, was yet another reality check. In reflecting on his mom and those last days in Chicago during a 2016 interview at his home in Calistoga, Seaver said that, for a lot of reasons, his instincts were telling him he needed to take stock of his career and his life.

"There were multithings that I didn't like," he said. "I remember it was my mother's birthday. I was in a hotel on the road, and I picked up the phone and called her, and said, 'Happy birthday, Mom.' She said to me, 'Where are you?' And I looked around the room and said, 'I don't know, Mom. I don't know where I am.' After I hung up, I said to myself, 'This is not good.' I've got two daughters, they're in high school or whatever, you know, and I said, 'Time to go home, Tom.'"

Sarah Seaver remembered getting phone calls from her father at Boston College, each time sensing a trace of loneliness in his voice. "He'd call me from the road, wanting to know what I was doing," she said, "and then his voice would crack. He was homesick. Back home in Greenwich, he'd thrown himself one hundred percent into his projects, creating all that space for his little orchard in the back, trying to figure out why there was no fruit on his plum trees. He had to neglect all of that when he went to Chicago."

Around the middle of June '86, Seaver called me from Chicago. After going six straight starts without a win, Seaver had asked White Sox general manager Ken "Hawk" Harrelson to see if he could work out a trade to get him home to New York. Harrelson's first call had been to Frank Cashen, who was interested even though he had a full contingent of young quality starting pitchers, led by Dwight Gooden, Ron Darling, Bobby Ojeda, and Sid Fernandez, who were in the process of taking the Mets to their first World Series since '73. But Cashen's manager, Davey Johnson, rejected the idea of bringing back Seaver.

"I need your help," he said to me. "I'm trying to get back to New York. Hawk's talked to the Mets, I think, but they're not interested. Could you call George for me and tell him I need to get home, and I would love to finish my career as a Yankee?"

I was still covering the Yankees for the *Daily News* and, as part of the job, had cause to frequently check in with the principal owner George Steinbrenner. I told him I'd relay his message to Steinbrenner, adding that upstaging the Mets' drive to the pennant by bringing Seaver back to New York, but in the Bronx, was right out of the Boss's playbook. "I can't imagine he won't jump at this," I said.

Much to my surprise, and for reasons Steinbrenner never explained, he was lukewarm to the idea, and negotiations between him and Harrelson eventually got hung up on a six-foot-six Yankees shortstop prospect from Venezuela named Carlos Martinez. "I can't trade him," Steinbrenner told me. "The kid's our shortstop of the future."

"George," I pleaded, "we're talking about Tom Seaver here! Plus, the scouts all tell me Martinez is too big to play shortstop and will eventually have to move to first base."

Harrelson called me June 29 to say the deal was not going to happen. Steinbrenner would not relent on Martinez, so instead he'd worked out a trade with Red Sox general manager Lou Gorman: Tom Terrific for infielder Steve "Crazy Horse" Lyons. (Apparently the mercurial Steinbrenner changed his mind about Martinez—and quickly—because just one month later, Harrelson got his wish: Martinez and Yankees catcher Ron Hassey in exchange for big bat Ron Kittle and two other players. Martinez would spend seven years in the majors as a journeyman part-time designated hitter, third baseman, first baseman, and outfielder. But not once as a shortstop.)

It wasn't New York, but as far as Seaver was concerned, Boston was close enough. "I know my age," he said candidly, "and I know my record this year"—2-6, with a 4.38 ERA and just one complete game in twelve starts. "I just question Lou Gorman's judgment for bringing me here. Physically, I'm fine. I have to prove I can pitch to my new teammates." The swap also reunited him with his former manager in Cincinnati, John McNamara.

Seaver made 16 starts for Boston from July 1 to September 19, winning 5 of them to run his lifetime total to 311. In mid-September, however, his right knee began balking every time he took the mound. The Sox were comfortably in first place the day he joined them, and although the Yankees, Orioles, and Blue Jays all came within striking distance at points, Boston pulled away with an 18-8 September, then overcame a three-to-one-game deficit to beat the California Angels in seven in the ALCS and land in the Fall Classic against a certain team from New York. But Tom Seaver wouldn't be returning to the World Series for the first time since 1973: After two straight subpar starts in late September in which he failed to get out of the fourth inning, he had to shut it down. X-rays on his knee revealed a torn cartilage, which was going to require surgery. "If I tried to pitch now, I'd either totally tear the knee or hurt my arm," he said.

It was therefore a cruel destiny that, on October 18, 1986, Seaver found himself back at Shea Stadium, in uniform, for another Mets World Series. Instead of standing on the mound preparing to throw the first pitch of game one, however, he was sitting in the visitors' dugout, clad in a Red Sox warmup jacket and relegated to the role of spectator.

Nevertheless, during the pregame introductions of the players, he received one of the loudest ovations. He would always be Tom Terrific—the Franchise—to Mets fans. A week later, the last time he would ever be in Shea Stadium as a player, he watched with bittersweet emotions as the Mets came from behind for the second straight game to defeat the Red Sox in game seven, 8–5, for their first world championship since the miracle year of 1969.

CHAPTER 12

Lord of the Grapes

THERE WOULD BE ONE MORE SEAVER-METS REUNION—SORT OF.

In late February 1987 Dave Anderson, the sports columnist for the *New York Times,* visited Tom's home in Greenwich to gauge the forty-two-year-old pitcher's thoughts about his career—in particular, whether he thought it might actually be over. It had been nearly four months since Seaver watched disconsolately from the top step of the visitors' dugout at Shea Stadium as his new Red Sox teammates blew the 1986 World Series by allowing the Mets to come back from a two-run deficit with two outs and no one on in the bottom of the tenth inning of game six to win, 6–5, forcing a seventh and deciding game. In that game, the winning run came home when Red Sox first baseman Bill Buckner famously allowed a ground ball to go through his legs. In the interim, Seaver had undergone arthroscopic surgery to repair the torn cartilage in his right knee that had benched him for the postseason and turned down a $500,000 one-year offer from Boston to come back in 1987.

Now Seaver was just waiting, while also offering a hint as to why he spurned the Red Sox' offer.

"Two outs, two strikes, nobody on, showed me a lack of killer instinct," Seaver mused about that traumatic game six. "When you're up by two runs, within one pitch of winning the World Series, you have to win. If you don't, you don't deserve to win."

Seaver was granted free agency November 12, 1986, but because the Red Sox had made him an offer, they were entitled to a first-round amateur draft pick as compensation from whichever team signed him. This caused the Yankees to back off after initially expressing interest in signing him. After that, no other team called.

"I really haven't made a decision," Seaver told Anderson. "Not that there's a decision to be made if somebody doesn't show any interest. I could go out and get a television job tomorrow. But from a business standpoint, is that prudent? If I don't play, I'll miss the pitching, although I won't miss working seven days a week and six nights out of seven, and I won't miss the travel. My idea now is to take some time off before jumping into something else."

But it was also the first time in twenty-one years he was not in spring training, and this was something he clearly was missing.

"I've learned," Seaver said with a sigh, "that every team thinks it has enough pitching on February 20, but every team starts hunting for pitching on March 20."

That was the precisely the case with his old team, the Mets, only it was at the end of May, not March, when he received a call from Frank Cashen, who was looking for a starting pitcher—*and* perhaps also hoping to rectify his mistake that had led to Seaver's unceremonious second departure from New York in 1984. Bobby Ojeda, one of the Mets' primary starting pitchers, who'd gone 18-5 for the '86 championship team, had been felled by an ulnar nerve issue in his elbow that was going to require season-ending surgery.

"How are you feeling, Tom?" Cashen asked.

"Well," said Seaver, "I'm not sure. My knee is fine after the surgery, but I haven't thrown a pitch since last September."

"Are you up for a comeback try?" Cashen asked.

Seaver thought about that for a moment.

"I could be," he said, "but only with you guys. I had kind of resigned myself to the fact there weren't going to be any offers, and I want to be close to home."

The next day, Seaver drove to Shea Stadium to meet face-to-face with Cashen. They agreed on a one-year contract for $750,000. From there, he was to go down to the Mets' Tidewater Tides Triple-A team in Norfolk, Virginia, to work himself into shape. The plan was for him to pitch one game against the Tides, then join the Mets on their road trip to Chicago, Pittsburgh, and Montreal in mid-June, during which he would pitch a couple of simulated intrasquad games against the Mets' backup players. Unfortunately, none of that went very well.

Granted, there was a lot of rust on that right arm after eight months of inactivity, but Seaver could sense the loss of velocity and not enough crispness to his pitches after being hit hard by the Tidewater minor leaguers—and it was much the same in the simulated skirmishes with the Mets' reserves. As Seaver told Jack O'Connell of MLB.com many years later: "I joined the Mets on that trip, and I remember flying to Chicago, getting into O'Hare Airport at one o'clock in the morning, and then taking that long bus ride on the expressway to downtown. I'm looking out the window of the bus and saying to myself: 'I don't want to do this anymore.'"

The roughing up Seaver took from the Mets' reserves in Montreal a few days later, which culminated with second-string catcher Barry Lyons hitting a long home run off him, clinched it for him. He was not going to be a Met again, but at least this time it would be on his terms.

With his 311-205 career record, 2.86 ERA, 3,640 strikeouts, and 61 shutouts, he and the Hall of Fame immortal Walter Johnson were the only two pitchers in history with 300 wins, 3,000 strikeouts, and an ERA of under 3.00. So, no, there was nothing he'd left unfinished.

Seaver called Cashen to inform him of his decision, and it was agreed the Mets would hold a gala Tom Seaver retirement press conference at Shea Stadium the following Monday, June 22, an off-day for the team. With Nancy by his side (no tears this time), Seaver told the assembled media: "Now I can live the rest of my life and say it was no longer there. Now I can say I got every ounce out of it.

"I would love to help this team win another championship, but when I realized I couldn't do a thing to help them, I didn't want to create a logjam if they have to go out and get another pitcher. I have been getting paid since the fifteenth of the month, and I could have continued to get paid right up until September 20 if I'd wanted. But this was a good-faith contract, and when I realized I couldn't do it, I decided not to go any further. There are no more pitches left in this arm."

As he got up to leave, he shook Cashen's hand and hugged Buddy Harrelson, who'd been sitting in the front row, when a reporter had one more question for him. "Who was the toughest batter you ever faced, Tom?"

A grin came over Seaver's face. "Barry Lyons," he said.

It would not be until the following year, July 24, 1988, that the Mets feted Seaver with a day in his honor at Shea Stadium. Among the dignitaries saluting Seaver was Bill Shea himself, who, along with Joan Payson, had spearheaded the return of National League baseball to New York with the birth of the Mets in 1962 and for whom the stadium was named. Sitting in the dugout were Seaver's closest former teammates: Rusty Staub, Jerry Grote, Jerry Koosman, and Harrelson, all of them retired for several years by now. They wore white caps emblazoned with a blue-and-orange number 41, which was being officially retired by the Mets as part of the ceremonies.

Longtime Mets broadcasters Bob Murphy and Ralph Kiner performed the masters of ceremonies duties, with a video backdrop of Seaver's career accompanied by a slow, moving musical rendering of "Take Me Out to the Ballgame" on the center-field scoreboard. There were gifts aplenty, including a case of wine presented to Seaver by current Mets favorites Gary Carter, Mookie Wilson, Lee Mazzilli, and Keith Hernandez (the latter of whom spoke proudly of being Seaver's three thousandth strikeout victim "on a hanging slider up and away—a helicopter waiting to be clobbered"). All the while, the sellout crowd of 46,057 remained standing, applauding and applauding. Their 1988 Mets were riding high, heading toward a division championship and a hundred wins; since Davey Johnson took the reins, the club had averaged ninety-eight victories per season over five years.

"Nobody else in the history of baseball ever had this dramatic an impact on a franchise," said Cashen to reporters. "Everybody wants to talk about Babe Ruth and the Yankees, and certainly you have to do that. But if you talk about Ruth, you have to talk about Lou Gehrig. Before Tom Seaver, there was no one here. This team was a laughingstock. He was Moses, leading them to the promised land."

In his column for the *Daily News* the next day, Mike Lupica wrote: "Seaver did not make up to New York for what Walter O'Malley and Horace Stoneham did. He did not bring back the Dodgers and Giants. But he was the first to make it hurt less."

When it was time for Seaver to approach the microphone, he talked first about Gil Hodges, "who taught me how to conduct myself as a professional," and, pointing to Nancy, daughters Sarah and Annie, and his dad, Charlie, sitting in chairs alongside him, "being blessed to have the family I have." He thanked Cashen and the Mets' owners, Nelson Doubleday and Fred Wilpon, and lastly, to a crescendo of cheers, the Mets' fans. He concluded his speech by saying: "I have always been asked how I would really thank everyone if there was ever a thing such as Tom Seaver Day."

With that, he whirled around from the microphone and dashed out to the pitcher's mound, put his foot on the rubber and began bowing, this way and that, to the biggest sound of the day from the adulating crowd.

"No one knew I was going to do that," Seaver said later. "Nancy didn't know. My dad didn't know. Nobody. It was just something I wanted to do. To say thank you from the mound. I was always happiest there."

For Seaver, it was a warm and wonderful afternoon in which he once more basked in the outpouring of love from the Mets' fans. And after that, nothing. He would not set foot in Shea Stadium for another eleven years.

He and Nancy spent the rest of the summer and fall enjoying life and each other. They traveled to Europe, played tennis regularly, and Tom continued work on his long-envisioned pet project: a spectacular, sprawling woods garden in the backyard of their Greenwich home. It was during that project that he contracted Lyme disease. Although it was treated successfully at the time, there would be devastating consequences from the disease thirty years later. Over breakfast in the mornings, he perused the *Daily News* and the *Post* for the sports news before attacking the *New York Times* crossword puzzle, and in the afternoons he played squash.

"Once I realized he was definitely ready for retirement, I was one hundred percent for it," said Nancy in 2017. "We could travel in the summer like normal people, not just in November. We played a little doubles tennis. We went biking together, and Tom had his garden, which he loved. Every once in a while, though, he would become a little quiet, and I could see the wheels turning. I thought: 'This is transition time,' and he was just transitioning."

They both knew he needed to get back to baseball, and in February 1989 Seaver was hired by NBC to replace Joe Garagiola in the broadcast booth alongside the venerable Vin Scully for the network's Saturday *Game of the Week*. He had previously announced postseason games for both NBC and ABC while he was still a player, so this, as Nancy saw it, was a natural part of that transition. "I've done a lot of television through the years," Seaver said, "and I feel comfortable with it. I've enjoyed a two-year period where I could really reflect on what had been a lovely twenty-year career. Now I'm anxious to get back to work."

At the same time that NBC hired Seaver, Bill White, the former Giants and Cardinals first baseman who had been working as one of Phil Rizzuto's partners in the Yankees' WPIX-TV broadcast booth since 1971, resigned to become president of the National League. Now the Yankees, too, were in the hunt for a broadcaster.

"When Bill White left, we needed a replacement, preferably someone with a New York identity," said Marty Appel, WPIX's executive producer at the time. "I had liked Tom's work at NBC and was a fan of his. We'd done a couple of books together and had a good working relationship. It turned out well. Tom and Rizzuto came to like each other a lot, and commuting from Greenwich to Yankee Stadium was easy for Tom and got him back in the game. But although he brought a lot of knowledge to the booth, I had the feeling Yankees fans never warmed up to him as I'd hoped they would. I can only suppose it was his ID as a Met."

Seaver's contract with WPIX was for $125,000 a year—the same as Rizzuto's—which, when the Scooter found out, did not sit well with him; the Yankees' fan favorite had been working in the WPIX booth since 1957, as well as on radio until just recently. But before Seaver could launch his second career, he was suddenly confronted with a fearful crisis at home. In late March, his daughter Sarah, who had just turned eighteen, was diagnosed with cancer.

"He was terrified," Sarah remembered. "He had just lost his mother to cancer, and now this. He and my mom were in shock. I was supposed to go to Italy on a spring trip, and instead I had to have surgery. I told him: 'You owe me a trip!' which he came through on the following spring."

"I remember her doctor telling me she probably wouldn't be able to have kids," Seaver told me in 2016. "I looked at him, and I said: 'You don't know my daughter!'"

"My dad did a great job of keeping things normal for me," Sarah said. "It was my senior year in high school. He let me drive to school just as if nothing was wrong."

As it turned out, Seaver was right about his daughter. Sarah went on to get married and have three boys.

The NBC *Game of the Week* gig lasted only one year for Seaver, when the network's contract with baseball expired. He did get to broadcast the 1989 All-Star Game and the National League Championship Series, and he often said one of the greatest experiences of his life was his season working with Scully, then in his fortieth of sixty-seven season as the voice of the Brooklyn–Los Angeles Dodgers, with whom he also broadcast some golf. On the other hand, the Yankees games with Rizzuto were a whole different trip, frequently involving more storytelling than actually describing the game.

"I never knew where Scooter was going to take us on any given night," Seaver said. "We must have celebrated a thousand birthdays and anniversaries, and there was constantly boxes of cannolis, and cakes and bottles of Sambuca being sent up to the booth from God knows who. Phil would veer off the game with his stories, and I just went along for the ride. That was a fun time for me."

The Mets, meanwhile, were said to be furious with Seaver's decision to cross over to the other side, but he didn't care. According to Seaver's closest associates, he never felt the Mets truly appreciated him and what he meant to the franchise. So it was especially embarrassing for the Mets when the Baseball Writers' Association elected Seaver to the Hall of Fame in January 1992—by the largest plurality (98.8 percent) in the history of the voting at that time—and he spent the entire summer celebrating the honor with Rizzuto in the Yankees' broadcast booth.

"I don't suppose this is really going to hit me until I walk into the halls of Cooperstown next August," Seaver told me the day after the election. "There were few times in my career I was speechless, but the magnitude that goes with the Hall of Fame and the numbers . . . I'm in total disbelief at the percentage of the vote."

Among the hundreds of congratulatory telegrams he received was this succinct one from Bill Denehy, his former Mets pitching sidekick with whom he shared his 1967 Topps rookie baseball card: "It's about time you did something to uphold your half of the card!"

For the 1992 induction, the Hall of Fame moved the ceremony from its customary site adjacent to the National Baseball Hall of Fame Library (which was under construction) to a vast twenty-acre pasture behind the high school gymnasium on the outskirts of Cooperstown. It was a good thing. When Seaver came to the microphone to accept his Hall of Fame plaque, following his fellow inductees—Oakland A's relief pitcher Rollie Fingers, wartime Detroit Tigers pitching ace Hal Newhouser, and the late umpire Bill McGowan, whose son accepted for him—the green pasture had been transformed into a sea of blue-capped Mets fans, the majority of them wearing "41" Mets jerseys. The crowd was later estimated to be in excess of fifteen thousand, the second largest ever to attend a Hall of Fame induction to that point, just behind 1989, the year his Reds buddy Johnny Bench and Boston Red Sox legend Carl Yastrzemski were inducted.

Seated behind Seaver were thirty-two returning Hall of Famers, including Yogi Berra, Bob Gibson, Jim Palmer, and his former Cincinnati Reds teammates Bench and Joe Morgan, while in the family section, directly in front of the podium, were Nancy, Sarah, Annie, and his dad. A few rows behind them sat the gang from Fresno: Russ Scheidt, Larry Woods, Don Reinero, and company.

After waiting a minute or so for the *"Sea-ver! Sea-ver! Sea-ver!"* chants to subside, Seaver began reliving the journey that had taken him to this stage for baseball's highest honor. He started by thanking Scheidt, his boyhood Fresno neighbor and Little League teammate ("who started it all for me by showing me how to wear a uniform"), before acknowledging "one of my very best friends, Buddy Harrelson," along with his other former teammates in the audience, Jerry Koosman and Tom Hume. He thanked his former pitching coaches, Rube Walker, Bill Fischer, and Dave Duncan, as well as his three main catchers, Jerry Grote, Johnny Bench, and Carlton Fisk, and talked about the relationship pitchers have with their shortstops, citing his own with Harrelson and Ozzie Guillen. That allowed him to segue and also acknowledge his broadcast partner, Yankees shortstop great Rizzuto, which evoked another cascade of cheers.

Then it was on to the heavy part of the speech, beginning with his dad, whom he pointed to in the front row.

"The man who gave me my foundation, gave me the work ethic, gave me the direction; the man who was always there as the pillar of strength throughout our entire family, was my father, Charles. My dad and I spent many hours in the backyard playing pepper, playing pepper, playing pepper, and one of the reasons I had such excellent control and was such a lousy hitter was that I did all the pitching. The groundwork of what it's all about started when I was eight, nine years old in my backyard in Fresno."

Next were Nancy, Sarah, and Annie. "My family is all in front of me here today," he said. "My two daughters, Sarah and Annie, twenty-one and sixteen years old. And . . . Nancy Lynn Seaver, my wife." He paused to keep his composure. "I have been very blessed, from the time of my marriage, from the time of that, as I stand here with this fraternity behind me. Family is the heart and the essence to the soul of our very lives."

As he reached the conclusion, his voice began cracking. "The only two people that are not here today whom I would want to be here and miss very much . . . the one guy who taught me what it was like to be a professional and what to do when I got here, Gil Hodges . . . the most important man in my life from the professional standpoint of my career, and, God, I know that you're letting Gil look down here today . . . and the other person who is watching now, God love her, my mom."

Later, back at the Otesaga Hotel, Seaver told a couple of the New York writers: "I knew at the end I wasn't going to last much longer because I knew 'Mom' was coming. That was my stopping point. I knew that five years ago when she died."

One notable late arrival at the inductions was Seaver's older brother, Charles, who showed up on Sunday looking very frail but happy and excited. Unbeknownst to Tom, Charles had been diagnosed with terminal lung cancer. At Charles's instructions, the family kept it from Tom so as not to cast a pall over his big weekend, and it wasn't until Monday, as Charles prepared to head home to Massachusetts, that he told his brother the grim prognosis.

Whenever Seaver talked about Charles, who died February 6, 1993, at age fifty-four, he couldn't help himself from becoming very emotional—as he did in a conversation we had in the Calistoga vineyard in September 2017.

"Charles just wanted to know what it was like, pitching in front of fifty thousand people. He would want to know what it feels like, and it was very difficult to explain. He was a teacher, a poet, a sculptor, and what I did was something he was in awe of. He once made a metal sculpture of a pitcher in his motion. It's my most prized possession. He was one of my most favorite people in life. My big brother. He was a swimmer at Cal, beautiful like my mother. God, I adored him."

"What happened?" I asked.

"Never smoked. Got the cancer when he was redoing apartments in Lower Manhattan. Asbestos. God, it was awful. One of the things I do when I'm down in this vineyard, one of the best parts of my day, is that I talk to Charles, and I talk to my mom."

Once ordained into the Hall of Fame fraternity, Seaver became fully engaged in the entire Cooperstown operation. He'd always been a student of the game and its history, but in the ensuing years, whenever he was there, he'd spend hours walking the halls of the museum and marveling at the archives in the basement. And every year when he would attend the inductions, he'd make sure to spend a few minutes in the Hall of Fame plaques gallery in front of the first-year class of 1936, which included Christy Mathewson, the iconic New York Giants right-hander who won 373 games from 1900 through 1916, and Walter Johnson, the Washington Senators' legendary "Big Train," winner of 417 games from 1907 through 1927. Seaver felt a special kinship with the college-educated Mathewson, who was regarded in his day as the consummate gentleman and most respected player in the game. "I always have to make time to talk to my boys, Christy and Walter, touch their plaques," Seaver told me. "We'll chat, and I'll point to my plaque across the room and tell them, 'I'm right over there, boys. Such an honor to be with you.'"

It was also not long before Seaver took on the role of unofficial Hall of Fame ambassador. During the year, he'd make calls to various fellow Hall of Famers, checking on their well-being and impressing on them the importance of returning every year to the inductions ("baseball's high holy day of obligation"). At the Sunday-night Hall of Famers–only dinner at the Otesaga Hotel, when the new class is officially welcomed to the club, Seaver presided over an exclusive "pitchers-only" table at which all the invitees—Gibson, Palmer, Sutton, Carlton, Koufax, and Fingers—were required to each bring a bottle of their favorite wine. (Later, Seaver made one exception to the club by allowing Carlton Fisk to sit at the table.)

There was no mistaking the Hall of Famers' titular leader. One year when Baseball Commissioner Bud Selig, who was there to make the plaque presentations at the ceremony, asked that the time of the

Sunday dinner be moved up an hour because he had an early flight the next day, Seaver said to him, "You're just a guest here, Commissioner. We dine at eight. If that's too late for you, you're free to leave early."

Three years after his induction, Seaver was elected to the Hall of Fame's board of directors. Hall Chairman Jane Forbes Clark had come to lean heavily on him as her liaison with the other Hall of Famers as well as with the baseball writers. Of particular interest to Seaver was the Veterans Committee, which was charged by the Hall to vote on managers, executives, umpires, and those players who'd failed to attain the necessary 75 percent for election to the Hall after fifteen years on the Baseball Writers' Association ballot. While he lobbied hard every year for Gil Hodges (to no avail) and Marvin Miller (inducted, at long last, in 2019), Seaver conferred often with Clark about the importance of the Veterans Committee maintaining the exclusivity standards of the Hall.

But much as he was enjoying both working with Rizzuto in the WPIX booth and his ever-increasing involvement with the Hall of Fame, Seaver still felt unfulfilled. He considered inquiring of George Steinbrenner about the Yankees' general manager job, which had become a revolving door in the late eighties and early nineties, but then thought better of it. And he desperately had wanted to be considered for one of the league presidencies, if only because, he felt, it was there that he could most have an impact on baseball's future direction. He still regarded himself as a baseball purist and wondered why the people running the national pastime "didn't have enough confidence in the sanctity of the game that we feel we have to do all these things—wild cards, more playoffs—just to compete with other sports."

"I could see he was searching, and he became more and more unhappy. And that's the word I would use, because that's what he was," said Nancy. "He wasn't being challenged. He wasn't being creative. And then all of a sudden, he sprung it on me—this was like being traded; I never saw it coming. He said to me over breakfast one morning: 'I think we should move to California. I want to create a vineyard.' You could have picked me up and scraped me off the kitchen floor. I couldn't believe what he was saying."

Seaver wanted to go back to California, buy a piece of land in the Napa Valley, develop it from the ground up, plant grapes, and create a vineyard to produce wine. Nancy listened as he went on, and tried to get a grip on what was suddenly about to happen to her life.

"I was definitely not agreeable to it at all," she said. "We were having such a good time in Greenwich. But I said, 'Okay I'm going to listen.'

"He wouldn't go into therapy," she said with a laugh. "He wasn't talking about trading me in for a younger wife. So, we came to an agreement: we would go to California and look for land and see what happens. Once again, his intelligence took him to a deeper level. He's such a great planner—he's a great organizer, you know—and if he couldn't build a championship baseball team, he was going to build a championship wine."

Seaver's time as a Yankees broadcaster came to an end after the '93 season, when Steinbrenner entered into a fifteen-year, $493.5 million deal with the Madison Square Garden Network to televise the majority of the team's games on its own Sports Channel. As a result, WPIX was reduced to televising just fifty games a year and looking to slash costs on talent. But instead of negotiating with Seaver, the station didn't even offer him a contract. While he was miffed at being dumped, around the same time, he had also signed a lucrative deal with Chemical Bank—ironically, the Mets' chief sponsor—to do commercials and appearances.

And Seaver was also deep into the planning of his vineyard project. He'd read countless books on vineyards and wine making and consulted often with Rusty Staub, who'd attained legendary status within the California wine industry. After numerous trips to California and even Washington State, Seaver wound up purchasing 155 acres of dense trees and brush atop Diamond Mountain in Calistoga.

It was Staub who introduced him to Jim Barbour, the preeminent vineyard manager in Napa Valley. Before he would agree to take on Seaver's project, however, Barbour needed to be assured that this retired baseball player was serious about learning the wine business from the ground up, as he insisted he was, and was not just doing this as a vanity project to buy his way onto the cover of *Wine Spectator* magazine.

One day Seaver and Barbour began traipsing their way together through the thick brush of Seaver's property in what Seaver said was an exercise in "literally needing to see the forest from the trees.

"As I was interviewing Jim, I didn't realize he was interviewing me," Seaver recalled. "As we pushed our way through all the trees and brush, I climbed up a tree to get a better view of the property and saw this slope. Jim looked at it and looked at me and said, 'How the hell did you find this? This is what people kill for around here: a south-by-southeast slope.'

"Obviously, the guy I bought it from didn't know what he had. I told Jim how much I loved Zinfandel and how much I'd like to grow Zinfandel grapes, and he looked at me aghast. 'With this piece of property,' he said, 'you don't plant Zin! On Diamond Mountain, with this piece of property, the only thing we're growing here are Cabernet Sauvignon grapes.'"

· · ·

"Well, look what the cat drug in."

The morning sun had just risen over Diamond Mountain, but Seaver, now seventy-two, was already a couple of hours into his daily rounds of strolling up and down the rows of his vineyard along with "the Rowdy Boys"—his three black labs, Major, Brix, and Bandy Boy—inspecting the grapes and pruning the excess vines when he spotted me approaching. He was clad in jeans, a red, plaid long-sleeve shirt, and work boots, his pruning shears attached to his belt, and wearing a maroon cap inscribed "Seaver Vineyards." I, on the other hand, was wearing shorts, a short-sleeved knit shirt, and sneakers.

"You look like a real rube, Madden," Seaver said. "You'll never make it out here dressed like that. If the sun doesn't get you, the snakes and the poison oak surely will. This is not a playground. It's a place of work."

Ever since he'd begun the second chapter of his life as the proprietor of his own wine business, Seaver had been pressing me to come out and see firsthand his whole operation. "You might learn something," he said.

He laughed when I noted that this was going to be another hundred-degree day in Napa Valley, before plucking a grape off one of the vines and handing it to me.

"In another month," Seaver said, "we'll be harvesting all of these and taking them over the mountain to Outpost, the crush facility owned and operated by my winemaker, Thomas Brown. Like Jim Barbour, Thomas Brown is the preeminent winemaker in his field. You'll like this too: his uncle is Bobby Richardson, the Yankees' second baseman in the sixties. Never hurts to have a baseball connection."

"The harvest must be an exciting time for you," I said.

"Exciting and a little sad," Seaver said, pulling off another grape.

"These are my babies. They start in the spring, and I'm out here every day checking their progress. I'm one of the worker bees here, right along with all the other vineyard hands. It's always a little sad to see the empty vines after the grapes have all been stripped and trucked over to the crusher. The harvest is my World Series now.

"I'm just fascinated by this whole process. In my previous career, I knew I could throw a baseball sixty feet, six inches. I didn't transfer that perception to the vineyard. It would be very presumptuous of me to think I'd be just as good at this. I'm just the caretaker here."

At the far end of the vineyard, we came to a lawn chair nestled under a Douglas fir tree. On the seat were folded copies of the *San Francisco Chronicle* and the *New York Times*. "This is one of my offices," Seaver said. "I'll sit here, take a break, and read the papers, check the box scores, and do my crossword puzzle."

"So, you're still following baseball every day," I said.

"Not the way I used to," said Seaver. "It just bugs the hell out of me what they're doing to starting pitchers now. Bugs the hell out of Gibson. Bugs the hell out of Marichal. Bugs the hell out of all of us. Pulling these kids out of the game after five, six innings? These kids aren't being given the chance to learn how to pitch. They don't know what they're missing, you know, and they're afraid, and maybe so. Look, I'm not there. I'm a farmer now. But they've got a computer there making the decisions about how many innings they're going to pitch."

"It's all about pitch counts now," I said. "A hundred pitches, and you're out of there. How many times did you throw more than a hundred pitches in a game?"

"Every time I went out there," Seaver said. "I had my own pitch count, probably 135. Koosman was probably 140 to 145, and Nolan Ryan was probably 150 to 155. During the course of the game, I knew how to save pitches for when I'd need them in the eighth or ninth. I'm not going to waste eight pitches on the number-nine hitter. I feel for these pitchers today. I think they have the heart, the guts, but they just won't let them get out of the corral."

We had completed my brief tutorial on the growing, nurturing, and harvesting of grapes, and Seaver led me up the hill from the vineyard to a large garage full of farm equipment where he deposited the Rowdy Boys. From there, we hopped into an SUV with the California license plate "GTS CAB" (*GTS* being his initials; *CAB* for Cabernet), and Seaver drove about a thousand yards farther up the hill to his house, which sits atop a vista overlooking the vineyard and a fabulous view of Napa Valley off in the distance. As he parked at the front door, he pointed to a flower bed that draped the sidewalk.

"You see that?"

"See what?" I said. "What am I supposed to be seeing?"

"The sculpture, you dummy," Seaver said. "Right there."

Tucked among the flowers was the metal sculpture of the pitcher in his throwing motion that his brother, Charles, had made for him.

"I put it right there," Seaver said, "so every time I come home I can say hello to Charles."

The Seavers' seven-thousand-square-foot California contemporary house, with its high ceilings, panoramic windows, poured concrete floors, and wide open spaces, with one room flowing into another, offered little hint of the ostentation or ego one might expect of a Napa Valley wine baron. On one wall was a photograph of the Andy Warhol painting of Tom, surrounded by a few colorful slashes of paint that was part of the silkscreen artist's Complete Athletes Series, commissioned in 1977. (The original is in the Hall of Fame.) Seaver then pointed to two identical paintings of a spade from a deck of cards, one in vivid colors and the other in black and white. "Richard Diebenkorn," Seaver said. "My favorite artist. How I wish I could paint like him."

From the front foyer, we strolled down the hallway to Seaver's office, where, on one section of wall opposite his desk, his entire career was displayed: his three Cy Young Awards next to nine thin glass shelves, each holding twelve baseballs. "There's a ball from every important game I ever pitched," Seaver explained, adding: "You see that first ball on the bottom shelf? That's the ball from my three hundredth win. But right next to it is the ball from my three hundred first. It was just as important."

"A real baseball fan could get lost just looking at all these balls and the Cy Young Awards," I said.

"Maybe," said Seaver, "but I'm not that Tom Seaver anymore."

Seaver often said his passion for gardening and now grape growing was in his blood, going all the way back to his dad in the raisin business in Fresno. Charlie had moved from Fresno to his beloved Pebble Beach—where he was a bigger legend than most of the latter-day golfers who played in the annual AT&T Pebble Beach National Pro-Am classic there—and whenever he visited Diamond Mountain to observe the progress on the vineyard, which was completed in 2001, he could not help but see the pride in his son's eyes. But he never got to see the fruition of Tom and Nancy's great adventure: the first vintage of GTS (for George Thomas Seaver) Cabernet Sauvignon in 2005. "I didn't want the name *Seaver* on the wine," Tom explained. "I wanted it to stand on its own."

On October 25, 2004, Charlie Seaver died of what Tom said was acute leukemia. He was ninety-three. A few days later, there was a private memorial service in the Little Chapel by the Sea in Pacific Grove, a suburb of Pebble Beach, where he was cremated. Besides Tom and Nancy, Seaver's two older sisters, Katie and Carol, were there, along with childhood friend Larry Woods and his wife, Penny, and Russ Scheidt and Gary Kazanjian, who drove over together from Fresno.

As they entered the chapel, they were handed a card with Charlie's picture on one side and, on the other, a poem by Tom's late brother, Charles, in which he wrote in part: "Like white kites tied together in the wind, their secret eyes *aligned* / oh I wish you could have been here on that day to share the feeling we felt to see them fly away / our breaths were taken in the rush of God's eternal glory."

Afterward, the funeral party drove to nearby Monterey for a lunch at a favorite Italian restaurant of Tom's. Upon the group's arrival, Tom brought Woods, Scheidt, and Kazanjian to a small bar upstairs. As they sat down, he gently placed a framed eight-by-ten photo of Charlie on the bar along with a mahogany box containing the ashes.

"Scotch and soda all around," said Seaver to the bartender.

His Fresno pals understood. When the drinks arrived, they raised their glasses and touched Charlie's picture with them, in a final toast to Seaver's dad, with Charlie's favorite drink and favorite song.

Around the time Seaver moved permanently from Greenwich to Calistoga in 1999, the Mets sought to get it right with their greatest player and finally bring him back in the fold again—by making him an offer he couldn't refuse. In February 1999 they decided to cut ties with their long-term, popular TV announcer Tim McCarver, purportedly because of ill will between him and Mets manager Bobby Valentine, whom the highly opinioned former catcher had criticized frequently on the air. They needed an even more popular replacement, and while Seaver was already envisioning his new life as a grape farmer, the Mets made it well worth his while to return to the fold. His contract called for a salary of $250,000, plus first-class airfare to and from California for the broadcasts and, when he stayed in New York, a suite at the Waldorf-Astoria.

In the six years since he'd been dropped by the Yankees and WPIX, there'd been periodic columns in the New York papers questioning why the Mets had not reached out to him and brought back their "Franchise." Two months before he signed the new contract with the Mets, Seaver told Wally Matthews of the *New York Post*: "Basically, I have no relationship with the Mets." He also said in the same article: "The one thing the Yankees do well and the Mets don't is the Yankees understand the importance of their history to the fans."

He would work six years in the Mets' TV booth, during which time he formed a lasting friendship with his broadcast partner, Gary Thorne. By 2002, however, the vines were in the ground on Diamond Mountain, and Seaver's true passion was now with them. "Tom was ready to move on," said Thorne. "When we'd have dinner on the road, all he talked about was the vineyard. He couldn't wait to get home. He'd also gotten to a point where he couldn't put up with the crowds and the city, and there wasn't much of an attachment to the Mets. He'd gotten so used to the serenity of strolling the vineyard every morning with his dogs and tending to his grapes."

The year 2005 marked both the first vintage of GTS and the end of Seaver's TV work. In January 2006 he signed a six-year "special ambassador" contract with the Mets, which required him to make a number of appearances every year for the club and its chief sponsor, Chase Bank, which had merged with Chemical. Initially, there'd been discussion about the bank increasing its advertising with the Mets to help offset some of Seaver's salary. But when Seaver heard about that, he erupted. "I don't want to be paid by you," he told one of the bank officials. "Let the Mets pay me themselves!"

Among the special events he attended for the franchise were the fortieth anniversary of the 1969 team in August 2009, the closing of Shea Stadium on September 28, 2008, and the inaugural game at Citi Field on April 13, 2009. He was especially moved by the reception he received at the Shea finale when he and Mike Piazza, the recently retired Mets catching great, teamed up for a ceremonial "final pitch" after the conclusion of the regularly scheduled game. Amid tens of thousands of flashbulbs lighting up the doomed Shea, Seaver bounced his pitch to Piazza, but it didn't matter. It was an indelible moment. As soon as he gloved the ball, Piazza rushed to the mound, where he and Seaver embraced before walking to the outfield arm in arm, waving to the ebullient and tearing crowd as Louis Armstrong's "What a Wonderful World" boomed from the stadium sound system.

"It was the happiest I ever saw Tom at any event," said Seaver's longtime memorabilia agent, Molly Bracigliano. "Everywhere he went in the stadium that day, he was treated like royalty. The king of Shea. Afterward, on the way to his car with Nancy, there must have been a hundred fans standing behind the barricades cheering him. But instead of walking on past them, he stopped and started signing autographs. He signed for every one of them, laughing and talking to them. He was truly loving it."

On the other hand, at the opening of Citi Field the following April, in which he and Piazza reprised their ceremonial duties with the new stadium's "first pitch," the Seaver-Mets relationship began souring again. It had always bothered him that the Mets were seemingly so indifferent to their own history, and when he walked into Citi Field for the first time, he was flabbergasted. Mets owner Fred Wilpon, who grew up in Brooklyn a devout Dodgers fan, had turned his new ballpark in Queens into a shrine to long-demolished Ebbets Field in Brooklyn.

"Tom walked into the Citi Field rotunda and the first thing he saw was this huge '42' in commemoration of Jackie Robinson," one of Seaver's closest friends related to me in 2020. "He was furious. He said to me, 'With all due respect to Jackie Robinson, he was one of the all-time great players and trailblazers, but I don't remember him playing for the Mets.' There was nothing commemorating Tom or their history. They didn't even have a room for the Mets Hall of Fame until a year or so later. And, of course, there was no statue.

"Tom was acutely aware that all the new stadiums that had gone up in baseball over the previous few years—Comerica Park in Detroit, Turner Field in Atlanta, the new Busch Stadium in St. Louis, the new park in Pittsburgh—were all built with statues of the franchises' greatest players—Al Kaline, Hank Aaron, Stan Musial, Roberto Clemente—in front of them. He had really never gotten over the M. Donald Grant trade in 1977 or being left unprotected in that draft in 1984, but now he'd really had it with the Mets."

Seaver never said anything publicly about the oversight, but in a June 2016 telephone interview with Eric Barrow of the *Daily News*, Nancy expressed her dismay at the Mets' neglect for still not having a statue of her husband at Citi Field. "I'm embarrassed for the Mets, I really am," she said. "They should have a statue for all the numbers they have retired on the outfield wall: Tom, Piazza, and Gil Hodges."

As part of the fiftieth anniversary of the 1969 Mets celebration, June 27, 2019, at which his daughters, Sarah and Annie, represented him, the Mets renamed the street running in front of Citi Field to "41 Seaver Way" as the official new Mets address, and announced plans for a Seaver statue "in the near future." But by then, it was too late. Seaver had ceased traveling three years earlier, and he would never reconcile with the Mets.

Into His Own

"Now I think of my life as vintage wine . . ."
—Ervin Drake, "It Was a Very Good Year"

IT WAS MOLLY BRACIGLIANO, HIS MEMORABILIA AGENT SINCE 1999, who first began to notice something wasn't right.

She talked with Seaver every day, keeping him updated on the doings of the Mets as well as on her many other clients: his fellow Hall of Famers Johnny Bench, Ozzie Smith, Robin Yount, Carlton Fisk, Joe Morgan, Tony Perez, Steve Carlton, Rollie Fingers, Jim Rice, Don Sutton, Jim Palmer, Andre Dawson, Bob Gibson, and Willie McCovey.

"He loved to tease me about not making enough money for him, and I'd protest, and then he'd burst into laughter," Molly related in a 2016 interview. "He loved breaking my chops: 'Don't forget which one of us is the Hall of Famer here.' And, of course, he loved his life out in the vineyard and never stopped talking about every aspect of it."

Always, he was in good humor.

Then, around the time of his sixtieth birthday, in November 2004, Molly began noticing a subtle change in Seaver's demeanor. Maybe it was all just part of his gradual withdrawal from baseball; he seemed uninterested at times when she'd talk about the Mets and their various trials and tribulations, and his recall of events from when he was a player—which had always been spot-on with detail—had suddenly become a bit vaguer. He was forgetting things. She asked Bench, his closest friend, if he noticed that Seaver was starting to have some memory issues, and he laughed her off. "Molly, dear," Bench said, "we're all just getting old. You've gotta bear with us."

But privately, Bench, too, suspected something was amiss with his friend, though it was not until a 2017 interview at the Hall of Fame that he expressed his awareness of Seaver's gradually deteriorating condition, remembering how he'd previously always attempted to make light of it. "He pitched for the Mets and the Reds and all that stuff," Bench said. "What does it matter? He's, you know, a great wine grower now. He gets on his tractor and walks with the dogs. And he talks to the grapevines these days. I understand. I'd punish him by not calling him as much, and the great thing is, when I did, he didn't remember. You know. All those grapevines. I think he's smoking those grapevines."

It was at the surprise sixtieth birthday party Molly threw for Seaver at his daughter Sarah's house in Connecticut that she first observed the mood swings. He'd been uncharacteristically ornery all day. That night at the party with his friends and family, over many glasses of wine, he teared up often—something he almost never did, except when he talked about his late brother, Charles—and intermittently cackled with laughter over nothing.

When Molly mentioned her concerns to some of the people who'd been at the party, they dismissed her. "They said they didn't see anything out of the ordinary with him," she recalled.

Over the next few years, he would become more and more forgetful and less and less the ever-jovial Tom. There would even be occasional flashes of anger, about the scheduling of a signing event or after being reminded of something he'd forgotten. The signing events themselves were gradually becoming a major problem. In his signing prime, Seaver could methodically sign as many as 1,300 autographs in a two-hour session, but now he found himself increasingly engaged in conversation with the people on the line, to the point where he was sometimes unable to complete his quota.

After a couple of hours of signing the wholesale stuff in the back room, witnesses said, he'd start to get cranky and tired before declaring abruptly, "That's it. I'm done!" Even in those private sessions, it could take him as many as six to seven hours to sign four hundred items.

This was not a matter of getting older, as Bench had suggested half jokingly. Something was very wrong with Tom Seaver. And it wasn't just mental. Unbeknownst to almost everyone, he wasn't feeling well physically, either. He'd experience headaches, muscle pain, and spells of nausea during the daytime. Occasionally he'd lose his equilibrium, or his speech would be slightly impaired. He told me later that he was terrified. So was Molly, who was afraid to leave him alone when he'd come to New York for one of her autograph shows.

At the Baseball Hall of Fame in Cooperstown in July 2011, Molly was frantic when Seaver was a no-show for his two o'clock autograph session at the Tunnicliff Inn off Main Street. He had always been a model of punctuality when it came to the signings, often waiting at the front door of the hotel lobby for her to take him to where he had to be.

She drove frantically to the Otesaga Hotel, where the Hall of Famers were all staying. After calling his room and getting no answer, she dashed through the hotel lobby and out onto the back veranda that overlooks picturesque Lake Otsego, asking everyone if they'd seen Seaver.

That was when someone said he was downstairs in one of the

conference rooms doing an interview with ESPN. "Unbelievable," Molly thought. "He doesn't even *like* to do interviews." He had totally forgotten his signing session. Considering he routinely pulled in twenty grand for the Hall of Fame weekend, this was no small memory lapse.

And then, on January 22, 2012, it all came to a head at the Baseball Assistance Team's annual dinner at Manhattan's New York Marriott Marquis Hotel. Seaver had not wanted to go to the dinner—by this time, he was thirteen years into his California home and vineyard, and he didn't like leaving his domain, especially for New York in wintertime. But BAT, a nonprofit charitable organization that provides various forms of assistance to baseball retirees in need, was honoring the Mets for their fiftieth anniversary, and after much cajoling, they finally prevailed on the Franchise to attend. Molly made it more worth his while by arranging an autograph show with dozens of former Mets at Citi Field the Sunday before the dinner. The show was a disaster. Seaver could barely accommodate half the fans who had waited hours for his autograph, and Molly and her assistants had to haul cartons of photos, baseballs, and other various memorabilia back to Seaver's room at the Marriott Marquis in hopes that he could sign them the next day.

He wasn't feeling well when he arrived at the dinner Tuesday night, and that put him in a bad mood. At first, the other six patrons at the $25,000 premium table didn't seem to notice, even though Seaver was talking on, somewhat incoherently, slurring his words. "They thought he was drunk, but he wasn't," Molly said. "He'd hardly had anything to drink because, by then, he'd started losing his taste for wine. He was sick. More sick than anyone realized."

Then, just before the program began, the man next to Seaver asked him to sign his dinner program. Seaver erupted, screaming and cursing with a flurry of f-bombs as everyone else at the table looked on in shock. Realizing the situation had suddenly gotten totally out of control, Molly and Lorraine Hamilton, the Mets' longtime special events director, rushed over to Seaver, coaxed him out of his seat, and quickly escorted him away from the table. As they pushed their way through the crowd, patrons at the other nearby tables, who had heard the commotion, began mumbling.

"It's okay!" Molly shouted. "He's okay! He's just not feeling well." They got him up to his room, and the next day, the Mets had someone pick him up and drive him to the airport.

"Despite all the witnesses, we were able to keep it under wraps," said Joe Grippo, then the executive director of BAT. "It would have been terrible if it had somehow gotten into the papers. This was Tom Seaver, after all."

Back home in Calistoga, a few days after the BAT dinner, Seaver learned that his 2008 GTS Cabernet had received a 97 rating from the *Wine Spectator*, which was almost as good as the 98.84 plurality he'd gotten from the Baseball Writers' Association for his election to the Hall of Fame. "It's an honor," he said, "but the real honor belongs to my winemaker, Thomas Brown. I'm just a poor old dirt farmer." At the same time, friends said, Seaver was becoming more and more reclusive, seldom dining out with Nancy in public; his phone calls with Molly now more like two or three times a week instead of daily. When she mentioned the BAT Dinner incident to him, he insisted he had no memory of f-bombing the guy at the table. She believed him.

On June 1, 2012, Johan Santana, in only his eleventh start since coming back from serious shoulder surgery, became the first Mets pitcher in history to hurl a no-hitter. Santana had been the Mets' ace his first two seasons in Flushing, 2008 and 2009, and their number two starter in 2010 before missing all of 2011 because of the surgery. The feat quite naturally evoked memories of Seaver, the greatest of all Mets pitchers who'd come the closest with two notable near misses: losing no-hitters with one out in the ninth to the Cubs' Jimmy Qualls on July 9, 1969, and to the Padres' Leron Lee on July 4, 1972. With all the media trying to reach him for comment, Seaver issued a congratulatory statement to Santana in which he said: "I've never met Johan personally, but from what I've heard about him, is he has a big heart and is a huge competitor."

But if he thought that had successfully quelled the media's quests for interviews, little did he realize it merely set off more alarm bells about his mental state. For, as it was quickly pointed out in various media outlets, he had, in fact, met Santana before. During spring training in 2008, they'd done a half-hour special on SNY, the Mets' cable channel, talking at length about pitching strategies.

Not long after that, Seaver was sitting, drinking coffee in his kitchen one morning when his head vineyard foreman, who had been with him for seven years, appeared at the door. Seaver looked at him curiously but could not remember his name. That was when Nancy, having watched her husband's deterioration in frustration and shared his same fears for the past few years, finally decided this was enough. "We're going to the doctor to find out just what's wrong with you," she told him firmly.

Tom had been avoiding a diagnosis because he was afraid to know what was wrong; afraid that he was suffering from Alzheimer's disease or that he'd had a series of strokes. Either way, the prognosis was likely to be dooming, and that was something he just couldn't deal with.

After Seaver underwent an examination and a battery of tests that included a CAT scan, the doctors told him he did not have Alzheimer's disease and had not had a stroke. That was the good news. The bad news was that he was suffering from a recurrence of Lyme disease, which he'd first incurred from a deer tick back in November 1991 while tending to his garden in Greenwich. The initial case had been severe—and complicated by Bell's palsy, a temporary paralysis of the muscles in his face—but the doctors told him they would treat it with antibiotics that would effectively prevent it from returning.

But now it had, and the relief he felt about not having Alzheimer's was offset by the fact that the Lyme disease had progressed to stage 3. They could arrest it somewhat with medication, the physicians said, but they could not repair the brain cells that had been damaged by his failure to address it much sooner. He could expect his memory issues to worsen gradually.

Seaver began the medication, and, ever so slowly, he could feel improvement. The bouts of nausea, sleep deprivation, and chemical imbalance lessened. He was having more good days than bad days. His morning ritual, trudging up and down the rows of grape vines in the vineyard with his three black Labs, was once again invigorating. "It's great cardio," he said. He was beginning to feel alive again. He was still able to do his *New York Times* crossword puzzle, as well as read the box scores and then grouse about starting pitchers increasingly being taken out of games after six innings or less.

Nevertheless, with his short-term memory loss, interviews would always be dicey from then on, although Molly sensed her client was at least ready to come back into society again. "You need to tell the world what happened to you," she told Seaver. "You need to talk about the Lyme disease. Not only will it explain everything the past few years, it'll also help the thousands of people with Lyme disease."

"Okay," he told her. "But I'm only gonna do it with Madden."

I was at spring training in Tampa when I called him late Thursday morning, March 14, 2013. Even though it was eight o'clock his time, he was already in the vineyard with the dogs.

"What do you want, Madden?" he snapped. "Can't you hear I'm busy out here?"

"I want to know about the Lyme disease," I said. "I want to write about it because it needs to be written. People need to know what happened to you."

"I don't know. I'm not sure," he said hesitantly. "Why?"

"Because they care," I said. "We all care."

With that, Tom Seaver began deliberating on all that had transpired from the day he couldn't remember his vineyard foreman's name.

"I didn't know what was happening to me. Right now I could kill those doctors back in Connecticut who told me it wouldn't come back. I didn't know that once Lyme disease gets into your blood system, it causes real problems and never leaves your body. I'm taking these pills—twenty-four of 'em a day, plus one penicillin pill to get my chemical balance back. It's a cycle that kills off all the spirochetes in your body. There are days I'll still feel like I have a bad case of the flu. But these last couple of weeks, they've been less and less."

"What about wine?" I asked. "Can you drink with all that medication?"

"No," Seaver said. "But to tell you the truth, I haven't had a glass of wine or a beer in eight months. I don't miss it."

"If nothing else," I said, "it must be a great relief to you to know that you don't have Alzheimer's."

"Without a doubt. I was terrified. I didn't know what was happening to me. But now I feel like I'm a bunt hit away from feeling normal again."

Always with the baseball metaphors. It was good to hear him so up-beat, although after our conversation, I thought to myself, "God only knows how much of his memory was left forever in the darkness."

We would find out in the coming months. That July, he made what would be his last trip to New York, to throw out the ceremonial first pitch at the All-Star Game at Citi Field. This time his batterymate was David Wright, the Mets' fan favorite third baseman and captain. Clad in an orange National League All-Star jersey, Seaver stepped to the mound to another huge ovation, milking the moment by waving to the crowd and saluting the umpires, before unleashing his pitch—which was short and to the right of home plate, prompting Wright to spring to his feet to clutch it. His duty completed, Seaver walked off the mound toward home plate, seemingly uncertain where he was sup-posed to go, when a security guard came out on the field and whisked him away to Baseball Commissioner Bud Selig's private box upstairs.

In the elevator on his way up to the box with Nancy, somebody said, "Nice going, Tom. The pitch looked like a strike to me."

Rubbing his shoulder, Seaver smiled. "My arm might not be all the way gone, but your eyes sure are," he quipped.

He had not wanted to make the trip, particularly since Citi Field was not "his" ballpark. All his memories were buried in the parking lot across the way where Shea Stadium once stood. But he understood the symbolic importance of throwing out the first pitch at the first All-Star Game hosted by the Mets since 1964. How would it look if the great-est of all Mets wasn't there? More questions would be asked. So, he agreed to go, but Nancy set the conditions: No interviews. No press conferences. And that's how it was. By the end of the night, all anyone was talking about was Mariano Rivera, the Yankees' Hall of Fame closer, in his final All-Star appearance, retiring the National League in order in the eighth inning to get the victory. Seaver was just a footnote.

The next time Seaver was back in the public spotlight was November 15, 2013, when he was featured on the cover of *Wine Spectator*. He'd always insisted that was nothing he ever aspired to when he got into the business of growing grapes. In the accompanying article, his winemaker, Thomas Brown, said: "Tom's the easiest hands-on owner I deal with when it comes to the vineyard. It sounds like hyperbole, but he really is out there every day. With the vineyard being only one and a half acres, I don't doubt Tom has a personal relationship with every single vine out there."

My last trip to the vineyard was in May 2017. Seaver had stopped going to the Hall of Fame after the 2015 induction ceremony, when he'd spent most of the weekend in his room with Nancy and had trouble recognizing many of his fellow Hall of Famers. In the two years since, it was alarming to me how much his mental acuity had further deteriorated. The old Seaver sense of humor was still there, though, as we strolled the vineyard together, and he retold the old stories about his favorite foil, "McGraw"—Tony LaRussa—but he frequently found himself apologizing for having repeated the same thing he'd said a few minutes earlier. And he had almost no memory anymore about his career.

"The Lyme disease has been a big issue for us in this later day," Nancy said to me that day. "I'd like to say retirement, but we're not quite there yet. He's built this huge life, and, you know, with his memory issues, he's struggling more and more with the nuts and bolts of the life. Over the last five or six years, we've had more of a power transition—where he was always the engine that pulled the train, and now I'm doing more of the pulling of the train in certain areas. I have to tell him I love him every day so he won't forget."

I talked to Seaver a few times by phone after that visit, usually starting the conversations by deliberately provoking him—"You'll be happy to know that last night, Yankees manager Aaron Boone removed his starting pitcher, who was pitching a *no-hitter*, after just eighty-four pitches"—and we'd go from there. Suddenly, in October 2018, there was radio silence from Calistoga. Sometime shortly after the harvest of his grapes, Seaver's cell phone had been shut off, and Nancy wasn't returning any messages or texts from hers. It was not until the following spring that Seaver's friends and his hundreds of thousands of fans learned why. On March 7, 2019, the Baseball Hall of Fame issued a statement bearing sad news about one of its most prominent and admired citizens:

"The Seaver family announced today that Hall of Fame pitcher Tom Seaver has recently been diagnosed with dementia. Tom will continue to work in his beloved vineyard at his California home, but has chosen to completely retire from public life. The family is deeply appreciative of those who have supported Tom throughout his career, on and off the field, and who do so now by honoring his request for privacy. We join Tom in sending warmest regards to everyone."

Even though he'd already shut himself off from the rest of the world for more than a year, the statement sent shock waves through the baseball community. Tom Seaver, dementia? It couldn't be.

"I've known this was coming; I guess we all did," said Johnny Bench. "But I've been content to have those conversations with him in my mind. That's the way it's going to have to be because I can't envision him without that beautiful mind."

"So sad to hear Tom Seaver has dementia," tweeted Mike Piazza, who'd joined the pitching great in Cooperstown in 2016. "He will always be the heart and soul of the @Mets, the standard which all Mets aspire to. This breaks my heart. Do not feel worthy to be mentioned in the same breath, yet honored to be with him in the Hall of Fame."

Given the dire nature of his diagnosis and the finality of the statement, it was hard to imagine Seaver having one more victory in him. And yet there was—and against a most unlikely opponent. In early June 2019 a Boston law firm uncovered an application filed with the US Patent and Trademark Office by the management firm of New England Patriots' six-time Super Bowl champion quarterback Tom Brady attempting to trademark the nickname "Tom Terrific." The revelation evoked immediate howls of outrage, not just from Mets fans but also from New Yorkers as a whole, who viewed this as another provocation from the North in their long-standing sports war with Boston. One application by Brady's firm was for trading cards and posters, and another was for T-shirts.

As soon as the application was made public, the Patent and Trademark Office was deluged with letters of protest from New Yorkers documenting the many examples—news articles, T-shirts, Wikipedia, and other biographical references—in which "Tom Terrific" had been fully established as referring to Seaver.

After considering all the materials and arguments, on November 22, 2019, the USPTO rejected Brady's application, stating "it would falsely suggest a connection to Seaver" and that the "Tom Terrific" nickname "points uniquely and unmistakably" to Seaver. "Given the fame of the mark and use of the mark in connection with the applied-for goods, customers will falsely associate the applicant's name with Tom Seaver," the Patent Office concluded.

While it does not appear as part of his official record on Baseball-Reference.com or in any baseball encyclopedia, the 312th victory of Seaver's career was perhaps the most profound and definitive of them all.

After all, there was, and always will be, only one Tom Terrific.

On September 3, 2020, the Baseball Hall of Fame announced in a statement: "Hall of Fame pitcher Tom Seaver passed away in the early hours of Monday August 31. He was 75. Seaver passed peacefully in his sleep at his home in Calistoga, CA, of complications from Lewy body dementia and COVID-19." His wife, Nancy, and daughters, Sarah and Annie, were at his side.

In their game against the Yankees at Citi Field that night, the Mets players all bore symbolic smudges of dirt on the right knee of their uniform pants in tribute to Seaver's trademark drop-and-drive pitching delivery. "It's a sad day in Metsville," said Ed Kranepool. "We have lost our star and our leader."

ACKNOWLEDGMENTS

This book, certainly in its present form and depth of interviews, could not have been possible without the considerable contributions, assistance, and encouragement of Martin Dunn and Marie McGovern of Street Smart Video and of Teri Thompson, my former sports editor at the *New York Daily News.* It was Martin and Marie who had the vision to turn my relationship with Tom Seaver into a documentary, which resulted in the dozens of interviews we conducted together over the course of three years. Seaver and his wife, Nancy, graciously turned over their house in the vineyard in Calistoga to us and our crew and sat for hours of interviews on two separate visits in 2016–17. At the same time, Teri assisted on the documentary, and as Seaver's memory issues, the result of his Lyme disease, worsened gradually, she urged me to incorporate those interviews into a book.

"There needs to be a definitive book on Seaver," Teri said. "You're the guy to do it, but if you don't, I guarantee you, somebody else will." Once the process began, Teri served as my personal line editor for each chapter before I turned it over to my editor at Simon & Schuster, Bob Bender.

No book about the Mets or one of their foremost citizens would be possible without the help and cooperation of Jay Horwitz, the Mets' tireless, longtime publicist and now their official historian. Jay was invaluable to me on this project, putting me in contact with numerous former Mets and Seaver teammates.

During the course of writing this book, it seemed like there wasn't a week that went by when Bill Francis, research historian at the Baseball Hall of Fame, wasn't providing me with material filling in various aspects of Seaver's career. I am sure I am not the only author who has said Bill Francis is the Hall of Fame's most valuable resource.

I also want to thank Robert York, the editor in chief at the *New York Daily News*, and Mike Dabin, the photo editor at the *Daily News*, for affording me full access to the *Daily News* photo library for use in this book. Of course, the photos still had to be tracked down, and that task fell to Vincent Panzarino, who presides over the *Daily News*'s library and has been of enormous assistance on all of my books. Once again, thanks, Vinny!

For the chapter on Fresno, I am most grateful to Larry Woods, one of Seaver's lifelong pals, who provided pertinent insight on their friendship as well as Seaver's other relationships. Larry and Jeff Ring, another Fresno cohort, also contributed photos of Seaver in his youth with his high school friends and teammates. In addition, I want to thank Melissa Scroggins of the Fresno County Public Library, who spent hours combing through the 1950s editions of the *Fresno Bee* for Seaver's Little League game stories and box scores, and Tom Sommers, the unofficial Fresno historian, who provided me phone numbers and other contact information for many of Seaver's former coaches and friends. One of my guideposts for the Fresno chapter was Malka Drucker's 1978 children's book *Tom Seaver—Portrait of a Pitcher*, co-authored with Seaver, which detailed his formative years, from Little League through high school and college. Forty years later, Malka was most generous sharing her notes and remembrances of the time she spent with Seaver and his parents.

It is not possible for anyone to write a book on baseball without making liberal use of Sean Forman's Baseball-Reference.com. It is the consummate statistical resource. In addition, Bob Waterman and John Labombarda of the Elias Sports Bureau were of constant assistance in providing statistical information for this book.

I also want to thank Ira Berkow, a valued friend, for providing me copies of correspondence he had with Seaver on projects on which they worked together for News Enterprise Associates (NEA).

Also, I need to thank Simon & Schuster for assigning Philip Bashe as the copy editor for this book. Of all the books I've written, I've never had a more meticulous copy editor and stickler for detail and accuracy. We never actually met, but I could tell that even though Phil is a Yankees fan, he is above all a devout baseball fan who strove to make this the best book it could be. Thanks, Phil.

And special thanks to Bob Bender, my editor at Simon & Schuster, who was somehow able to shed his Yankees pinstripes and take on a book about the greatest of all Mets. Bob was a true "writer's editor" who encouraged me throughout.

Lastly, I again have to salute my longtime agent, Rob Wilson, for finding a great house for Seaver's story in Simon & Schuster and a great editor in Bob Bender. To Rob, this is merely the continuation of a beautiful friendship.

BIBLIOGRAPHY

Drucker, Malka, with Tom Seaver. *Tom Seaver—Portrait of a Pitcher*. New York: Holiday House, New York, 1978.

Lang, Jack, and Peter Simon. *The New York Mets—Twenty-Five Years of Baseball Magic*. New York: Henry Holt, 1987.

McGraw, Tug, with Don Yeager. *Ya Gotta Believe! My Roller-coaster Life as a Screwball Pitcher and Part-time Father, and My Hope-Filled Fight Against Cancer*. New York: New American Library, 2004.

Seaver, Tom, with Dick Schaap. *The Perfect Game*. New York: E. F. Dutton, 1970.

Swoboda, Ron. *Here's the Catch—A Memoir of the Miracle Mets and More*. New York: Thomas Dunne Books, 2019.

Williams, Dick, and Bill Plaschke. *No More Mr. Nice Guy—A Life of Hardball*. San Diego, New York: Harcourt Brace Jovanovich, 1990.